IT'S A DON'S LIFE

Books by the same author

Saint Radegund, 1925.
The Lyfe of Saynt Radegunde (edited), 1926.
Saint Giles, 1928.
Slowly Forward (with S. Fairbairn), 1929.
Oar, Scull and Rudder, 1930.
South Mymms, the Story of a Parish, 1931.
Latin in Church, 1934 (revised edition 1955).
The Medieval Latin and Romance Lyric, 1937 (new edition 1969).
A Short History of Jesus College, 1940.
Babylon Bruis'd and Mount Moriah Mended (with B. L. Manning), 1940.
Bernard Lord Manning, 1942.
Arthur Quiller-Couch, 1948.
'Q' Anthology, 1948.
Tales of South Mymms and Elsewhere, 1952.
Mostly Mymms, 1953.
A History of Jesus College (with A. Gray), 1960.
The Jesus College Boat Club (with H. B. Playford), Vol. I 1928, Vol. II 1962.
Guide to Cambridge
The Penguin Book of Latin Verse (edited), 1962.

FREDERICK BRITTAIN

by Narraway

It's a Don's Life

AN AUTOBIOGRAPHY BY
FREDERICK BRITTAIN

HEINEMANN
LONDON

Heinemann Educational Books

LONDON   EDINBURGH   MELBOURNE   TORONTO
SINGAPORE   JOHANNESBURG   AUCKLAND   KUALA LUMPUR
IBADAN   HONG KONG   NAIROBI   NEW DELHI

ISBN 435 32140 4

© M. Brittain 1972

First published 1972

Published by
HEINEMANN EDUCATIONAL BOOKS LTD
48 Charles Street, London WIX 8AH

Printed in Great Britain by W. Heffer and Sons Ltd, Cambridge

Contents

Illustrations

Preface

In writing this autobiography I have tried to bear in mind that some of its readers may have little or no previous idea of the life and work of a don and may wish to know more. With them in view, I have gone into details about academical life with which other readers may already be thoroughly familiar. If they are, I trust that nevertheless they will not find my details tedious. Perhaps they will not, because just as no two universities are identical in their ways, so no two colleges in one and the same university are replicas of each other and no two dons in one and the same college have an identical reaction to their environment.

I wish to record my thanks to those of my friends who kindly read through the typescript of the book and gave me the benefit of their advice: the Rev. Ralph Gardner (who was the instigator of the book), the late Mr Gerald Woods and Mrs Woods, the late Dr F. J. E. Raby, Mr L. N. Battersby (who has given me much valuable advice ever since we were undergraduates together), and Prof. I. Ll. Foster. I also wish to thank my wife, Mrs Vera Lucas, and Miss Janet Rich (Mrs Jeremy Gotch) for typing my manuscript and for being so patient with it.

F.B.

Knowing that Alan Hill, a devoted member of Jesus College, had pressed F.B. to write his memoirs, it was natural that on Freddy's death I should offer this manuscript to Heinemann's.

I could not have wished for a more sympathetic publisher, and the encouragement given to me by Reuben Heffer also helped to make the book possible.

Muriel Brittain

1972

I

Although I have travelled a good deal in Europe and beyond, I have spent most of my life within twenty-five miles of that quiet and little-visited part of south-east England where my ancestors lived for centuries, probably from time immemorial. It was here that both my parents were born, and it is here that scores of my relations still live, working mostly on the land, as farm labourers, market gardeners, or farmers, like their ancestors throughout the ages.

This piece of country lies partly in Hertfordshire and partly in Bedfordshire. Its southern boundary is the bare Chiltern Hills, where in spring the purple pasque-flower blooms and in summer the chalky fields and lanes are bright with the vivid sky-blue flowers of the tough-stalked succory. Its northern boundary is the less elevated Greensand Ridge which runs across Bedfordshire a few miles away from the Chilterns and is covered with pine-woods, holly, bracken, gorse, and heather.

The land between these two ranges is given up almost entirely to farming and market-gardening and contains no town of any size. It is watered by such little streams as the Hiz, the Ivel, and the Flitt — tributaries or sub-tributaries of the Great Ouse — and dotted with ancient village churches standing for the most part on little knolls. Those along the foot of the Chilterns are built of flint-stones dug out of the chalk, and those nearer the Greensand Ridge are of the local red ironstone.

All these churches contain monuments to men and women of local or occasionally national eminence, and the churchyards contain many scores of gravestones commemorating village worthies; but until the twentieth century opens one may search in vain among them for even the simplest memorial to any of the Brittains or the other families from which I am descended. Hewers of wood and drawers of water for people more fortunate, more clever, or less scrupulous than themselves, they were too poor to afford even a gravestone.

Robert Bloomfield, the shoemaker-poet who spent his last poverty-stricken years in this area soon after the close of the Napoleonic wars, might have had any of my ancestors of his time in mind when describing the hero of his *Farmer's Boy:*

Giles must trudge, whoever gives command,
A Gibeonite, that serves them all by turns.

Richard Jefferies, too, might be writing the obituary of any one of them in the vivid last chapter of *Hodge and His Masters*, where he traces the life of a typical nineteenth-century farm-labourer from his birth in a thatched hovel, through long years of poverty and unremitting toil to the inevitable workhouse and a pauper's grave:

> ... and the very grave-digger grumbled as he delved through the earth hard-bound in the iron frost, for it jarred his hand and might break his spade. The low mound will soon be level, and the place of his burial shall not be known.

So must have lived and died many generations of men and women whose blood runs in my veins. The modest provisions of the Welfare State, at which some persons born with silver or silver-plated spoons in their mouths sneer as 'undermining the independence of the working class,' would have seemed untold wealth to them. They made the mistake of being born too soon, into the penury (for them) of the Unfair State. My heart goes out to those generations of dead men and women whom I never knew, but to whom I owe an incalculable debt. Peace be to their ashes!

All eight of my great-grandparents lived in the district which I have described, within fifteen miles of each other. Two of my great-grandfathers worked on the land, the other two were village craftsmen. One of these, Robert Brittain, was a tailor at the Bedfordshire village of Clophill. He taught his trade to his three sons, William, Mark, and Frederick, all of whom left home in early manhood to set up business for themselves in villages a few miles away. Mark, who was my grandfather, settled at Stondon, a parish which is only five or six miles from Clophill and borders on Hertfordshire. Soon after his arrival there he married Eliza Hibbott, the daughter of a farm labourer in the same parish.

All four rooms of the cottage in which they passed the whole of their married life, and in which all their eleven children were born, were small. The front door of the living-room opened straight on to the road and had no porch of any kind. It was the only room in the house that possessed a fire-grate: the so-called kitchen adjoining it was consequently used only for storage and for washing. There was no tap: all the water had to be drawn from a well at the back of the house. A staircase led straight from the living-room into the back bedroom, and it was necessary to go through this bedroom to get to the front bedroom.

The living-room was always called 'the House' — a name which puzzled me greatly when I was small. Like all the other rooms in the cottage, it had a low ceiling, which could easily be touched with the hand. The tiled floor was partly covered with strips of coconut matting and partly with a home-made hearth-rug. The middle of the room was occupied by a square table. The one small window was fitted with a wide shelf packed with geraniums and fuchsias. Next to it stood a mahogany arm-chair, padded with horsehair, but no one ever sat in it: it was a show piece. All the other chairs in the room were hard and unpadded. The space to the right of the fireplace was occupied by a china-cupboard stretching from floor to ceiling. On the other side of the fireplace there was a low cupboard, on which stood a clock and several ornaments, including two pink vases with cut-glass pendants hanging all round them and dried grasses in them. On the wall above the clock there hung a framed black-edged memorial card with some under-taker's verses about a member of the family who had died in infancy. The other chief ornaments of the room were a maple-framed German oleograph of Christ entering Jerusalem, a wall-clock which never went, and a side-table on which stood my grandmother's work-box, flanked by two oil-lamps standing on home-made woollen mats.

Mark Brittain was a little man, standing only about five feet four inches high, with a white skin, keen light-blue eyes, and toothless gums. Clean-shaven except for a 'monkey frill' round his throat, he possessed an abundant head of hair all his life. Although he was a tailor, his trousers and jacket were generally in need of repair and had a button or two missing. He wore a cap at all times — in or out of doors, at meals and at work, from the moment he got out of bed in the morning until he got back into it at night. Endowed as he was with a sympathetic and generous nature, a keen sense of humour and a gift for story-telling, his company was much sought. He was an incessant talker and his loquacity was sometimes too much for his wife, who would cut him short with a 'Shet yoor ol' chank, man, doo.'

When Mark set up in business for himself at Stondon he worked for about twenty years in the 'kitchen,' which possessed only one tiny window and all his sewing was done by hand. Then, having managed to save some money, he had a workshop built on his already small garden, a few yards from the back door of the house, and a year or two later he had a treadle sewing-machine installed in it. The shop had brick walls and floor, a pantiled roof with a house-leek growing on it, and a window running nearly the whole length of the wall farthest from the door. About two-thirds of the room was occupied by 'the board,' waist

high, on which Mark sat cross-legged to do his hand-sewing, or at which
he stood when cutting out or pressing clothes. In this shop all his
business was done, from the preliminary measuring of the customer to
the trying-on of the finished garments.

Mark's daily routine varied but little from year to year. When he
came downstairs (rather late) in the morning he drank a cup of tea,
took down his shop shutters, lit the stove which kept the shop warm in
winter and at which he heated his irons all the year round, and settled
down to work. Soon after ten o'clock he went into 'th' 'ewse' for his
'bayver', which consisted of a slice of bread and a 'mossel o' cheeäse'.
He sometimes started to toast his bread, holding it on a knife in front
of the fire, but invariably lost patience in a few seconds and petulantly
exclaimed, 'There's no 'eeät in the gallus foire at all'; to which Eliza
would reply, 'Yew should git up sooner, man, and 'ave breakfast, loike
other fooälk, afoore the foire's maäde up.'

Within ten minutes he was at work again, singing aloud in a good
tenor voice to the quick hum of his sewing-machine or to the slow
rhythm of his needle or his pressing-iron. He would sing *Whack-fal-de
day*, bringing his iron down smartly at the 'whack'; or he would sing

> If you knew the 'aardship
> You'd never pooäch agaain;

or *Polly Perkins:*

> As beautiful as a butterfloy and as prewd as a queeän
> Wor my pretty little Polly Perrkins of Padd'n'ton Greeän;

or the old ballad on the death of Nelson:

> 'Twor in Trafalgar Bay
> We saw the Frenchmen lay.
> Each 'eeart were bewndin' then:
> We scorned the furreign yooäke;

or (perhaps most frequently of all) *The Farmer's Boy:*

> Though little Oi be, Oi will laabour 'aard
> If you will me emply-y-y-y
> To plough and sow, to reeäp and mow
> And be a faarmer's by-y-y-y,
> And be a faarmer's by.

About half past twelve he would be called indoors to dinner, at
which he scorned to use a modern fork, preferring the old-fashioned
'three-tined' (or, best of all, 'two-tined') steel fork with a bone handle.

He would eat whatever was put in front of him, sometimes jocularly complaining that, though he had no teeth, 'Liza allers 'as gone me the booänes to chaw.'

After dinner, Mark and his wife enjoyed 'forty winks', sitting in their hard 'elbow cheers', one on each side of the fire. Mark's chair, as it had to leave room for the upper door of the china-cupboard to open, had a very low back, so that he had to sleep with his elbow resting on the arm of the chair and his chin on his hand. He slept very lightly; for one reason, he was afraid of missing anyone who might pass by the house. Often, in his half-slumber, he would hear the trot of a horse in the distance. As the sound grew louder, his face was a study, even though his eyes were shut: it showed the struggle going on inside him between his desire to sleep and his desire to see who was passing by. The sound grew louder and louder, then began to grow obviously fainter. At this point, Mark used to hurl himself suddenly from his chair to the door and throw it open just in time to see a horse and trap before they disappeared round the bend. He would then shut the door and go back to his chair; but not before Eliza, with her eyes still closed, had asked, 'Who were that, Maark?' and he would answer, 'Th' ol' paarson,' or 'Tom Simpkins, gooin' t' Shill'n'ton,' or 'Muster Pooästgaate, gooin' t' th' staation.'

After a siesta of about twenty minutes Mark used to go back to his shop, where he worked until half past four. He then drew water from the well for the house, chopped some fire-wood, and went in to tea. This consisted invariably of a slice of bread and butter, a piece of cake, and two cups of tea, and was his last meal of the day. By half past five he was back in his shop. He enjoyed his evening work more than either his morning or his afternoon work, particularly during the winter, for then he was almost certain to get a number of visitors, attracted by the cosy warmth of his stove and oil lamp, and some of them might stay the whole evening. He welcomed them all — even those to whom his wife, if she happened to peep in, gave a stony glare, and audibly stigmatized as 'a lo' o' ol' galluses'. In this category she included 'Naailus Brucks' (Cornelius Brooks), the village ne'er-do-well, whom she considered an all-too-frequent visitor. The warm shop was a delight to him after the stable or pig-sty where he normally slept, and the stove was very handy for baking his potatoes on. If he did not contribute much to the discussions that went on between the other visitors to the shop he at least enjoyed listening to them; and Mark, unlike Eliza, suffered his company gladly.

Mark generally stopped work for the night at about half past eight. Having dismissed his visitors (whom he was to meet again elsewhere a few minutes later), he put out his oil lamp, locked his shop, and went to one of the three inns in the village. He usually went either to the *Red Lion* ('Tommy Burr's') or the *Horse Shoes* ('Emery Cooper's'), and only occasionally to the third inn, which had once been thatched and was unofficially called *The Thatched House*. The brewers had rebuilt it in brick, with a slate roof, and renamed it *The New Inn*, but the local inhabitants ignored this new-fangled style and invariably referred to the inn either as 'Jack Kitson's' or as 'The Thecked 'Ewse'. Whichever inn he visited, Mark was the undisputed president of the company gathered there. It was he who welcomed visitors from neighbouring villages or from far-away Bedford or Luton, and he who led the discussion on such favourite topics as crops, the weather, births, marriages, deaths and funerals. He stayed until closing time at ten o'clock. When he got home, Eliza's caustic remarks on 'traailin' dewn to th' blaamed ol' aale-us' did not prevent her from asking who had been present or from listening closely to her husband's summary of the conversation. He generally went to bed within half an hour of his return from the inn, though occasionally he went back to his shop and worked for another hour or even two hours.

He worked six days a week. On Fridays and Saturdays he left his shop about six o'clock, put on his best suit, shouldered a bundle of patterns and finished garments — sometimes his fiddle as well — and walked on Fridays to Shillington and on Saturdays to Meppershall one week and Henlow the next. In each of these villages he held a clothing club in one of the inns. His method was simple. If, for instance, a pair of trousers cost fifteen shillings, fifteen men would pay a shilling each for as many weeks and Mark would make a pair of trousers each week, the order in which the customers received them being decided by lot. He thoroughly enjoyed these gatherings, at which his social gifts were a great asset; but, as he met many old friends at them, he often returned home the worse for drink, noisy, and with much less money in his pocket than he should have had. Eliza, though she was very angry, did not waste much time on recrimination, for sad experience of hard times had taught her a far better way of dealing with the situation. She therefore got her husband to bed and asleep at the earliest possible moment, took all the remaining money from his pockets, hid it in a place known only to herself, and doled a few pence out to him each day during the following week — just enough (but no more) for him to buy as much tobacco and beer as would keep him in a good temper. His sense of humour and his respect and affection for his wife were such that he accepted the situation with a very good grace.

His rare holidays included a few visits to one of his sons at Yarmouth. It was there that, on catching the first glimpse he ever had of the sea, he mistook it for 'a gallus gret turmut field'.

When he paid his first visit to London and made his first acquaintance with a public convenience he was astonished and delighted with its lavish display of marble, the like of which he had never seen. On returning to the street he begged the whole company to go downstairs and gaze at such magnificence.

After his eightieth birthday he dropped the making of new garments and did only repairs. When his last illness came he went to live first with one daughter at Stondon and later with another daughter at Pulloxhill, where he died, leaving fifty-seven living descendants. He was buried at Stondon, and his wife was buried beside him in the following year. When I last visited his grave there was some speedwell growing near it, its flowers almost the colour of his eyes.

Friends who call on me in my college rooms at Cambridge are often amused (and strangers are startled) to find me sitting on the floor or on a settee with my legs crossed and hidden under me – like a Buddha, as they put it – and my work lying round me. To sit like that for a long time does not cause me the least discomfort. I sometimes wonder whether I inherited the knack from my tailor grandfather, and I at least like to think that it is so, for there was a great affection between us.

2

My father was the seventh of the eleven children of Mark and Eliza Brittain and was born at Stondon in 1866. In those days parents in country districts did not bother very much about such matters as the registration of births, and my father's birth was never registered. In due course he was taken to Stondon parish church to be christened, for the Brittains appear to have been Anglicans always. He was given the name Elijah but disliked it so much that, when he grew up and left Bedfordshire, he changed it to William, skilfully reinforcing the change by appropriating the birth certificate of his brother William, his junior by a year or so, who had died in infancy.

After attending Stondon village school somewhat desultorily until he was seven years old, my father began to work for a firm of coprolite diggers for a few pence a week, while still nominally attending school each morning. At the age of ten he left school altogether and worked on a farm for six full days a week, from six o'clock in the morning till half past five in the evening, for three shillings a week. A few years later he gave up farm work for gardening, for which he had a passion that was lifelong. When he was in his early twenties he met and fell in love with my mother, Elizabeth Daniels, who was two years his junior.

My mother was the eldest of the twelve children of Thomas and Sophia Daniels and was born in 1868. Thomas Daniels was a son of Daniel Daniels (commonly called 'Double Dan'ls'), a carpenter at Maulden, adjoining Clophill, and followed his father's trade. His wife, Sophia Anderson, was the daughter of a shepherd at Clothall in Hertfordshire. This tiny village, which is seven or eight miles from Stondon, stands high up in the chalk hills to the south of Baldock, surrounded by cornfields. My mother was born there and was christened in the rugged stone font, some eight hundred years old, in which her mother, grandmother, and probably many generations of her ancestors back to the twelfth century had also been christened. She was brought up at Clothall by her grandparents, who were anxious to help their daughter Sophia in her difficult task of rearing her large family, nine of whom survived infancy and ultimately reached old age.

My mother enjoyed her time at the tiny church school at Clothall. Her grandparents, being (like most country people of their generation) illiterate, wanted her to become 'a good scholar', so that she could read to them. For that reason, and also because they were devoted to their grand-daughter, they allowed her to stay at school until what was then (for the children of the poor) the unusual age of fourteen. She would have liked to have become a teacher, but the poverty of her parents and grandparents made that impossible. The result — almost inevitable for a girl of her social class at the time — was that when she left school she drifted into domestic service, becoming a few years later cook at Stondon rectory. There she met my father and became engaged to him. They left Stondon soon afterwards, one after the other, to take employment at Barnet, on the southern border of Hertfordshire, she as a cook, he as a gardener. After working for one or two other people, my father settled down under an employer with whom he stayed for many years. This was a solicitor who had an admirable taste in gardens. My father's working hours were from 7 a.m. to 6 p.m. on six days a week, with two or three hours' work on Sundays and Bank Holidays, and his pay was twenty-four shillings a week. On the strength of this, in 1891 he married Elizabeth Daniels at St Albans, where he had a brother living at the time.

Their marriage was a very happy one, even though husband and wife possessed many dissimilarities, as was obvious at a glance. My father, a rough diamond, had a good brain but cared nothing for appearances and at times even seemed to despise the graces of life. To the end of his days he remained an untutored, dialect-speaking countryman. My mother, on the other hand, who kept her good looks until she died at the age of eighty-two, spoke English as perfectly as she wrote it. When she came to see me from time to time at Cambridge in later years she was assumed, by those who did not know otherwise, to be a university graduate. Her interests were more intellectual than my father's but both were great readers when opportunity allowed. My father liked good fiction and books on travel and natural history. He had read most of the works of Scott, Dickens and Thackeray. My mother preferred history, biography, and works on sociology. She loved music, which he almost hated. Neither of them cared for poetry, which is not surprising, as they had never been trained to appreciate it.

Both my parents were wonderfully quick and hard workers all their lives, and soundly practical. My mother was a first-class housekeeper, equally good at catering for a family on the most meagre allowance, at cooking, at making clothes, and at bringing up children. My father could do anything that was wanted in the house: glazing, carpentry, boot-mending, house-painting, rug-making, furniture-repairing, picture-framing, fruit-bottling, jam-making, wine-making — all seemed to come as easily to him as gardening. In religion my mother was a practising Anglican, but she did not go to church nearly as often as she would have liked, as my father was virtually an agnostic. He was strongly anti-clerical, and his church-going was limited to attending family weddings, funerals, and (if he was unable to escape) christenings. The Anglicanism of all his ancestors in John Bunyan's county, where feeling between church and chapel ran high, was reduced in him to little more than a mistrust of any Nonconformist until he found him trustworthy.

Obviously, it was not from my father that I inherited my lifelong veneration and affection for the Church of England and its services. In later years, indeed, he used to lament that I was 'always stuck in church'. Nor was it from either of my grandfathers, but rather from my mother, from my grandmothers, and from previous generations. I inherited also from all my ancestors that love of the country which the proximity of the insatiable metropolis to my native district has converted into a passion. I inherited my mother's love of music and could say, with W. H. Hudson, that 'like Sir Thomas Browne, I am so sensitive to it that I may be moved to tears by even the common and tavern sort of music.' I inherited from neither of my parents — nor, so far as I have been able to discover, from any of my grandparents — my strongly dramatic temperament or that habit of dramatizing almost every situation which I consider to be one of my outstanding defects. Although I have always been very fond of acting and have even been told that I missed my vocation through not making the stage my career, I cannot act when off a stage, being too emotional to conceal my real feelings — a characteristic which has often proved a disadvantage and a source of embarrassment to me.

Barnet, at the time of my parents' marriage and for long afterwards, was a small, sleepy market town at the top of a hill eleven miles from London on the Great North Road, about 430 feet above sea level, and completely surrounded by fields. Houses now link it on the south with New Barnet and Whetstone, and so with London; yet, even today, it looks across open country to the north, east, and west. During the course of centuries the town had overflowed on the north into the parish of South Mimms. This overflow area, which was known (according to the point of view of the speaker) as Barnet Side, South Mimms, or as Mimms Side, Barnet, was served ecclesiastically from about the middle of the nineteenth century by Christ Church, a daughter of the medieval parish church of St Giles, South Mimms. It did not become a separate ecclesiastical parish until the year 1900, though much the same area was formed into the civil parish of South Mimms Urban soon after my birth. It was here that my parents made their first home, at 33 Bruce Road.

The house consisted of five tiny rooms, two upstairs and three downstairs, the living-room measuring less than ten feet by seven. The rent was seven shillings and sixpence a week — nearly a third of my father's wage of twenty-four shillings. The so-called garden at the back of the house was a mere drying-yard, about thirty feet long. Consequently, in order to grow vegetables and make ends meet, my father was forced to rent an allotment of twenty square poles of ground, about three-quarters of a mile from the house, though we moved nearer to it later. He cultivated it in the evening with the greatest zest until he was ninety (after which he sublet half of it), so that his working day for most of his life lasted until nightfall throughout the year.

It was at 33 Bruce Road that my elder sister was born in 1892, and I on October 24th, 1893.

Soon after my birth I was taken to Christ Church and christened, and in due course began to attend the church day-school for infants. I was by nature left-handed and the teachers allowed me to continue so, except that they forced me to use the right hand for writing. To this day, although I am ambidextrous in many things, I prefer to use the left hand for everything except writing. It is only if I have a broad empty road (or preferably a field) to manoeuvre in that I can perform such feats as mounting or dismounting from a bicycle on the usual side.

I began to attend Sunday school about the same time as day-school. My father, despite his anti-clericalism, approved of this, because I was a noisy talkative child and he was glad to get me out of the way on Sunday afternoons, so that he could read or sleep undisturbed for an hour or two.

A third child of the family, my brother John, was born in 1896 but lived little more than a year. One of my earliest datable memories is hearing the doctor say to my mother, 'I am afraid he is going to die.' I did not know what he meant at the time, but I can still see and hear my mother crying and pleading, 'Oh, don't say that!' A fourth child (a second girl) was born a few months after John's death. By this time we had moved from No. 33 to No. 41 Bruce Road. Our rent was now nine shillings a week, but the new house had a third tiny bedroom over the scullery. That, indeed, was why we had moved. My father's pay was raised some time after this by a whole shilling a week, from twenty-four to twenty-five shillings. My parents thus had some fifteen shillings a week for feeding and clothing themselves and their three children. Impossible though it may seem, they also managed to insure the whole family for some small sum, to pay into a sick-benefit club for my father, and to put by a few pence each week against a rainy day.

Whenever there was any illness in the house I must have been an intolerable nuisance with my chatter, and at such times neighbours would often help my mother by taking me to their homes for an hour or two, or for a walk. Once, when my mother was ill, one of her friends, who belonged to the Plymouth Brethren, took me to the chapel that she habitually attended. The prayers were all extempore, and an elderly bald-headed man who was called on to lead the congregation in prayer went on for a very long time. Apparently he was an expert at praying, because members of the congregation, after the custom of their sect, kept encouraging him with cries of 'Amen! Amen!' To me, however, who knew only the services of the Church of England, the word 'Amen' meant that a prayer was ended. I was therefore delighted with the interjections, taking them as well-deserved hints to the elderly man to stop praying; but, to my astonishment, the more they seemed to ask him to stop the longer he went on, and I thought it very rude of him.

In 1900, when I was six, I was promoted from the infant school to the boys' school. When I consider how congested the building was, and how short of equipment, I am amazed at the good work accomplished by the teachers. There were only seven of them in addition to the headmaster, and there were very nearly 400 boys to teach, packed tight in classes of from fifty to sixty each, with either two or three classes in each room. Individual teaching was therefore clearly impossible, and a good deal of the masters' time had to be devoted to keeping discipline or to hearing the boys recite multiplication tables, word-spellings, or pieces of poetry in chorus, with two classes often competing against each other in one room. The school had no wash-place and only a minute stony playground, in which the boys merely rushed about in a cloud of dust and screamed at the top of their voices during the ten-minute interval that was euphemistically called playtime. Organized games were obviously out of the question in such a confined space, and our only physical exercise was Swedish drill, which I detested, as no doubt the teachers did too.

I also detested religious instruction as laid down by the diocesan authorities, because so much of it consisted of reciting, day after day, week after week, and even year after year, things we already knew backwards. Thus I came to loathe the Catechism and hate the very mention of the Ten Commandments. I hated the Second Psalm, too, and it still seems to me almost incredible that so incomprehensible a composition should have been selected for children to learn by heart. ('Kiss the Son, lest he be angry, and so ye perish from the right way: if his wrath be kindled, yea, but a little, blessed are all they that put their trust in him.') It was fortunate that we had to learn only a few of the Prayer Book collects by heart, because I conceived against those few a prejudice which lasted a very long time. It was many years, for instance, before I came to appreciate the magnificent English of the Collect for Advent Sunday, with its sweeping rhythm, ringing in the church's year as with the blast of a trumpet, rising and falling, echoing and re-echoing.

The teachers at Christ Church were, however, kindly and humane men, who deserved great sympathy in their struggle with obstacles for which they were in no way responsible – the serious lack of equipment, the gross overcrowding, and the noise that inevitably resulted. That they overcame these defects, which were common to most church elementary schools at the time, was in no small measure due to the inspiring leadership of the headmaster, John Brown.

John Brown was one of the most remarkable men I have ever known. Tall, erect, prematurely grey, with strongly marked features and steady eyes, he would have been picked out of a crowd of hundreds by a complete stranger at a first glance as no ordinary man. He was a born teacher and a born organizer, but he was something much more than that: he was a man who was completely devoted to duty – to his school as an institution and to his boys as individuals. They all realized that, without ever being told it. As a result, they extended to him a respect and a fidelity that were lifelong – even those of them whom he found it necessary to punish once, twice, or many times. Many of his pupils did well in life. Whether they did well, moderately, or badly, they came back Christmas after Christmas for what was officially termed an Old Boys' Reunion but was in fact a Society for the Veneration of 'Gaffer', as he was affectionately called. To me, as to so many others, he was an inspiration, and I had the privilege of his close friendship until he died in 1951.

John Brown was a talented musician, being an accomplished pianist and organist and the possessor of a fine baritone voice. In addition to being headmaster of the boys' school, he was for ten years organist and choirmaster at Christ Church. As I had inherited my mother's love of music and possessed a singing voice of the required standard, he had me in his choir from an early age, so that, like the prophet Samuel in the Old Testament, I was brought up to the service of the temple almost from infancy. It was exacting work. In addition to the singing lessons included in the ordinary time-table of the school, we had a choir practice immediately after afternoon school every Monday, Tuesday and Wednesday – sometimes after morning school as well; and on Wednesday evenings, after attending service in church, we stayed behind to practise with the men. We sang both from ordinary notation and from sol-fa, and were taught to translate the former into the latter at sight.

I enjoyed singing in the choir at Christ Church but never acquired the least liking for its services. They had too much of the solemn and over-earnest atmosphere of old-fashioned Evangelicalism to appeal to my temperament. Although it was a daughter of St Giles's, South Mimms, it was the reverse of being *matre pulchra filia pulchrior*; for whereas the mother church was well known for the beauty of its interior decoration and its services, the daughter was almost as plain and bare as the church of primitive Christianity must have been; and I, who from a very early age have felt a great love for 'the beautiful things that will never grow old', found nothing in Christ Church to satisfy my longings.

My membership of the choir nevertheless instilled into me a knowledge of the liturgy of the Church of England which grew into a love for it in later years. The Anglican Communion to me, as an American convert expresses it, 'represents Christianity in its most rational, most Catholic, and most beautiful form.' Sceptical though I have been at times about some of the articles of the Christian faith, the church has never failed to hold and fascinate me. There is nothing for which I am more profoundly thankful than I am for having been born in the Church of England and trained to her service from boyhood.

One of my difficulties in early boyhood was to get books to read. The day-school possessed no library – not a single book that could be borrowed – nor was there a public library for children within miles. It is true that the Sunday School possessed a small lending library, but it seemed to consist mostly of such nauseating works as *Jessica's First Prayer*. Fortunately, my father managed – I do not know how – to buy second-hand copies of some of the usual boys' books of the time, by such writers as Henty, Kingston, and Ballantyne. I read these with much pleasure, graduating from them a few years later to Scott, of whose novels my father possessed almost a complete set. He had bought them second-hand in his single days, at threepence a volume, recovering them with cloth cut from the covers of his father's discarded pattern-books. He also possessed Anne Pratt's two charming little illustrated volumes on English wild flowers, which I read with avidity. They were the first of a long series of books read in the course of my life on wild flowers, trees, and country life in general — subjects which absorbed me more and more as time went on and culminated in a devotion to the works of four writers of whom I can never tire — John Clare, Richard Jefferies, W. H. Hudson, and Edward Thomas.

Nothing, however, would induce me to read a book of a very different kind, which I had noticed in the family bookcase from the time I first learned to read. Its title frightened me: *Dead Man's Rock, a Romance*, by Q, and I did not dare to open it. Something of that feeling survived in me for years, even when I had grown up, so that *Dead Man's Rock*, Sir Arthur Quiller-Couch's first novel, was one of the last of his numerous works that I ever read. It naturally did not occur to me in childhood to wonder who 'Q' was, but I did wonder how a man could have a name consisting of a single letter.

3

Although there were no television or wireless sets in those days, and few books and no gramophones for the poor, we boys did not lack entertainment. There was, for instance, the market every Wednesday, with its lowing cattle, squealing pigs, and bleating sheep, bringing with it a chance that some obstinate animal would break away from the herd when being driven out of the market, take a wrong turning, and cause an exciting chase. There was the forge where we could stand and admire the blacksmith's skill while he mended our iron hoops. There were the long processions of heavily laden haycarts moving slowly up the Mimms road by twilight, on their way to Covent Garden, each with its driver apparently asleep on his little slung seat but in fact quietly encouraging the attendant greyhound to reconnoitre for a rabbit or a hare. There were Parliamentary elections, with a chance of two rowdy open-air meetings in one day, because Chipping Barnet and South Mimms Urban were in different constituencies. There were the barrack-square concerts and church parades of the 7th (Militia) battalion of the King's Royal Rifle Corps, which had its headquarters at Barnet. During the hunting season there were occasional meets of the Enfield Chase Staghounds in the market place. The hunt kennels were at Old Fold Farm, just outside the town, and now and then I would walk out to them with one of my school friends, Tim Turner, whose father was huntsman. During the Boer War there were big bonfires on Hadley Green to celebrate the relief of Ladysmith and Mafeking, and volunteers returning from the War would be lifted into cabs at the railway station and man-hauled through streets lined with cheering crowds. Early in 1901 Queen Victoria died and the new king, Edward VII, was seriously ill at the very time fixed for his coronation. I remember a woman who lived near us saying one day 'What I say is, "Let the Queen go to the Abbey to be crowned, and let the Archbishop go to the King and crown him in his bed".' Her advice, if proffered to the right quarter, was not taken and the delayed coronation was performed in the usual way in 1902, with more bonfires and the singing of

Oh! on Coronation Day,
When they give the beer away.

Now and then, often quite unexpectedly, a circus procession would delight us by parading the streets with its caged lions and tigers, stately elephants, and grumpy camels; or a German band or a one-man band would play round the streets; or an Italian would appear with a hand-organ and a monkey; or a man with a poor chained bear, which he would sometimes reward for dancing by giving it a drink of beer from his tankard; or Walford Barnard, 'the finest dentist in England', would extract teeth free of charge on a van in the market-place; or 'Sequah, the cripples' friend', wearing cowboy dress, would extol the virtues of his medicine, compounded of 'snakes' heggs and 'edge'og ile'. Every First of April we tried to make fools of everyone we met. On Whit Mondays we watched long processions of Boys' Brigades from London march from the railway station to Wrotham Park, the Earl of Straf-ford's seat, just outside the town. Every July we piled pieces of broken tile into a circular wall a few inches high, decorated it with nasturtium flowers, put a lighted candle inside it at dusk, and asked passers-by to 'remember the grotto.'

By far the greatest entertainment of the year, however, for all the children for miles round, was Barnet Fair, held early in September for three days and one of the biggest fairs in the kingdom. It was held on the London side of the town, on the slopes of Barnet Hill − the horse and cattle fair on the east side of the main road, the pleasure fair on the west of it.

The camp-followers of the fair extended their operations right into the town, in which no house was left unvisited by gipsies trying to sell clothes pegs and other small articles, and no public house was without 'nigger' minstrels singing and twanging banjos and guitars outside the door for a considerable part of the day. All the way from Barnet parish church to the fair, the main road was lined on both sides with pavement artists, with vendors of noisy toys for children, ash walking-sticks for men going to the horse fair, 'ticklers' and bags of confetti for both sexes, and with stalls selling winkles, cockles, mussels, and whelks, over all of which viands the eaters shook vinegar liberally out of a bottle with a hole bored in the cork. At every street corner there was a performance being given by a conjuror, a weight-lifter, a contortionist, a swallower of swords, watches, and tin-tacks wrapped in blotting-paper, or an expert at escaping from knotted ropes. When the 'rope king' had been apparently well trussed up by someone in the crowd (usually a confederate), his assistant would go round the ring of spec-tators with a collecting-tin, announcing that the performer would stay as he was, with the ropes cutting into his flesh, until a certain amount of money had been subscribed. If the money was slow in coming in, the performer would try to go white and blue in the face, exclaiming in an agonized voice, 'For God's sake, ladies and gentlemen, don't keep me waiting much longer.' Meanwhile, the Salvation Army band, which seemed to be on duty all day during the fair, would go blaring and banging by, and would stop at the next corner to do a little 'Gospel grinding', as my father called it.

Hundreds of sheep and cattle were brought to the fair, a few donkeys, and thousands of horses. The horses were brought from all over the British Isles and the dealers seemed to come nearly as far, Welshmen being particularly noticeable. For the mere spectator, a great part of the fun consisted of seeing the horses being ridden up and down by prospective buyers, or rearing up into the air when red flags tied to long sticks were flapped in front of their eyes by dealers, or racing across the fair-ground at tremendous speed harnessed to a trap, and sending the onlookers flying in all directions.

Much pleasure could also be got by studying the hangers-on of the horse fair. There was, for instance, the three-card trickster, who arranged his cards on an open umbrella, so that he could shut up shop in a fraction of a second if a police constable came in sight. There was the philanthropist who sold what looked like gold watches for ridiculous sums, 'just to advertise'. There was the other philanthropist who sold for half-a-crown a piece of crumpled paper into which he appeared to have thrown three half-crowns only a second before; and there was the vendor of jellied eels, which seemed to be the staple food of so many visitors to the horse fair. He took the greatest pride in his eels. He would watch a customer devouring them and exclaim, 'They're grand, ain't they, mate?' and the customer would spit the bones to a distance and grunt 'Ah.' When he had gone, the jellied-eel man (if anyone was watching him) would dip the empty cup into a can of water which was probably changed every day and would refill it without wiping it, in readiness for the next customer.

The pleasure fair came into its own after dark, when thousands of flaring naphtha lamps were hung along its streets of stalls selling fried fish, rock, and trinkets of every kind; when the long row of coconut shies was doing a roaring trade; when the steam-driven organs on the roundabouts and switchbacks were competing against each other with simultaneous renderings of *Ta-ra-ra-boom-de-ay, Dolly Gray, Bluebell, Where did you get that hat?, Skylark,* and *Soldiers of the King,* and when 'Professor Elliott', standing on the platform outside his booth with his team of brawny boxers, nearly burst himself blowing a big trumpet to attract attention, and then proceeded to challenge anyone in the crowd to stand up to his champions for more than a single round. There was always someone in the crowd who answered the Professor with insulting remarks about his 'lot of rabbits', assuring him that he would pulverize any of them in less than no time. The innocents in the crowd thereupon paid their money and swarmed inside, hoping to see bloodshed, only to find that the bellicose 'stranger' was merely a docile member of the Professor's troupe after all.

There were numerous rivals to the boxing booths, ranging from such small fry as the performing love-birds, the pony that could count, the five-legged pig (guaranteed to be alive), the pigmy couple, and the fattest woman in the world ('doctors and nurses admitted free') to big shows like Biddall's Mexican knife-throwers. Most of these performances were displaced for some years by cinema shows – called 'bioscopes' then – but when permanent 'picture palaces' were established all over the country the knife-throwers and their colleagues came back into their own at the fair. There were many other things to see – the helter-skelters, for instance, the swings, the cake-walk (good for the liver), the shooting-galleries, and innumerable games of skill and chance, with pieces of tawdry china for prizes. There were also the beggars, among them a blind organ-grinder who stood in the gutter under the railway bridge, playing the same four or five tunes year after year on a little box-organ. All but one of the tunes were well known; but that one, sweet and plaintive, I could not recognize. I feel sure that it occurs in some Italian opera; but, although I have heard many Italian operas since then, I have not yet succeeded in identifying it. I hope that I may do so some day, for the tune haunts me still, as does the face of the blind man who played it.

After Barnet Fair was ended and the conker season had gone by, the next event of importance in the children's calendar was November 5th, when we made guys, lighted small bonfires, and let off fireworks if we could get them, or big matches with coloured flames, called 'harbour lights', if we could not. At Christmas we went carol-singing from door to door. Then, if the weather was severe, we saw the year out with tobogganing on toboggans made from old boxes.

That was the time of year when the pinch was most keenly felt in Bruce Road. It was a completely working-class road, most respectable and industrious; but many of the men followed seasonal occupations, like house-painting and brick-laying. They were consequently out of work for a great part of the year, particularly in winter; and there was no unemployment pay in those days. Our own family, with a bread-winner in constant employment (provided he kept well), was in comfortable circumstances compared with some of the others; but even we rarely tasted milk except in tea – and it was, of course, always separated milk. How some of the other families managed to get through the winter I cannot imagine. Even in summer, many of the children had nothing but bread and dripping, or bread and lard, for dinner. In winter it was plain bread, with a little help once or twice a week from the charity soup-kitchen.

One of my ineffaceable memories of winters in the early years of this century is of long columns of unemployed men, marching four abreast through the streets with haggard faces behind a drum-and-fife band. Whenever I hear a member of the middle-class delivering one of the easy speeches that comfort comfortable men, and declaring – as I have even heard some of the best among them thoughtlessly declare – that what the working classes want is a dose of unemployment to make them work, my mind goes back to those sad processions. Then I in-voluntarily clench my fists, and I see red.

In the autumn of 1904 we left Bruce Road for 16 Puller Road. This was another completely working-class street, running straight downhill into the fields in the direction of South Mimms village.

Our new home had the same number of rooms (three up, three down) as the old one, but they were bigger. There was also a con-siderably bigger garden, some of which was still left for cultivation after my father had built a greenhouse on it, and taken over a coal-shed and a hen-house and a run from the previous occupier. The rent was ten shillings and sixpence (ultimately fifteen shillings) a week. My father's pay was raised to twenty-five shillings about the same time, becoming twenty-seven and sixpence some time before 1914 and thirty shillings during the war. On the other hand, my mother's eldest brother came to live with us for a year or two, and by the time he left us my elder sister was earning a little, having left school at the age of thirteen. For some years she worked in a local factory from eight o'clock in the morning until nominally six (but normally until eight) on five days a week, and from eight to two o'clock on Saturdays; yet she managed in her spare time to become a very proficient pianist. After the war of 1914 she became a maternity nurse and married a few years later.

We had been living in the new house only a few months when the fifth and last child of the family, a boy, was born. I well remember the family discussion about what he was to be called. Being eleven years old, I naturally had a number of suggestions to make, all of which I thought were good; but I was silenced with the remark (not new to me) that small boys should be seen and not heard. The discussion ended with a decision to call the baby Frank. As none of our family had a second Christian name, I at once realized the disadvantage that would accrue to myself later in life from being one of two brothers named F. Brittain; but, having been rebuked already, I did not dare say anything. Some weeks after the christening, a visitor, on learning the baby's name, said, 'But won't it be awkward for the two brothers, when they have grown up, to be both F. Brittain? Won't it be confusing?' – 'Yes,' I burst in, 'it will, and I thought of that at the time.' Whereupon – such is human injustice – those who had silenced me on the previous occasion turned to me and demanded, 'Then why didn't you say so?' Many years later, for a jest, I started to spell my Christian name with two small ffs. This became so generally accepted that a pupil once called on me in distress and with profuse apologies for (as he thought) incorrectly addressing a letter to me in which he had spelt Frederick with a single F.

It was very soon after our move into the new house that I began to take an interest in Hertfordshire. My interest was much stimulated through reading a little book by H. R. Wilton Hall, who lived at St Albans and came over to teach at Christ Church School for some months, travelling backwards and forwards by train every day. He was a charming man and a real scholar, and he befriended me until he died. I still treasure a copy of his *Hertfordshire: a Reading-Book of the County*, as he modestly called it, which by good fortune we used at school and which I came to know almost by heart. Long since out of print, it gives an admirably succinct and attractive account of Hertford-shire, and no subsequent book has ever equalled it as a brief intro-duction to the topography and history of the county. Wilton Hall obviously knew and loved his Hertfordshire, and he and his book certainly planted a love for it in me. I studied his map of the county avidly, until I could draw its very irregular boundary from memory and insert the courses of its eighteen little streams, together with their charming, thoroughly English names, mostly monosyllabic: Lea, Mimram, Beane, Rib, Quin, Ash, and Stort; Colne, Ver, Gade, Bul-bourn, and Chess; Brent; Ivel, Hiz, Oughton, and Pirrell; and the Cam, which has its beautiful source at Ashwell, on the Cambridgeshire border.

In my childhood we of course could not afford ever to go away for a paying holiday, but I often stayed with relations in Hertfordshire and Bedfordshire. Sometimes I went to Clothall, which my mother naturally revisited from time to time to see the grandparents who had brought her up and to visit other relations and old friends after her grandparents had died. One of my chief interests there was listening to the local dialect. I was delighted to hear it still spoken undiluted by some of the older inhabitants when I revisited Clothall many years later. That was during the winter of 1940-41, when my mother, seeking some respite from the frequent air-raids at home, was staying in the village temporarily with her sister. There was a hard frost one morning, and I overheard a brief exchange of comments between two farm-labourers, one of whom was my uncle by marriage. 'That's coold enew t' flee ye',' said one. 'Ah! that's frore proper shaarp,' the other answered.

I also stayed occasionally during my boyhood at the little Hertfordshire town of Hemel Hempstead, to which my mother's parents had moved from Maulden in Bedfordshire. I like the ancient borough, with its tiny River Gade and its Norman parish church. I was taken to the church on Sundays; for the Danielses, like the Brittains, were all Anglicans, even though there were many members of both families who supported the church only from the outside — buttresses rather than pillars of the church, as Lord Melbourne described himself. I remember staying at Hempstead once or twice with my grandparents and once with my mother's sister Anne, and her husband, Harry Floyd. He was a corn-chandler and kept a pet piglet which followed him about like a dog.

I never got to know my maternal grandparents well, as they died while I was still quite young; but I knew most of my mother's brothers and sisters very well. Her two younger brothers, Henry and George, made their mark in very different careers. Henry had a very clear vocation to holy orders but was unable to gratify it in England, for financial reasons. He therefore emigrated to Canada and the United States, saved enough money at farm work to enter a theological college, was ordained in the American Episcopalian Church, and ultimately became Bishop of Montana.

His brother George, who had a good business head, went into the service of the Pearl Assurance Company and rose to be a divisional manager. During the early part of his career he lived for a few years at St Albans, where I often stayed with him. On Sundays he used to take me with him to services in the Abbey, thus introducing me to cathedral music and to the grandeur and beauty of a building which I was to haunt later in life. No other cathedral ever supplanted St Albans in my affection, and Ely alone came to rival it. Once when I was staying with him at St Albans he took me to the County Hall Theatre to see my first professional play. It was a wonderful melodrama, called *Her Love against the World*. The actor who played the villain was so good at his part that every time he appeared on the stage he was hissed loud and long; whereupon one of the attendants in the auditorium, apparently thinking that the actor might feel hurt, protested loudly to the audience, 'It's all in the play. It's all in the play.'

The place to which I went most often for my summer holiday, however, was the village of Stondon, where I stayed with my paternal grandparents.

I came to know Stondon and its inhabitants well, and soon achieved proficiency in the Bedfordshire dialect — a proficiency that I have never lost. Most of the men and boys in the village, including two of my uncles and a number of my cousins, were farm labourers, and their life was hard. They worked from six in the morning till half past five on six days a week, including all Bank Holidays except Christmas Day and Boxing Day, and they had no other holidays. Even though the rent of their bare gaunt cottages was often no more than two shillings a week, that represented one fifth of their pay, which stayed at ten shillings a week right down to the 1914 war. In harvest time they worked from four in the morning till eight at night. For this they received double pay, but it was swallowed immediately by the annual rent and the buying of essential clothing to last them till the next harvest. Apart from this harvest pay there were no extras of any kind, whether of money, food, or drink; and in wet weather at any time of the year the men were 'stood off' without pay. I noticed that few of them possessed overcoats: they had nothing better than old sacks to keep out the weather. Farm labourers and their children seldom tasted meat, except for their Sunday dinner.

4

The Education Act of 1902, important in many ways, took the first step towards bringing secondary education within the reach of working-class children. It empowered local authorities to grant a few scholarships each year to enable boys and girls to go from elementary schools to secondary schools. I was an early beneficiary under the Act. In the summer of 1906, after a written examination at Barnet and an oral examination at Hatfield, I was awarded a Hertfordshire County Scholarship to Queen Elizabeth's Grammar School, Barnet. I entered it in September the same year and spent five most happy years there.

The school, which had been founded in 1573, possessed some agreeable old buildings as well as some less attractive modern ones. The ivy-clad Hall, where we assembled every morning for prayers, and the ceiling of which was supported by a long disused whipping-post, was the original school building. The pleasant library was added early in the seventeenth century. It was reached from the Hall by a spiral staircase, and its walls were covered with wistaria. The spaciousness and quiet of the school and its big playground, with a mulberry tree in the middle of it, were most striking after the overcrowding at Christ Church School, with its nearly 400 boys.

Although, less than twenty years before, the Grammar School had had 160 boys on its roll, there were now only 70. (If the ratio of boys to buildings and playground had been as high as at Christ Church there would have been 700 or 800.) All but six of the boys paid small fees and were the sons of local tradesmen, superior clerks, or small professional or business men. The six scholarship boys included Alec Randall, afterwards British Ambassador to Denmark and the Vatican, who was my senior by a year or so and very kind to me. We received free education, plus a grant of £5 a year, without which my parents could not have kept me at school as long as they did. The school was divided vertically into six Forms and horizontally into four Houses, named after worthies connected with its history. These were Underne, Rector of Barnet at the time when the school was founded; Leicester, the earl who obtained the school charter from Queen Elizabeth; Stapylton, a prominent nineteenth-century Governor; and Broughton, an Old Elizabethan who in 1836 became the first bishop in Australia. I was in the House named after him. We were one of the first day-schools in the country to adopt the House system, which proved a great asset to our corporate life.

The headmaster, William Lattimer, who entered the school in the same term as myself, was a mathematical graduate of Clare College, Cambridge, and came to Barnet from Brighton College, where he had been an assistant master. He was wonderfully neat and tidy in his personal appearance, his speech, his handwriting, and his methods of teaching and administration. I have never known so remarkable a disciplinarian: he kept perfect order without the slightest effort. Some of his assistants were very far from being his equals in that respect, but one silent look from 'Old Bill', as we called him, was enough for any boy. He seldom punished except for laziness or what he sometimes mistook for laziness; and, although he did not abolish corporal punishment, he spared the rod without spoiling the child. Extra work out of school hours was his usual form of punishment and was the only one that he allowed his assistants to inflict.

There was no bullying in the school and little snobbery, though there was one master who would occasionally sneer at a scholarship boy before the whole class, addressing him as 'You who do not even pay your own fees,' as though the possession of money were a virtue. Another master, in order to express his contempt for one of my classmates (who happened to be a fee-payer) told him one day that he possessed the mentality of a domestic servant. The boy resented this as an insult, and a heated argument took place between him and the master. I thought of my mother; and to this day I feel ashamed at not having had the courage to rise from my seat, denounce master and boy as a pair of cads and walk out of the room.

Games were compulsory at Barnet Grammar School; and on our two weekly half-holidays, which were on Wednesday and Saturday, we were expected to play Association football in winter – the school had not yet gone over to Rugby – and cricket in summer, or to watch school matches if we were not selected for a team. Never having played a game in my life, I took up football with trepidation. I soon came to enjoy it, but was never a good enough player to be on anything better than the fringe of the first eleven. I was also fond of cross-country running – down the fields to Fold Farm and Knightsland, splashing through the brook at Dyrham Park, and back again. On the other hand, I have always been hopeless at any game played with a small ball: my eye cannot follow it quickly enough to make me even a passable player; and

C

so, to escape being a laughing-stock on the cricket field (as I felt I was certain to be) I became the score-keeper. I enjoyed the occupation and was even considered a benefactor to the cricket club, as I was one of the few boys who could bother to keep a bowling analysis correctly. Occasionally I played fives (a much more secluded game than cricket) with my bosom friends, Tom Guyatt and Kenneth Williams: they always beat me 15–0, or 15–1 at best, except when they deliberately gave points away.

When I entered the Grammar School I had to start to learn French and Latin from behind scratch, so to speak. On the other hand, the high level of John Brown's teaching in two other subjects was at once apparent; for although I was classed with boys older than myself I had to mark time for over a year at algebra, and at singing I marked time (or rather went backward) for the whole five years that I spent at the school. At Christ Church, where no boy stayed after he was fourteen, there had been a high standard of voice-training and three-part singing. At the Grammar School, where boys might stay until they were eighteen, there was no voice-training at all, and nothing but the ragged shouting of simple national songs in unison – what is now called 'community singing'.

I was placed in the third Form to start with. Here we were taught French by the new 'direct' method, with the aid of *Dent's First French Book*, which we all disliked. We learned our Latin (with the old pronunciation) from Kennedy's *Latin Primer*, supplemented by other works. After two terms I was promoted to the fourth Form, in which I spent only one term. My second year was therefore passed in the fifth Form, in which we began the study of German, though we were unfortunately allowed to drop it three years later. (I have, however, continued to use German script all my life, finding it convenient as a sort of mild cypher for diaries and private notes.)

During my second year at the school, my Form read Caesar's *Gallic Wars* with Mr Lattimer, who (not illogically) tackled any Latin text as though it were a mathematical problem. It was about this time that our new reforming headmaster made the whole school change over to the new reformed Classical pronunciation of Latin. The change was inevitable and right, but it caused consternation to our somewhat elderly and very conservative Latin master, G. W. N. Harrison, and bewildered those of us who had already started to learn Latin with the old pronunciation.

Although I had worked through two Forms in one year, I was by no means a model pupil. I was too talkative and exuberant to be that – so much so that G. W. N. Harrison (whom we loved and referred to as 'Hoggy') sometimes ejected me from his class as 'an intolerable nuisance'; and W. A. Freeman, the English master, once refused to have me in his class for a whole fortnight. On all such occasions I went to the school library and read. The result was that, being separated from my cronies, I did much more work than if I had stayed in the classroom. It has since occurred to me that 'Hoggy' and 'Waff' knew quite well what they were doing when they ejected me from their classes.

'Hoggy', like the eponymous hero of Ernest Raymond's *Mr Olim*, was fond of calling us by derogatory names, though he meant no harm by them. 'Cowboy', 'ploughboy', 'potboy', 'guttersnipe', and 'East Ender' were among his favourite names for us; and I remember his saying to one boy, 'Now, you vulgar bounder, get up on your hind legs and tell me what reasons we have for believing that St Matthew wrote his gospel for Jewish readers.' He used what might be called visual aids to the teaching of good manners. Once, for instance, when a boy addressed him with a pencil in his mouth, Hoggy picked a big book from his desk, thrust one corner of it into his wide-open mouth, and made inarticulate noises. Then, putting the book down, he said, 'I talks to you as 'ow your manners is.' The demonstration was effective.

In addition to being a nuisance, I was also lazy at times. For a whole term, I did no work whatever at Divinity, which we were supposed to prepare during the week-end. During that particular term, we were examined in it at nine o'clock on Monday mornings by the headmaster himself. At the end of the hour he read out the marks, and I scored nil out of twenty every week, unless now and then I scored a mark or two from general knowledge. The headmaster said nothing; but I knew, from the grim way in which he looked at me, that he was waiting for me to come out bottom in the examination in Religious Knowledge at the end of the term. This would have seriously affected my position in the Form list for the term; and 'Old Bill' knew, as well as I did, that trouble would ensue for me at home. I was determined to disappoint him. Accordingly, during the fortnight or so before the examinations, I got up early every morning and started to concentrate on Religious Knowledge at 4 a.m. In particular, I learned the headmaster's admirable cyclostyled notes on the Second Book of Kings and the Gospel of St Luke practically by heart. The result was that I did very well indeed in the examination and kept my place in the Form list easily. I cordially (though of course secretly) agreed with 'Old Bill's' terminal report:

'Religious Knowledge. He did better in the examination than his term's work had led one to expect.'

In my third year at the school (1908-9), when I was in the lower sixth Form, I began to show a propensity for acting; also a literary bent, as was revealed by my becoming the founder, proprietor, and editor of a periodical (published at irregular intervals) called *Hogwash*. I need hardly say that it circulated only in manuscript and was written in inks of several different colours. A term or two later it was renamed and became less satirical. When this important paper came to an end I started a third manuscript periodical which was much more sober and elevated than its predecessors; but it was equally short-lived. We possessed a school magazine, *The Elizabethan*, but it was edited by one of the masters and, being severely annalistic, had hitherto published nothing by boys. I therefore felt that I had achieved something when, in my last year at school, I appeared in print for the first time in my life, with an article on the Waverley Novels published in *The Elizabethan*.

Literary composition, and indeed homework of any kind, was not easy for me during my school days, partly because I had no room to myself, partly because my little brother inevitably made a great deal of noise in the house, and partly because the bricklayer who lived next door was very fond indeed of playing a concertina. He was particularly trying in the winter, as he was out of work most of the time, and – poor man! – played his concertina for long hours to keep his spirits up. The day came when he and his family were turned out into the street for non-payment of rent, and when my little brother wept, imagining that we were going to be evicted too. The next occupiers of the house had a lodger, a shop-assistant, who was learning to play the cornet. It sounded very doleful, but we heard much less of it than we had heard of the concertina, because the shop-assistant was at work from 7.30 a.m. to 8 p.m. on Mondays, Tuesdays, and Wednesdays, from 7.30 to 2 o'clock on Thursdays, from 7.30 a.m. to 9 or 10 p.m. on Fridays, and from 7.30 a.m. to 11 p.m. or midnight on Saturdays. Still, he was as free as the air for the rest of the time. Yet he did not seem to appreciate this freedom, for he spent a considerable part of his small amount of spare time trying to organize a local branch of the Shop-Assistants' Union, which asserted that the lot of shop-assistants was capable of improvement. Those were the good old days of Free Enterprise.

One of our near neighbours was Philip Robinson, who had a small grocer's shop at the corner of Puller Road. Although I never knew him to go inside any place of worship until he was involuntarily taken to church for his funeral, he was an ardent supporter of the Church of England and its close ally, the Conservative Party. Liberal Nonconformists were consequently his pet aversion and he never attempted to hide his feelings, even at the risk of losing custom. When boys were going home from school they took a natural and almost daily delight in knocking down a pile of empty orange boxes which stood outside his shop door awaiting buyers of firewood. Philip's reaction to this jest was always the same. He knew the boys must be of Nonconformist parentage. 'There they go again,' he would exclaim, 'those damned chapel-going kids. They've no respect at all for property. They're not taught it in their chapels.' After the great Liberal victory of 1906 he became, in one respect, Addison's fox-hunting Tory in real life, for he blamed all subsequent bad weather on to his political opponents. If any of his customers complained about excessive rain or snow he would say, courteously but frankly, 'Can you be surprised, sir? It's the judgement of the Almighty on the nation for returning a Liberal Government to power. That will be two-and-ninepence. Thank you, sir. Yes, sir, the judgement of the Almighty. Good morning!'

Philip Robinson's son, Vincent, who was his only child, had been very severely brought up but was as generous as his father was miserly. He helped in the shop and, although he was now a grown man, was treated as if he were still a boy. Being of an artistic temperament, and hating trade, he gave his spare time to painting but had to practise the art secretly, as his father considered it a waste of time. He kept specimens of his work in his pocket or in a safe corner of the shop, among the innumerable packing-cases with which it was almost completely blocked. If Philip was out with a bucket, collecting horse-dung for his garden, Vincent used to show some of his pictures proudly to selected customers; but if he saw or heard his father returning they were whipped out of sight instantly and he began to talk about either the weather or the iniquities of the Liberal Party, both of which were approved subjects of conversation. When I grew older, he used to arrange for me to meet him when he was on his way to the *White Lion* to fetch his father's supper-beer. That was the only outing he was allowed, except to go to church on Sundays, and he liked to spend his few moments of freedom reciting passages of Tennyson or Matthew Arnold to me in his hoarse voice. Our friendship lasted until his death half a century later.

5

When I entered Barnet Grammar School at the age of twelve I was beginning to take a great interest in the surrounding country and its inhabitants. I think it was in my first year at the school that an older friend of mine, who had just become a very junior clerk in a Barnet solicitor's office, invited me to walk with him to South Mimms Vicarage one evening, in order to deliver a summons on the Vicar, the Rev. Allen Hay. I had often heard his name mentioned, generally with strong disapproval — sometimes for his High Church practices, at other times for alleged offences that would be shocking even in a layman. The summons was probably for nothing more serious than failure to pay a dog licence within the prescribed time, but to me a summons was a summons and therefore a dreadful thing.

It was accordingly with feelings compounded of curiosity and horror that I accompanied my friend on what was to become the most familiar stretch of all roads in the world to me. We did not see a car all the way, or any other vehicle except an occasional hay waggon or a pony and trap.

When we called at the Vicarage we were told that the Vicar was taking a choir practice in church. We waited for him in the churchyard and in a few minutes he came out, wearing cassock and biretta. He was a tall, finely built man, about forty years old, and even at my age I could tell that he was handsome. He was not at all the monster I had expected to see, and I even thought there was a twinkle in his eye. He read the summons, it seemed to me, with suitable gravity, thanked my friend for taking it, and wished us a genial good-night. I came away feeling that he could not be as black as he was painted; but I had, naturally, no idea that my life was afterwards to be closely linked with his until his death nearly fifty years later.

I did not see Allen Hay again, as far as I can remember, for another two or three years; but meanwhile I was exploring, more and more thoroughly and farther afield as time went on, the undulating country between Barnet and Ridge Hill, with its farms whose very names will always be sweet symphonies to me: Old Fold, Kits End, Knightsland; Valentines, Dancers Hill, Bridgefoot; Deeves Hall, Summerswood, Rabley, and many others, with their meadows and cornfields large and small, hedged with blackthorn, hawthorn, and bramble, and with an elm, an oak, a hornbeam, or an ash rising from the hedgerow here and there.

I was enamoured above all of Mimms Wood, which spread its two or three square miles of elm, oak, hornbeam, beech, ash, birch, cherry, pine and larch over Ridge Hill in the shape of a great swallow-tailed butterfly. To me, as to Richard Jefferies, 'the Immortals are hiding somewhere still in the woods'; and I can add, with him, 'even now I do not weary searching for them.' I explored Mimms Wood at all hours of the day and often after dark, in every month of the year and in all weathers, sometimes with friends, but generally wandering alone for hours, dodging the gamekeepers in boyhood, making friends of them in later years. I found the sweet-scented spurge laurel flowering while it was still winter; I watched the larches breaking into 'not foliage, but emerald fires' in early spring; I spent hours walking among the wind-swept anemones; I found the corner where wild daffodils grew; and one day in May, when I was still quite young, I saw for the first time the astonishing unearthly beauty of a great carpet of bluebells stretched 'like a sky-lit water' under the beech trees. For a long while I stood there, gazing at them as though spellbound; happy, and yet at times afraid, half expecting a spirit to appear; and then I felt a physical pain as I realized that all this beauty must soon die. I came back to the bluebells day after day that spring; and in after years, when I had to be away for the greater part of the year, I tried to get to Mimms Wood at least once a year in bluebell time if I possibly could.

One day, soon after my first sight of the bluebells, I felt that I must go to the very top of Ridge Hill, which was a little farther on, in order to see what lay on the other side. I found what proved to be the ideal viewpoint — a bare open field just above the *Waggon and Horses* inn. The field adjoins the main road but rises higher and gives a far wider view than can be got from the highway. I walked excitedly up the bare slope, with only the sky above it, until suddenly a grand panorama appeared over the top. It was the landscape of which I had caught mysterious isolated glimpses now and then from a more distant view-point ever since early childhood; and I gazed at it for a long time, as silent as Cortez upon his peak in Darien.

I find that view as delightful and as absorbing now as on the day when I first discovered it. In front spreads the broad valley of the Colne. On a hill five miles away — not, as C. E. Montague says in his *The Right Place*, 'just spied on the horizon' — rises St Albans, its vast cathedral dominating the whole scene. Round it are grouped the wooded hills, the little green river valleys, and the 'fruitful fields of pleasant Hartfordshire'. In the background, a dozen miles or more beyond St Albans, one can see the dim outline of the Dunstable Downs and other high points in the Chilterns along the meandering Hertford-shire-Bedfordshire border.

I have often spent hours on end drinking in that scene, yet turning round every few minutes to study the far less extensive but (to me at least) equally absorbing landscape to the south. Here the view extends only five miles, being limited by the high ridge which carries Barnet and Hadley and shuts London, 'the great wen', out of the picture; but it displays the whole of the parish of South Mimms, with its cornfields, meadows and farms, and its parish church rising above the village street down below, in the middle of the scene. One might be a hundred miles from London, instead of within sight of its outskirts.

'There are places,' says Hudson, 'as there are faces, which draw the soul, and with which, in a little while, one becomes strangely intimate.' That strange intimacy has long existed between the field at the top of Ridge Hill and myself. It is when I am there that I realize, perhaps more than anywhere else, how deeply, how unreasonably, how desperately the clay of this pit whence I was wrought yearns to its fellow-clay in me.

I must have been to that field hundreds of times since my first visit, and I have nearly always gone alone. If it is a year when the field is given up to grazing I often have the company of a flock of sheep. They get used to me after a few days and stand staring intently at me from a few yards away while we carry on an inaudible conversation. Sometimes, instead of sheep, there are cattle in the field. One afternoon, when I was sitting on the grass, a bullock came running up to me from the herd, slackened its pace as it came nearer and nearer, and finally pressed its muzzle against my nose several times. Another came up, apparently with the intention of doing the same thing, but the first bullock pushed it away, glared at it as though saying, 'This two-legged creature is my property', and repeated the nose-pressing process.

Before I had been to the top of Ridge Hill many times I stopped one day on my way there and went into the village church at South Mimms for the first time. I stayed there a long while, because I found so much to see. The building was small, but it was full of interesting things and resplendent with colour, and all its ornamentation reflected the admirable taste of Allen Hay. What struck the eye first was the carved wooden screen between the nave and the chancel, with a crucifix standing over it. To the left, separating a side chapel from both the chancel and the north aisle, were medieval screens carved with the leopard's head of the Frowykes — the leading family of South Mimms in the Middle Ages, whose canopied tombs and memorial brasses were to be seen in various parts of the church. I studied the high altar, with its six tall candles, its flowers, and the three twinkling red lamps hanging from the roof in front of it; the banners standing round the chancel walls; the side altar with pictures painted on its panels; the mural tablets, one of which had a carving of a human skull as its chief ornament; the remains of the medieval glass in the aisle windows; the Norman font; and the coloured pictures of the fourteen Stations of the Cross hanging all round the walls of nave and aisle. The church fascinated me so much that I resolved to go to a service there as soon as possible.

Accordingly, one Sunday in July I walked down the St Albans road, between fields where the new-mown hay lay in long swathes and the unripe wheat was a lovely bluish green, to Evensong at St Giles's. There I entered a new and dazzling world of beauty — not natural beauty this time, but man-made loveliness. It seemed almost too beautiful to be real. The church, viewed from my seat at the west end of the nave, seemed to come to life, and I revelled in every detail of the service. It struck so many of the strongest chords of my being simultaneously — the aesthetic, the dramatic, the musical, the literary, the historical, the religious. A brilliant evening sun poured through the west window on to the carved screens, the dresses of the congregation, and the monuments. It lit up the nameless medieval tomb in the sanctuary and made the flames of the six altar candles turn pale and ghostly. It shone on the black-cassocked members of the choir as they sang motionless in the chancel, on the red-cassocked acolytes as they moved about the sanctuary to light even more candles, and on the clouds of sweet-smelling incense-smoke, redolent to me of another world, which poured out of the censer at the *Magnificat*.

Except for two or three hymns sung later in the service to modern tunes, all the music was plainsong, and it moved me profoundly, as plainsong has done ever since, with its atmosphere that is at the same time of the medieval world and yet not of this world at all. It was the Dedication Festival, and I envied the men and boys of the choir as they sang with such obvious enjoyment the hauntingly beautiful and yet utterly simple words of the Prayer Book version of the Eighty-fourth Psalm:

O how amiable are thy dwellings: thou Lord of hosts.
My soul hath a desire and longing to enter into the courts of the
Lord: my heart and my flesh rejoice in the living God.

After the Second Lesson there was a baptism. In preparation for it,
John Gerken, the churchwarden, tossed kneeling-pads to the christening
party as they came to their places at the font, while Allen Hay, pre-
ceded by a cross-bearer and two small bare-footed acolytes holding
candles, came slowly down the nave to the singing of a hymn. The
baptism was very much a family affair, all the congregation turning
round to face the font while it was being performed and taking the
liveliest interest in it. At the end of it, the procession went back to the
chancel singing the *Nunc Dimittis*. A sermon came later, and the service
ended with a procession down the north aisle and up the nave, the
servers carrying the banners of St Giles, St Alban, and Our Lady, and
Allen Hay bringing up the rear in his white cope,

> While clouds of incense mounting veiled the rood,
> That glimmered like a pine-tree dimly viewed
> Through Alpine vapours.

When I came out of the church that evening I knew that I would
rather attend service there than in any other parish church as long as I
lived at home — and the thought that I might ever live away from home
had not then entered my mind. I have travelled much since then and
acquired many new interests; but from that day to this the church of St
Giles, South Mimms, has been the Gate of Heaven to me. After all these
years, it seems as beautiful to me now as on the day I first entered it.

Thus I became and have ever since remained a member of the congregation of a village church — a privilege which has always been a great
delight to me. I am by heredity and by nature 'a villager with the village
outlook', as Hudson said of himself, and I threw myself whole-
heartedly into the life of South Mimms village, socially as well as
ecclesiastically.

6

In my fourth year at Queen Elizabeth's School I was made a sub-librarian — a pleasant office, as it had few duties and gave me the run of the school library. It enabled me to read fairly widely in English literature and also gave me a room in which I could read and write in comfort and quiet for an hour or so after school.

I nearly had to leave school in the summer of 1910, because my parents, for all their skill and self-denial, were finding it practically impossible to make ends meet. Fortunately for me, a beneficent Governor of the school, Mr F. A. Milne, offered scholarships to enable two boys to stay a year longer at school, and I was awarded one of them. I was thus enabled to stay for a fifth year, to read Horace's *Odes* and *Epodes* with G. W. N. Harrison, to acquit myself well in the Oxford Senior Local Examinations, and to finish as head boy of the school, with a copy of Q's *Oxford Book of English Verse* (which I had much coveted) as a prize. It is clear to me now that Mr Milne's generosity made a turning-point in my life, and that without it my subsequent career would in all probability have been very different.

Nevertheless, when I left school in 1911 my prospects were narrow. I had a great desire to go to a University, preferably Oxford or Cambridge, but that was financially impossible. The two old universities were still beyond the reach of working-class boys, because such scholarships as were available did not meet the whole cost by any means. The talk which still circulates about the 'numerous poor boys' who had gone to Oxford and Cambridge in past centuries is humbug. Those so-called poor boys were members of the middle-class — sons of parsons and other professional men who could at least keep them during vacations. They were poor merely by comparison with the wealthy Fellow Commoners. A study of any of the ten volumes of the *Alumni Cantabrigienses*, which give brief biographies of all men who entered Cambridge University between its foundation and the year 1900, will soon convince anyone that the number of working-class boys who managed to get there before the beginning of the twentieth century was almost negligible. The few who went were geniuses or near-geniuses with private patrons. It was the Education Act of 1902 that began the process of bringing Oxford and Cambridge within the reach of the working-class, but by 1911 the process had not gone very far.

Even London University was out of the question for me financially. My parents and I therefore decided that I should become a school-teacher, but even a two-year course at a day training-college was impossible, for the same reason. I therefore became a student-teacher at Christ Church School for a year, during which the Hertfordshire County Council paid me the sum of £20, on which I managed to live. At the end of the year I became an assistant master at Christ Church, at a salary (if I remember rightly) of £70 a year.

I liked teaching, and I believe the boys liked me. Yet these three years are the part of my life to which I look back with least pleasure. The only part of my work that I really enjoyed was teaching history by means of short plays which I wrote for the boys to act, and taking them for rambles, as I was occasionally allowed to do in lieu of the abominable Swedish drill. On these pleasant outings I taught them the names of trees and wild flowers and let them swim in the stream at Mimms Wash.

My two great consolations at this time were closely interwoven with each other. One was 'the beautiful and deathstruck year' of nature. The other was the liturgical beauty of the services at St Giles's, where,

>   in set career,
> As through a zodiac, moved the ritual year.

From the quiet of Advent, when the bare trees and fields seemed to harmonize so well with the liturgy of the season, we moved on to Christmas, when the church was decked with berried holly, ivy, yew, and laurels brought from Dyrham Park. We loved the Midnight Mass, the gaily decorated crib, the carols, and the evening office hymn, 'From east to west, from shore to shore', with its plainsong running up and down the scale in a glorious riot of melody.

Soon after Christmas came Candlemas, when the Vicar blessed candles, which we lighted and carried in procession round the church, singing 'All prophets hail thee' to the charming Bayeux melody in the *English Hymnal.*

In Lent flowers were banned from the church, but hedgerows were all silver and gold with blackthorn, willow-catkins, coltsfoot, and celandine. After Evensong every Friday until Easter we performed the Stations of the Cross − a simple service that has never lost its appeal to my simple mind − singing the *Stabat mater* as we moved slowly round the cold church from picture to picture, 'from pain to pain, from woe to woe'. Palm Sunday morning brought the blessing of palms. We went

down the north aisle of the church carrying palm branches, out into the
churchyard by the south door, with the wind billowing our surplices
out like sails, and came back through the west door singing 'All glory,
laud, and honour'.

On the following Wednesday, Thursday, and Friday evenings we sang
the lengthy office of *Tenebrae* unaccompanied. The service consists, for
the most part, of a wonderful anthology of Hebrew poetry, selected in
past centuries for use in Holy Week; but from the time when Latin
became a dead language *Tenebrae* had been incomprehensible to
ordinary people for a thousand years. The unknown 'Ritualists' who
introduced it into Anglican churches in vernacular dress about the
middle of the nineteenth century did a greater work than has yet been
recognized, for *Tenebrae* in the English of the Prayer Book and the
Authorized Version of the Bible is, no less than *Tenebrae* in the Latin
of St Jerome, a literary and liturgical masterpiece.

The little band of us who sang *Tenebrae* at South Mimms every Holy
Week for over forty years certainly loved it. We did not weary of the
fifteen psalms which we sang each evening from Coverdale's superb
version:

Thou has laid me in the lowest pit;
In a place of darkness, and in the deep.

The Lessons from the Book of Lamentations acquired new pathos when
sung to a sorrowful melody instead of being read in a spoken voice:

Is it nothing to you, all ye that pass by?
Behold, and see if there be any sorrow like unto my sorrow.

The Old Testament canticles, too, sprang to life when sung. One
evening it was the triumphant Song of Moses:

With the blast of thy nostrils the waters were gathered together,
The floods stood upright as an heap,
And the depths were congealed in the heart of the sea.

Another evening it was the magnificent Song of Habakkuk:

The deep uttered his voice,
And lifted up his hands on high.
The sun and moon stood still in their habitation:
At the light of thine arrows they went,
And the shining of thy glittering spear.

Finally, we sang the *Miserere* in a darkened church, the candles and
lamps having been put out one by one during the singing of the psalms

and the *Benedictus*, and we made our way down the nave and out into the churchyard by the light of a solitary candle brought out from its hiding-place behind the altar.

The brief flowers and white vestments of Maundy Thursday were followed by the unveiling of the cross and the three hours' service in a naked church on Good Friday. On Easter Eve we worked all day polishing brass, bringing out every available candle and banner and vase of flowers; and in the evening we gathered in the porch in the mysterious spring twilight for the blessing of the new fire and groped our way up the dark nave to the chancel for the lighting of the Paschal Candle. Candle and candlestick together reached a good twelve feet from the floor, but only the top eighteen inches of the so-called candle were genuine. The rest was a curtain pole, round the top of which our ingenious sacristan had nailed a piece of tin to hold the real candle, and had painted the whole thing white. We held our breath during the difficult business of lighting the candle from a taper stuck in the end of a split cane, which in its turn fitted into the hollow end of a long bamboo pole. We breathed again as soon as we saw that the Paschal Candle, after several vain attempts to light it, was really burning.

After the elaborate ceremonies of Holy Week came the climax of Easter, with its profusion of daffodils, its cloth-of-gold vestments, its processions, and its triumphant music. A few weeks later came Rogation Sunday, when we went in procession round the fields singing the Litany, and the Vicar blessed the green corn. Close upon it, when

> Bluebells hid all the ruts in the copse,
> The elm seeds lay in the road like hops,

came Whitsun and its Golden Sequence. Early in July, before all the sweet-smelling hay had been carted, we kept our well-loved Dedication Festival.

On the 1st of September, when the leaves were beginning to turn colour, we kept the feast of our patron, St Giles, the Provençal hermit. Early in October, when the trees were aflame with scarlet and gold, we held our Harvest .Thanksgiving, and the church was full of farming people. We jocularly called it the Feast of St Mangold and All Wurzels, but loved it all the same. Close upon it came All Saints' Day, when we changed all the white hangings and vestments swiftly to black immediately after Evensong and stayed to sing Vespers of the Dead; then All Souls' Day and its requiems, with which the November landscape seemed so thoroughly in keeping, and very soon after that we were back again in Advent.

Allen Hay was naturally the central figure in this liturgical round, and yet he often forgot his part. It would be more correct to say that he never bothered to learn it and that he merely muddled through. I found before long that, although no one else was allowed to prompt him, I was permitted to do so. He and his wife had taken a liking to me from the first. South Mimms Vicarage soon became my second home and remained so until he died.

It had taken me very little time to discover that he was completely innocent of the serious charges which scandal-mongers had levelled against him, though they took years to die. He had his faults, of course, being human, but they were all very much on the surface. At times he infuriated even his best friends with his casualness, his thoughtlessness, his lack of tact, and his autocratic ways. Yet, as even one of his critics expressed it, he could charm a bird off a tree. His personality was so striking that he had been one of the best-known clerics for miles round ever since he went to South Mimms in 1898, and as time went on he became also one of the best liked. His style of churchmanship and his unconventional ways offended some, yet he influenced men and women whom no other cleric appeared able to reach. He had a wonderful bearing in church and possessed a fine clear voice, both in reading and in intoning. He excelled as an officiant at those services which bring a parish priest into most direct and intimate touch with homely people – christenings, weddings, and funerals. The pleasure that he derived from officiating at a wedding was delightful to see. He revelled in it: no matter how often he performed the ceremony, he always seemed to enjoy it quite as much as the bride and more than the bridegroom.

Allen Hay owed more than he ever admitted or realized to his verger and sacrist, Frederick Roland White, who had worked under him for some years in the East London parish of Plaistow and went to South Mimms with him. Frederick White was a born Levite, though the Vicar treated him rather as one of the Nethinim. He was a watch-maker by trade, but his heart was entirely in the church and its services and after he settled at South Mimms the watch-making existed in little more than name. It was a mystery how he managed to exist on the miserable pittance that he received from the church. Yet he was always happy, perfectly happy, because he had found his vocation as surely as any man who ever lived. Most of his time was spent in church, but he went home to eat and sleep, and made frequent journeys to the general shop to fetch paraffin for the lamps. He was consequently a familiar sight in the village street, with an overcoat and scarf over his cassock, a mildewed bowler hat crowning his white hair, and often an oil-can in his hand. He was so tall and thin that the choirboys called him 'Old Darner,' from his fancied resemblance to a darning needle. Yet the boys, like their elders, including the toughest non-churchgoers in the parish, all loved and revered him, so gentle was he in voice, in features, in every movement that he made, and above all in his dealings with others.

Frederick White was a mine of information on ecclesiastical matters, and I must have spent hundreds of hours with him in the vestry, learning from him and helping him in his work. Under his efficient and kindly training I very soon learned to move about the church completely at my ease, whether I was acolyte, chorister, altar server, cross-bearer, thurifer, or lesson-reader. Later, I became cantor, and also ceremoniarius whenever such an official was necessary – at big festivals, for instance, and throughout the elaborate ceremonies of Holy Week. Allen Hay liked to perform all these in full, but never remembered what to do next. I had to try to read his mind and anticipate his omissions, additions, or innovations, which he would sometimes introduce without the least warning, regardless of the printed text in front of him and of any consultations or agreements before the service.

We sang some hymns to plainsong, others to modern tunes. All the rest of our music – psalms, canticles, Masses – was plainsong. On Sunday mornings we used J. B. Croft's *Plainsong Masses*, the music of which was from post-medieval French sources – corrupt from the Solesmian point of view but undeniably tuneful and beloved by both choir and congregation. We sang the service antiphonally throughout, the two cantors' voices alternating, phrase by phrase, with those of the rest of the choir and the congregation. Evensong was also sung antiphonally, from Ravenshaw and Rockstro's *Ferial Psalter*, which dated from as far back as 1869 and could therefore hardly be expected to be technically correct throughout. It must nevertheless be accounted one of the most tuneful of all plainsong psalters, free from the boring monotony of some of the more correct rivals that have supplanted it in Anglican usage.

Our hymn book at all services was the *English Hymnal*, at that time a blithe newcomer into hymnody – decidedly suspect as a High Church product, and used in no other church for miles round. It was stamped with the thoroughly English Christian Socialism and liberal Anglo-Catholicism of its chief compiler, Percy Dearmer; and behind him, despite the book's reaction against Victorianism in so many ways, there loomed the gigantic shadow of John Mason Neale, the Victorian with the 'almost incredibly medieval cast of mind'.

Consequently, the *English Hymnal*, while characteristically Edwardian in its inclusion of numerous folk-tunes and its 'Mass and maypole' atmosphere, was at the same time the most thoroughly medievalized of all English hymn books that have ever been in common use. It provided translations of the medieval sequences and office hymns for all the seasons and festivals of the ecclesiastical year, including minor saints' days, and fitted them to their medieval tunes. Many of them were provided with alternative tunes from French 'church melodies' of the sixteenth and seventeenth centuries — coeval, that is, with J. B. Croft's Masses. These hymn tunes, although sometimes condemned by musical purists as bastard plainsong, provide in fact a most attractive half-way house between plainchant and modern music. They introduced a new and delightful lilt into English hymnody, especially when coupled with words written in the Sapphic metre, as in the office hymn for Michaelmas, *Christ, the fair glory of the holy angels*, which must haunt anyone who has heard it sung even once to the delightful Rouen melody with which it is coupled in the *English Hymnal*. The musical excellence of the book led to its gradual adoption in place after place, until it pervaded the Church of England; and, wherever it went, it subtly introduced the atmosphere and principles of High Anglicanism. No other book has ever done so much for the High Church cause.

Before the war of 1914-18 Evensong was choral every day of the year at South Mimms, and even on week-days there was a full choir of boys and a few men's voices. Although I have never been pious or devout — I am too fond of the world and the flesh to be that — I found the services so delightful, and Allen Hay's personality so irresistible, that I sang in the choir about five evenings a week until I left home in the autumn of 1914. From the cultural point of view, if from no other, I benefited greatly — first and foremost, perhaps, because I came to know the Prayer Book psalter almost by heart. It became, so to speak, part of me, and has remained so. It strikes me more and more as unsurpassed in the whole range of English literature for beauty and simplicity of language: the psalter in the Authorized Version is halting and prosaic by comparison.

Since we sang the ancient office hymns daily at Evensong, I also came to know by heart all the medieval hymns and their plainsong

D

melodies in the *English Hymnal* and could have sung most of them with my eyes shut. We sang, too, the medieval sequences which were a great feature of the book, including such enchanting compositions as the Advent Sequence and the Rosy Sequence, which are not heard outside the Anglican Communion nowadays, and in few churches even there. I can definitely date from this time the beginning − and a soundly practical beginning − of that love for the Middle Ages and medieval literature which was to be my chief academic pursuit in after years.

Life at South Mimms, however, was far from being all serious, for Allen Hay possessed a mercurial temperament and a strong and irrepressible sense of humour, which sometimes asserted itself even in church. It was still more apparent in the parish magazine which he started and edited, and in which we revelled, though it did not run for long. It was more like a school or college magazine than a parish paper. Sometimes the misprints in it, which were generally due to the editor's illegible handwriting − he had not yet taken to a typewriter − gave us unpremeditated pleasure, as when an intended reference to 'the feast of Corpus Christi' appeared as 'the feast of Cooper's Charities'. More often, it was the answers to imaginary correspondents that pleased us, such as this:

Concertina. − The Choir. They do their best. What more can they do?

or this:

Joe Burridge. − No. Insects are not burnt in this church, and never have been, unless by accident a poor fly or moth has got into a lamp. Perhaps you mean incense. If so, yes; but then we are Bible Christians. See Malachi i.11.

In addition to my numerous appearances at church, I continued to explore every field, copse, and lane in the parish, because from boyhood I have been, as one of my oldest friends puts it, 'Mimms mad'; and I entered with zest into the social life of the village. It centred on the parish hall, where there were periodic social evenings and dances, which I thoroughly enjoyed. Those were the days immediately before the introduction of jazz, when English dances, even if many of them were artificial commercialized products, were at least varied, and sociable. Quadrilles were almost out of fashion, but we still did the Lancers and such simple dances as the polka and the barn dance, supplementing them with the veleta and similar dances, a number of which seemed to be invented every year. The music, if it was not great, was at least lively and tuneful — very different from the monotonous moan that has usurped the name and function of dance music ever since the First World War. There were also classes in folk dancing, which I attended regularly, finding it good exercise and good fun if not taken too seriously.

Sometimes the parish hall, which had a small but effective stage, was transformed into a theatre, in which I performed in comedies like *Found in a Four-wheeler* and such old favourites as *The Area Belle*. At other times I wrote sketches of my own and produced them on the same stage. Later, I appeared there in my favourite role — as a pantomime dame.

7

In the days before the First World War we used to hold a church procession through South Mimms village once every summer, generally on a Saturday afternoon. We started from the school, which had been built at the top of the hill, at the very end of the village, so that it could serve the parish of Ridge as well as South Mimms. From the school we made our way through the village street to the church, sang Evensong there, and then went back to the school and dispersed. Once the procession was held at the beginning of August, to celebrate Lammas – so at least the Patriarch (as some of us called our Vicar) told us, but it was really held then because the Bank Holiday week-end was a convenient time for holding it. Once (because he forgot to hold it earlier) it was held at the beginning of September, in honour of St Giles, the patron of the parish; but it was usually held at the beginning of July as part of our Dedication Festival.

When the day arrived, those of us who were free were kept busy all the morning carrying from the church to the school everything that would be needed in the afternoon – cassocks, surplices, hymn books, copes, banners, candles, processional lanterns and crosses, censers, incense and charcoal. We arranged all these articles in the big schoolroom, with its ink-stained desks, its scrubbed floor, and its big coloured engraving which the suspicious old Mrs Trotter of Dyrham Park, always on the look-out for popery, once denounced as a portrait of the Pope; but it was in fact a copy of Bellini's well-known portrait of Doge Loredano of Venice.

In the afternoon everyone began to assemble at the school – men and women, boys and girls. Among them came Percy Penketh and Arthur Sherbourne from the Lower Village, Reg Bishop from the School House, the six Tracy boys and girls from St Giles's Avenue, the big family of the Picketts, and the numerous Powells from the Upper Village. Leslie, the eldest Powell, kept all his younger brothers in order with no trouble at all, just as he kept everybody in order at Chipping Barnet parish church when he became verger there in after years. (Members of that congregation used to say, 'Our Rector is Leslie Powell's right-hand man'.)

While we were getting ready in the schoolroom there was a good deal of confusion and a certain amount of noise. Half-muffled cries of 'Who's pinched my cassock?' were mingled with 'I do wish this candle wouldn't gutter', 'Look! the Vicar's burnt his cassock again', 'This lamp glass is cracked already', 'Olive Williams has got her hair in plaits, just like Faith and Phyllis Tracy', 'Why won't this wretched charcoal light?' 'Somebody's torn two pages out of my hymn book', and 'Get off my big toe!'

At last we were all ready — the men and boys in cassock and surplice, the women in their big picture hats, the girls in their white veils, the Patriarch resplendent in his cope and taking his last pinch of snuff before the procession. A complete hush fell as we filed out of the hot, stuffy schoolroom into the quiet village street — so quiet, because there were no buses within miles of us then, very few cars, and hardly ever an aeroplane. The air was full of the scent of new-mown hay, and the only sound to break the silence was the whirr of a mowing-machine as it ran along the meadow next to the school, and its click-click as it turned the corners. The wheat, full-grown and soon to be 'yellowing to the sheaf', stretched behind the hayfields to the top of Ridge Hill in a gently swaying sea of burnished blue-green. The sun shone brilliantly on it, and on the gaily-coloured banners and vestments;

> And in the perfect blue the clouds uncurled,
>   Like the first gods before they made the world
> And misery, swimming the stormless sea
>   In beauty and in divine gaiety.

When we were all correctly marshalled in pairs, with the censers and processional cross in front, the banners placed at proper intervals and the Patriarch bringing up the rear with his small barefooted acolytes, we began to move at a slow pace. Our first hymn was nearly always that naive but beautiful sixteenth century poem,

> Jerusalem, my happy home,
>   When shall I come to thee?
> When shall my sorrows have an end?
>   Thy joys when shall I see?

most appropriate to summer and to a Dedication Festival, and doubly so to a procession, being twenty-six verses in length. We sang it to the sweet plaintive tune by Staniforth, who has since been relegated to the appendix of the *English Hymnal* as a mere Victorian. It was remarkable how many verses of the hymn fitted particular scenes as we moved slowly through the village — the cottage, for instance, where a whole family was being wiped out by consumption:

In thee no sickness may be seen,
    No hurt, no ache, no sore;
In thee there is no dread of death,
    But life for evermore.

One verse seemed to be aimed at the more rickety cottages, difficult
to keep clean, and fit only for demolition:

Thy houses are of ivory,
    Thy windows crystal clear;
Thy tiles are made of beaten gold –
    O God, that I were there!

another at the occasional motor-car, filling our eyes, noses, and ears
with a great cloud of dust as it rushed rudely by us in those pre-tarmac
days:

Within thy gates no thing doth come
    That is not passing clean;
No spider's web, no dirt, no dust,
    No filth may there be seen.

Yet another verse fitted the roses, delphiniums, Canterbury bells and
sweet-williams in the front gardens of Rose Cottage, Ivy Cottage and
Rose View:

Thy gardens and thy gallant walks
    Continually are green;
There grow such sweet and pleasant flowers
    As nowhere else are seen;

and as we passed the Post Office and General Store, with old Mr Hollis
visible through the window, we used to hope that it would be our good
fortune to be singing just then

There cinnamon, there sugar grows,
    There nard and balm abound;
What tongue can tell or heart conceive
    The joys that there are found?

From 'Jerusalem, my happy home' we often went on to Sabine
Baring-Gould's equally beautiful and almost equally naive hymn on the
same theme:

Daily, daily sing the praises
    Of the city God hath made:
In the beauteous fields of Eden
    Its foundation-stones are laid.

How well this simple hymn suited the occasion, too! Our nostrils were full of the smell of incense wafted from the front of the procession as we sang:

> In the midst of that dear city
>   Christ is reigning on his seat,
> And the angels swing their censers
>   In a ring about his feet;

and when we reached the lime trees, resonant with the hum of myriads of bees visiting the honey-scented, honey-coloured, honey-laden flowers, we might be singing:

> There the wind is sweetly fragrant
>   And is laden with the song
> Of the seraphs and the elders
>   And the great redeeméd throng.

Yes, the procession was very enjoyable and very beautiful, but it had two drawbacks. One was the difficulty, even with the aid of a cornet or two, of keeping the voices together and of keeping them in tune, particularly if (as usually happened) the procession was made a long one by reinforcements from other parishes. The other drawback was that sometimes stalwart Protestants calling themselves Kensit's Wycliffe Preachers, if they heard that a procession was taking place, would come down from London and stand along the village street, distributing tracts and shouting, as we went by, 'A mockery of religion!' or 'Candles to light the Light of the World!' or (most often) 'No popery!'

We could not afford to hire a band, but one year the Patriarch had a sudden inspiration: he wrote to the head of the Salvation Army, General Bramwell Booth, who was a friend of his, asking if he could lend him a band for the procession. The General, if he knew what kind of procession it was to be, must have been rather startled at the request. Nevertheless, being a kind man, he decided to do what he could and called for volunteers from among his adherents. A few days later about a dozen uniformed bandsmen, with all the necessary music neatly copied out, came down to play in the procession.

It so happened that the Kensitites had chosen that particular occasion to make one of their periodical demonstrations. They accordingly took up their positions in the village street, armed with tracts; but they were astonished when, mingled with thurifers, cross-bearers, candle-bearers, banner-bearers, coped priests, and white-veiled girls holding banner-streamers in one hand and bunches of flowers in the other, there came a Salvation Army band, half-hidden in a haze of incense and playing John Keble's hymn

Ave Maria, Blessed maid,
Lily of Eden's fragrant shade.

At the sound of this, and at the sight, in such a setting, of the Salvationists' blue and red uniforms (which must have reeked of incense for weeks afterwards), the Kensitites were struck dumb and forgot to distribute their tracts.

So the Patriarch, who had set out to remove one of the two obstacles to a completely successful procession, accidentally removed the other also; or *was* it an accident?

8

It is a good many years now since Mrs Williams died at South Mimms, but I have never forgotten the night before her funeral. I well remember going with the rest of the choir to her house late in the evening and escorting her coffin to the church, where it was to stay until the burial next morning. I remember the Vicar suggesting — and his suggestions were practically commands to us — that her friends should keep watch over the coffin all night. If we took an hour each in turn, he said, it would be no hardship to anybody.

Now Mrs Williams had been kind and hospitable to me on many occasions and I felt in duty bound to take a turn in watching. I did not relish the prospect of being alone with a corpse in church at night, even for a few minutes, much less for a whole hour; and I remember hoping that my offer to take part in the watch would be refused. It was, however, accepted; and the prospect became even more unpleasant when I found that the hour allotted to me was from two o'clock to three. If it had been, say, from twelve o'clock to one, I should at least have had a chance of hearing a few living beings going up and down the village street now and then. That would have been some consolation to me; but between two o'clock and three there was no prospect even of such intermittent and unseen companionship as that. What made things even worse was that the night was very dark: there was no moon at all and the stars were blotted out by thick clouds.

A little before two o'clock I groped my way along the churchyard wall, and I entered the church just as the clock struck the hour. Our verger and parish clerk, Frederick White, had been watching since one o'clock. He was a man who lived for his work and generally stayed in the church much longer than was needed. I hoped that this time he would stay a whole hour; but to my regret he went into the vestry at once to get his hat, ignored the appealing look which I threw at him, and in less than two minutes the church door clanged behind him. The air was perfectly still at the time and I could hear him feeling his way out of the porch in the pitch darkness. I hoped that even now he would change his mind and come back; but he was soon out of the churchyard and into the street. The sound of his footsteps grew fainter and fainter and died away, and I was left all alone with the still-unburied dead and with the buried dead of nearly a thousand years.

I took up a position in a pew at the west end of the nave, between the tower and the main door, so that I could get out of the church quickly if need arose. The coffin rested on two stools just outside the chancel screen and was covered with a black pall. On each side of it stood three tall black wooden candlesticks, with big khaki-coloured candles burning in them. There was no other light in the church, except the tiny, almost negligible glimmer of the sanctuary lamps hanging from the chancel roof.

Even though nothing unpleasant had happened so far, I felt very uneasy in my loneliness. I tried to reassure myself by arguing, as the superstitious will, that the best way to keep the unpleasant at a distance was to keep everything (myself included) as it was; and so I sat perfectly still. For some time I kept my eyes fixed on the coffin, not daring to move even them; but after a while I felt safe enough to glance round the church, as far as I could do so without moving my head.

Here and there, in those parts of the building which were not blacked out in the great shadows thrown by the pillars, I could see monuments of every shape and kind — small and large, ancient and modern, artistic and inartistic, of stone, metal and wood, and with inscriptions in English, Latin and Old French; but it was the monument nearest to the coffin which interested me most. It was fixed to the south wall of the nave and its chief feature was a carving of a human skull, with an inscription underneath. I could not keep my eyes off it for long. From where I sat I could not read a word of the inscription, but I knew it by heart and it kept running through my head:

Yonge or oulde, look on. Why turn awaye thyne eyne?
This is no stranger's face: the phesnamey is thyne.

I repeated it to myself hundreds of times:

Yonge or oulde, look on . . .

and the candle-light shone on that horrible grinning skull and made its eyeless sockets glow with a ghastly gleam.

Every now and then the utter silence of the church was broken by faint noises, and whenever this happened I felt my flesh creep. Once there was a louder noise, which alarmed me greatly. I imagined for a moment that the woman in the coffin was not really dead, that she was regaining consciousness and beating at the coffin lid. Then, to my relief, I realized that the noise was caused by a movement of my own which had made the pew creak.

I had hardly settled down again when I heard a muttering behind
me, coming from the tower. Expecting to feel a skinny hand laid on my
shoulder at any moment, I dared not look round. The muttering grew
louder and louder. It turned to a rending, rattling sound. Was Thomas
Frowyke breaking out of his fourteenth century grave in the tower? I
could think of no other explanation. The rattle turned to a roar and to
a crash. I knew what it meant then; almost at once the clock struck the
quarter and I was calm again.

For the next quarter of an hour there was complete silence in the
church. I stared fascinated at the skull on the monument, while the
lugubrious

Yonge or oulde, look on . . .

repeated itself hundreds of times silently and maddeningly in my head.
Then, just after the clock struck the half-hour, I heard a slow, musical
wailing sound, repeated over and over again at short intervals:

Where had I heard that before? I soon remembered: it was the
opening notes of an antiphon which we had sung in the church when
we brought the coffin there in the evening. Yes, there it was again,
mingled with the accursed

Yonge or oulde, look on . . .

At first I tried to believe that what I could hear was merely a light
wind moaning, but I was very soon convinced that it was no wind, but
ghostly voices singing in the churchyard. I could hear the whole antiphon now; and before long, when the melody had been repeated some
dozens of times, I imagined that I could even distinguish the words:

and all the time the skull seemed to be muttering

Yonge or oulde, look on. Why turn awaye thyne eyne?

I had often — whenever I heard the 120th psalm sung — wondered where Mesech was. I realized now. Clearly it was the place of exile; the ghosts of the hundreds of men and women buried in the churchyard were complaining because they had not been given graves and monuments inside the church, but had been left outside.

The voices were terrifying enough, but there soon came something worse — the sound of footsteps moving up the churchyard path, footsteps so light that they could not be human. I heard them coming nearer and nearer along the side of the church. I trembled all over when I heard them stop just outside the porch. The voices had ceased now, and I broke into a cold sweat when the dreadful silence was broken by the sound of unearthly footsteps feeling their way through the church porch to the door. My teeth chattered when I heard a hand feeling all over the door to find the handle. Whose ghost could it be? Roger Ludford, slain on the football field in Queen Elizabeth's reign? One of the hundred or more Londoners who fled from the Great Plague only to find a nameless grave in our churchyard? William Ward, the highwayman, shot at Mimms Wash in the eighteenth century? Thomas Nicholson, who fell dead in our pulpit one Whit Sunday in Victorian times? I should soon know, for the searching hand in the porch had found the door handle and was turning it.

The other doors of the church were locked: there was no way out for me. I dragged myself to my feet, and with my knees knocking together I clutched the back of the pew in front of me and turned to the door to face my fate. The door opened. As it turned squeaking on its hinges the skull on the monument seemed to be screaming aloud at me:

Yonge or oulde, look on. Why turn awaye thyne eyne?

Then a face appeared at the door; but, to my inexpressible relief, it was the face of the living, not of the dead. Not understanding why lights should be burning in the church at this unusual hour, the constable on night duty had decided to peep in to see if all was well. He was wearing rubber-soled boots. In a few seconds he had gone, and I sat down again. The tense feeling had left me, and the rest of my watch was uneventful. From time to time I still heard snatches of the melody of *Woe is me that I am constrained to dwell with Mesech*, but there were no words to it now, and I felt sure that it was merely the wind moaning. I am inclined to believe that the medieval composer of that melody was deliberately trying to set the sound of a wind to music. Perhaps he composed it at night, watching beside a corpse in church.

9

It was about the time I left school that I became a convinced Socialist. It was not reading or listening to political talk, or anyone's personal influence, that decided my politics, but my own reflection and above all my observation of human life.

As far as I knew, every one of my relations was a Conservative. The Church of England, too, to which I have given my whole-hearted allegiance all my life, could at that time almost have been called the Conservative party in its Sunday clothes. Yet my observation told me that something was radically wrong with things as they were. Why, I asked myself, should my ancestors have been helots for generations? Why should most of my relations in Bedfordshire and Hertfordshire still be so? Why should my parents – honest, abstemious, hard-working, and intellectually gifted – be condemned to live just above the poverty line? Why should clever boys at the elementary school where I taught be deprived of a secondary education, while other boys of much inferior ability were able to go to the Grammar School just because their fathers possessed more money? Why should many of the inhabitants of South Mimms be living in squalid hovels? Why should some of the village children go barefoot during a great part of the year? Why should the church be packed on Christmas Eve with mothers bringing every child they could muster or borrow in order to get as many free loaves as possible from the Bradshaw charity? Why, at the very same time, should the so-called county families in the neighbourhood be living in luxury and magnificence and yet (apparently without even finding it necessary to thrust their tongues into their cheeks) simultaneously exhorting the poor to remember that duties come before rights?

All this sort of thing revolted me. It was clear that no adequate change could be expected from the Conservative party, for it was run by the 'county' families; and if it was true to its name it existed to keep things as they were, or at least to change them as slowly as possible. Improvement was much more likely to come from the new and struggling Labour Party, most of whose representatives in Parliament had been through the mill of poverty themselves. They alone among political leaders knew from experience where the shoe pinched, and I threw in my lot with them. It has stayed with them ever since. I have never read Karl Marx, or felt the need to read him. Socialism is to me the logical outcome of Christianity. I am sometimes told that the Conservatives now accept practically everything for which the Socialists used to clamour when I was a boy. It is indeed so; and it has been interesting to see how the Conservatives have all along, after an interval of time, caught the Socialists bathing and walked off with the very clothes which they used to revile them for wearing.

By this time I knew parts of Hertfordshire and South Bedfordshire well, as I had possessed a second-hand bicycle ever since 1910. I often cycled to St Albans and lingered round the Abbey, or wandered along the tiny River Ver, returning by the winding Fishpool Street, which must be one of the most charming streets in England. Then I would take tea with Wilton Hall at his house or go with him to St Saviour's church, of which he was the sacristan. My uncle George had now left St Albans for Luton, and I often stayed with him there during the school holidays, exploring the surrounding Bedfordshire villages by cycle and visiting my grandparents and other relations.

Until 1914, however, I had never been outside the three counties of Hertfordshire, Middlesex, and Bedfordshire, except for a day each at Southend and Littlehampton and a fortnight's convalescence at Bognor, during which I had made an excursion to Chichester. I was therefore delighted when one of my fellow-teachers, whose home was at Cambridge, invited me to spend the Whitsun holiday of a week or more with him there.

It was a wonderful holiday for me. I wandered, as in a dream, through many of the colleges, along the Backs, and up the Castle mound. I bought books at David's stall on Market Hill and called on my old school friend, Kenneth Williams, who was now an undergraduate at Trinity College. One day we went by train across the seemingly endless level of the Fens, with their straight willow-fringed roads and broad fields of black stoneless earth, to Ely; and the mighty cathedral, drawing nearer and nearer out of the distance, and rising superbly under the vast unbroken arch of the fenland sky, seemed to ride the sea of billowing green corn like a huge ship at anchor. We walked round the outside of the cathedral, then inside, and admired the curious tomb, carved with cocks' heads, of one of the bishops of Ely, John Alcock, who had founded Jesus College — one of the colleges which I failed to visit at Cambridge, because it stood somewhat away from the others.

That Whit Sunday at Cambridge I went, as in private duty bound, to

St Giles's church in the morning, and in the evening to St Clement's, to hear a sermon by the Vicar, the celebrated Canonist and Anglo-Catholic champion E. G. Wood, under whom Allen Hay himself had sat in his undergraduate days nearly thirty years before. In the afternoon I went to Evensong in King's College Chapel. I hardly dared enter so wonderful a building, with its fan-vaulted stone roof, its walls of glittering medieval glass, its beautiful carved organ-screen and canopied armorial stalls, and its world-famous music. Dr Mann was at the organ, and the choir sang Samuel Sebastian Wesley's immortal anthem, 'The wilderness and the solitary place shall be glad for them; and the desert shall rejoice, and blossom as the rose', with its almost painfully moving ending, 'and sorrow and sighing shall flee away', which always stirs me to the depths. After the service the Provost, Montague James, in surplice and the scarlet hood of a Doctor of Letters, was conducted from his stall to the west door by a chapel-clerk bearing a mace; and the riverside trees, with their spring foliage of vivid green, framed in the lofty open doorway, looked like stage scenery.

One week-day we went canoeing up the winding Granta, as far as the village of Grantchester and beyond it, into the beautiful, silent, unfrequented reaches above Byron's Pool. It was 'between the may and the rose': the forget-me-nots and yellow irises were in bloom along the river-banks, with masses of elder-flower hanging over them; the tall meadow-grass was full of buttercups, big ox-eye daisies, red and white campion, and sorrel; the first poppies had already opened their 'yawns of fire' in the green corn; and over the Granta, as (so it seemed) over Europe in general at the time, a few weeks before the murder at Sarajevo which precipitated the first World War, the sky seemed a perfect blue. I left Cambridge almost stunned by its beauty, and hoping that I might some day see it again.

In July that year, at the end of the school term, I gave up teaching and entered the Second Division of the Civil Service, an examination for which I had taken in the previous autumn. I was appointed to the Accountant-General's Department of the General Post Office at St Martin's-le-Grand and took up my duties there early in August, a few days after the outbreak of the First World War, travelling to and from the City daily in the smoky, dirty steam trains of the Great Northern Railway. The work was very boring, but I had only a few weeks of it. Late in September I applied for permission to join the forces, and enlisted in the ranks of the Royal Army Medical Corps. I was posted to the Second London General Military Hospital, which was stationed at

Chelsea, where it had taken over the premises of St Mark's College (a training college for elementary schoolmasters) and the adjacent girls' school.

I was plunged straight into ward work, and I loved it. I celebrated my twenty-first birthday that autumn by buying books on nursing, medicine, and surgery, and studying them diligently. After working about two months in medical wards I was transferred to the surgical side, where I found the work absorbing. On my weekly half-day off duty I got out of London as quickly as I could, took the St Albans bus to the top of Ridge Hill, and walked through Mimms Wood, regardless of the weather, before going home for tea. Apart from that weekly outing I was in the wards or the operating theatre all day seven days a week.

In August 1915, with about twenty others, I volunteered for Gallipoli, to replace men who had died when a transport, the *Royal Edward*, was sunk by a submarine with great loss of life in the Aegean Sea on its way to Gallipoli a few days previously. Those of us who volunteered were sent to a so-called rest camp on Southampton Common where we stayed about a fortnight while being equipped for foreign service and were put through an intensive course of physical training. One morning on parade we were rebuked (to our surprise) for not having our hair short enough. We therefore paid what seemed to us an unnecessary visit to the barber, only to be rebuked again the next morning, even more severely than before. Determined not to incur a third rebuke, we collaborated in buying a pair of hair-clippers, the closest clipping set obtainable in Southampton, and with them we cropped off every scrap of each other's hair close to the skin, at the front as well as the back, so that we looked worse than convicts.

When we removed our hats for hair inspection on parade next morning the orderly officer was decidedly startled. We were afraid at first that he would charge us with dumb insolence or some such offence, but he did not. On the contrary, we were all given embarkation leave and went home for the weekend. If we had suspected that this was coming we might have been less drastic with our hair. I was very head-conscious at church on the Sunday morning, when I performed my usual office of thurifer. It was not so bad at the beginning of the service, because then we moved in procession from the west tower to the chancel, and no one in the congregation saw me until I had passed by: but I was very embarrassed at the offertory, when I had to go to the chancel step to cense the people in the nave. As I stood there facing

Plate I

John (Gaffer) Brown

Mark and Eliza Brittain (grandparents)

Family Group, 1910
In front: William and Elizabeth Brittain (parents)
with Frank and Marjorie   *Behind:* Edith and
Frederick

Inside St Giles's Church, South Mimms

Plate II

F.B., The Bishop of Montana and
the Rev. Allen Hay, 1948

them, censer in hand, and bowed my cropped head to them, they forgot to return the bow and grinned from ear to ear instead.

On the last day of August, together with a contingent of thirty from Portsmouth, we were sent by train from Southampton to London where, at the Albert Dock, we embarked on the hospital ship *Egypt*. Our orders had been changed, because the Government were already contemplating the evacuation of Gallipoli. We were to stay on board as part of the ship's complement.

The *Egypt* was a converted Peninsular and Oriental liner of 8,000 tons, built on the Clyde in 1897. She was a graceful two-funnelled ship and we were always proud of her, even though we often asserted (as has no doubt been asserted of most ships) that in rough weather she rolled and pitched more than any other vessel afloat. She was lucky throughout the war, during which she suffered from nothing more than a little bombing and from a collision which split her bows open; but she was afterwards sunk in a collision off Ushant, when carrying a load of bullion.

At the time when we went aboard the *Egypt* the Admiralty had only just commandeered her, and had taken over the whole of the crew with the ship. Consequently, in accordance with P. and O. custom, the officers and chief petty officers were British, the petty officers and ratings Indians. Of these, the deck hands and stokers, who lived aft, were Punjabis, and Mohammedans to a man. The men of the purser's department on the other hand, who lived in the fore part of the ship, were from Portuguese India and all Christians. Unlike the Mohammedans, they wore European dress, and they all had Portuguese names, whether they possessed any Portuguese blood or not. They seemed to share only about three or four surnames among them, the commonest being Fernandez. Many of them spoke both Portuguese and Kanarese, their native Indian language.

The *Egypt* was my moving home for the greater part of the next three-and-a-half years. Under Commander George Montford we were a happy ship.

E

I O

While we were at sea I started and edited a ship's paper, *The Egyptonian*, which was printed entirely on board by my shipmate, Frank Rouse, who was a printer in civil life. He had nothing but a small hand-press, which had previously been used for the printing of official notices, and he was handicapped by shortage of type and by rollers which were apt to melt away when we entered the tropics; but, by the exercise of much ingenuity on his part, we managed to produce about two dozen issues at irregular intervals during the war, whenever circumstances allowed. At first the printing was done in the ship's office and the editing in the space (three feet wide and five feet long) that lay between a coal-bunker and a gangway on the main deck. Later, we were given a couple of disused bathrooms — one for the printer and the other (next door to it) for the editor. The ship's carpenter boarded the baths over and made a little furniture for us, and the cramped editorial office of *The Egyptonian* was a godsend to me. In it I did a good deal of writing and reading, entertained friends, and housed the books that I bought as we moved from port to port or that were sent to me from England.

My interest in languages was naturally quickened by foreign travel. Voyages to Malta, to Italian ports, and to Alexandria, where there was a large Italian colony, inspired me to take up the study of Italian, and I progressed with it until I was able to read Dante in the original. I still possess my first copy of the *Divine Comedy*, bought at Alexandria. It bears the marks of the teeth of rats, which lived in large numbers in the ship's hold and made foraging expeditions to the upper decks from time to time. An encounter with some members of the large colony of Spanish-speaking Jews at Salonica (where they published periodicals in their own language) led me to take up Spanish. Later, I studied Portuguese, so that I might be able to converse with those Goanese members of the crew who spoke it and practise the language with them. From there I went on to study the *Lusiads* of Camoëns, and then further back still, to the beautiful early Portuguese lyrics of the thirteenth century. One of the medical officers shared my linguistic interests. We used to work together, each in turn holding a grammar while the other conjugated verbs or translated.

Our first outward voyage ended at Alexandria. Next day we began to coal ship and, as the coaling was done by hand, it took two days to get 1,700 tons on board. The coal was brought out to the ship in lighters, which were moored alongside us. It was then shovelled into big rush baskets, carried up narrow planks on the shoulders of Egyptian labourers, and shot into the open scuttles all along the ship's side. The 'coalies' made a furious noise the whole time, shouting and gesticulating at one another. It was pathetic to see them sitting on the coal after dark and eating their supper of large round white cakes and lumps of dates. Except for their lips, their teeth, and the whites of their eyes, they were almost indistinguishable from the coal. Sometimes a grimy hand lay on a white cake for a moment, and the contrast was most marked. The meal was eaten to the accompaniment of a hideous din, almost every man pointing at his fellows with one hand, cramming his mouth with the other, and shrieking with a full mouth.

We were glad to get on shore for a few hours each day, away from the clouds of coal-dust that pervaded every corner of the ship; and I, who had not set foot on foreign soil before, can never think of Alexandria except with affection. It was there, in its stone-paved streets and dust-paved alleys, that I received my first experience of the romantic and highly scented East. It seemed unreal to be walking the same streets as men dressed in garments like night-shirts (chiefly blue, yellow, and dirt-coloured); to see grime-coated Egyptians, in baggy blue trousers patched with green and red, gazing intently at a cardboard figure of Charlie Chaplin which stood at the entrance to a cinema; to see money-changers sitting at almost every street corner; to see water-sellers carrying water in evil-looking goatskins, just as they did in the time of the Pharaohs; to see and hear an Egyptian band pass by, leaving behind it a weird noise from its three reeds and apparently innumerable drums; and to be taken back to the ship in a dhow, manned by a boy who set the sail and pulled the oar and by his obese parent, who sat at the tiller, directing operations with an occasional grunt and consoling himself in this labour by taking long puffs at a large and malodorous pipe.

When coaling was finished and the ship washed down, we stood by to receive patients. On they came — men with arms off, legs off, bandaged heads, shattered thighs, white with dysentery, yellow with jaundice; men who would never walk again, men who would never see again; mental cases, convalescents — the whole 500 were on board in four hours. We cast off from our moorings at once and began the homeward voyage.

The routine on that voyage was much the same as on many others — feeding seventy patients four times a day, making seventy beds, cleaning the ward, dressing wounds all the morning; assisting at surgical operations, washing seventy men, taking temperatures, giving medicines, and applying fomentations in the evening — not a minute's rest for fourteen hours, from six in the morning to eight at night, except during the intervals for meals. Yet I loved the work, even when the ship pitched and rolled heavily, scattering food and drink in every direction, and making it necessary to screw down the port-holes in an already stifling atmosphere to keep out the sea.

After a second voyage to Alexandria and back we left Southampton for Malta, where we arrived in the middle of November, and had one enjoyable day on shore before the return voyage. I was enraptured with the beautiful harbours, with Byron's 'cursed streets of stairs', with the church of St John and its tombs of the Knights of Malta, with the great fortifications; and almost asked, with René Bazin, 'And where are the Knights themselves?' I drove out into the country with some of my shipmates in an ancient cab, through miles of fields separated from each other by 'hedges' of big piled-up stones, the continued repetition of which gave a curious feeling that every field was an ancient fort. An hour's drive brought us to Musta, where we climbed to the top of the dome of the church — one of the world's great domes, larger than the dome of St Paul's, though Musta is only a village. From the top we enjoyed the wide view of Valetta, its suburbs and harbours, of St Paul's Bay, and of the island generally, with orange groves, lemon groves, and vineyards breaking the monotony of its walled fields, and here and there an ox at the plough.

We were at Malta many times after that. Once we were based on the island for more than a month, making a voyage meanwhile clock-wise round Sicily, calling at Palermo and going on through the Strait of Messina past smoking Etna to Port Augusta, near Syracuse. There we transferred our patients to the huge *Britannic* of 48,000 tons, which was sunk later in the year in the Aegean.

During one of our long stays at Malta in spring-time, I took the opportunity to explore the island thoroughly with some of my shipmates. On Lady Day we went to vespers at St John's, where the eloquent preacher paused now and then in his sermon to clear his throat noisily, spat audibly and visibly on the floor of the pulpit, took a sip of water and went on with his discourse. Sometimes we took the toy eight-mile railway to the orange gardens at Sant' Antonio and to the old capital, Melina, in the centre of the island. We went by horse-cab to visit the neolithic temples at Hagiar Kim and Mnaidra and to picnic in the Boschetto, and came back to Valetta to dance in the street with the revellers in the pre-Lent carnival, to take a whole box at the opera (top tier) for one-and-sixpence, or to go to the play at the venerable Manoel Theatre, reputed to be the oldest in Europe. March had not come in when we arrived and yet all the flowers of the year seemed to have come into bloom at once — peach, apricot, and geranium; pear and clover; hyacinth, violet and rose.

We spent the winter of 1915-16 in the eternal summer of the Aegean Islands, voyaging between Alexandria, Lemnos, Salonica, and Valetta. It was always a thrill to approach the Gulf of Salonica, especially early in the morning, and to see Mount Athos to starboard, like a huge pyramid, with its snow-capped peak rising above the clouds; to see, on the port side, the long black range of Pelion, with snow in its clefts; then Ossa, with its single snowy peak curved like a wave; next Olympus, with its grand field of snow, the sun glittering on its peaks and a white snow-like mist stretched along its base; then, finally, to drop anchor in front of Salonica itself, with its theatre-like slope to the sea, its numerous minarets and towers, and its long white wall running up the hillside and embracing the city; to go on shore, to walk down streets named after Socrates and Themistocles, and to visit the arch of Constantine and Justinian's great church at St Sophia, which had only just been converted from a mosque to a cathedral.

Our Mediterranean voyages were interspersed with a number of Channel crossings to bring back casualties from Calais, Boulogne and Dieppe. Sometimes there were so many of them that they had to lie in close-packed rows on the decks. It was as much as we could do to feed them and dress their wounds once before disembarking them at Southampton. We then turned round immediately and left again for France.

We returned to Alexandria many times after our first visit, the length of our stay there varying from a few days to over four months. We were given plenty of shore leave, and spent much time wandering round the streets of the city and watching the Egyptian craftsmen at work outside their little shops — silversmiths, coppersmiths, broom-makers, hat-makers, wood-workers shaping sandals and spoons with an adze, and turners making wooden bowls by the primitive bowstring method.

I also paid visits to some of the numerous churches which, in so cosmopolitan a city as Alexandria, where East meets West, had to cater for many different nationalities and rites. Sometimes I went to the French church, sometimes to the Italian. Generally, however, I went to one of the Eastern churches – Coptic, Greek, or Armenian – or to one of the Uniat bodies, such as the Melkites or the Maronites. At the Maronite church I was surprised to find women taking the collection and a layman reading the Epistle, in secular dress, from a 'made in Birmingham' kind of music-stand. This was forty years before laymen were allowed to do the like in England. More often than not, I went to the Coptic church. I acquired a great liking for the Copts, those native Egyptian Christians who had managed to survive centuries of persecution, and attended their services at Cairo and Suez as well as at Alexandria when the opportunity occurred.

During the latter part of the war, when we were making frequent voyages between Egypt and India, I used to attend the morning service at the little Coptic church at Suez whenever we spent a Sunday there. As at Alexandria, cymbals provided the only instrumental music that there was; the singing was led by a blind cantor; and the choirboys, in albs, purple stoles, and purple hats shaped like flower-pots, sat on benches running east and west outside the screen. The women of the congregation sat behind grilles in galleries, and the men stood in the nave: there were no seats for them. On the first Sunday that I went to the church the service was well under way when I arrived, and I stood just inside the door, among the men. As soon as one of the leading laymen noticed me – he was evidently a sort of churchwarden – he made some remarks to three or four men standing by him, and they all looked at me, nodded to him, and went out of the church. A few minutes later they came back panting under a big heavy high-backed padded armchair, a sort of gilt and red-plush throne in Second Empire style. Having deposited it on a low platform that stood just inside the west door, they made signs to me to sit in it. They had evidently heard that when an Englishman goes to church he must have a seat.

I told them in English, I told them in French – but Arabic was what they spoke – that I was quite happy as I was, but they would have none of it. I therefore stepped forward and sat enthroned, so to speak, with satisfied Copts standing all round and behind me. At the end of the service the celebrant, who was a bishop, came to the door of the screen and threw the contents of a bowl of water into the air. The choirboys, dodging it neatly, ran forward and knelt in rows along the steps outside the screen, and the bishop blessed them one by one, laying his hand on their heads. The men then went forward more sedately and were blessed in the same way — myself among them, at their special request; but the women stayed behind their grilles. After the service I was entertained to coffee at the clergy-house. When I went to the church a second time the gilt-and-plush throne was brought in as soon as I appeared. At my third visit it was already in position when I arrived.

Once, when in Cairo on leave, I inspected the ancient Coptic churches of Old Cairo, with their beautiful carved screens, inlaid with mother-of-pearl, and with ostriches' eggs hanging from the roof in front of them like lamps. On the Sunday morning I went to service at the Coptic patriarchal cathedral. This large modern building was on a much grander and more fashionable scale than the little church at Suez, and was furnished with pews and red carpets. Yet, as at Suez, there was no instrumental music other than cymbals, and the women sat behind grilles in galleries. The sermon was preached by a layman, wearing ordinary secular dress.

I made two expeditions to Cairo in the company of several of my shipmates. Our first visit inevitably included a tour of the Sphinx and Pyramids. After visiting the King's Chamber and the Queen's Chamber in the Great Pyramid we climbed to the top to enjoy the weird, unique view — on one side Cairo with its mosques and minarets, and the Nile with its narrow fringe of green; on the other, the Second Pyramid and the Libyan Desert with its limitless sand blown by the wind into the likeness of a tide moving up a gently sloping beach. Another day we took a train up the Nile to Badrachein, rode from there to the ruins of Memphis on donkeys, and out across the desert to Sakkara, with the sun and its reflection in the sand burning our faces. There we inspected the Step Pyramid (which must be one of the oldest monuments in the world), the tombs of the sacred oxen worshipped by the ancient Egyptians, and the so-called tombs of Mera and Tih. These were really underground temples containing thirty or more rooms, and their walls were carved and painted with illustrations of ancient Egyptian life and worship, as fresh and bright as if they had been coloured that year instead of some 6,500 years before.

We made many voyages in various directions across the Indian Ocean, with Suez and Bombay as our bases. Our first stay at Bombay was in May, and we found it uncomfortably hot. We nevertheless enjoyed our shore visits, when we inspected the city, walked along Back Bay, and watched the apparently endless procession of bullock-waggons laden with bales of cotton. We warded off beggars, bought mangoes, bargained in leisurely oriental style for silks and brass-ware, enjoyed the view from Malabar Hill during a green and blue sunset, and then went back to the ship. Our quarters were so stiflingly hot that we decided to sleep on deck, but no sleep was possible until two or three o'clock, on account of the innumerable cockroaches crawling over the decks and on to us.

Cockroaches were a pest in Indian waters and often got into the flour and were baked in the bread. As a consequence we used to slice our bread very thin, hold the slices up to the electric light and pick out the concealed cockroaches with a fork. The bread was often sour and mouldy, too. If anyone complained about it to Jim Bulbrook, the second baker — no one dared to tackle Bill Grant, the taciturn but forceful chief baker — he had two answers, according to the season. If it was outside the monsoon season he would say, 'Wait till we get into the monsoon, mate. It'll be all right then. See?' If it was during the monsoon his answer was, 'Wait till we get out of the monsoon, mate. It'll be all right then. See?' I never knew anyone to press him any further.

One day when we were on shore a small group of us were allowed to explore the gardens in which the Parsee towers of silence stood. We found the gardens beautiful, but did not enjoy the sight of the vultures waiting for a meal.

Sometimes we sailed in the ship's lifeboats to Elephanta Island to inspect the gardens and the huge statues of Brahma, Siva, and Vishnu. Sometimes we went further afield. One day a number of us went on an excursion up into the hills at Neral and Matheran, where we killed a snake and used it as a skipping rope on the way down. Arriving back at Bombay at three o'clock in the morning, and not being able to get a boat to take us out to the ship so early, we strolled about the streets, where hundreds of the poorer Indians were sleeping on the pavement, often with the family ox in the middle of the group.

On another occasion a party of us went up into the hills to Deolali for a few days' leave; and while we were there we had the unusual experience of attending a Hindu funeral. Hindus are normally cremated after death, but this man had been an ascetic and was therefore buried. The corpse, covered with coloured cloths and garlanded with flowers, was carried on a bamboo bier by eight men, while a ninth held a parasol all the time over the exposed face of the deceased. A band of drums and cymbals took part in the procession, incense was burned, and fruit was carried. Before the final prayers, which were read in an undertone in the grave itself, every hair was shaved off the dead man's head, beard, and moustache. What surprised us more than anything else was that several of the mourners smoked cheroots throughout the whole ceremony.

During our first stay at Bombay I became acquainted with the Anglican priests of the Society of St John the Evangelist (Cowley Fathers), who had a mission house at Mazagon. They very kindly invited me to regard their house as my home whenever we were in Indian waters. I often went there and attended services at their church of St Peter, which had a congregation of Europeans and Eurasians; but what I liked even more was their church of Holy Cross, Umarkhadi (another district of Bombay), which had an entirely Indian congregation and a service that reminded me greatly of South Mimms.

I twice stayed with another group of the Cowley Fathers in their mission house at Poona. One of my two visits was on sick leave after malaria. On arriving at Poona by train, I was informed by the military sentries that, owing to an outbreak of cholera, I could neither return to Bombay nor go through Poona City to Panch Howd, where the Cowley Fathers lived, but must remain in the cantonment until I was allowed to leave Poona. I escaped this unpleasing prospect by hiring a cab and, with the kindly connivance of the sentries, getting by a circuitous route to Panch Howd, where I stayed for four interesting weeks.

During that time I became friendly with a number of Indian Christians, some of whom I found to be ardent nationalists. They took me on a thorough exploration of Poona City and, as we went by, the inhabitants used to turn and stare at me, because I was the only European to be seen outside the boundaries of the cantonment, which formed a separate town. On Sundays I attended the Cowley Fathers' fine church of the Holy Name. As I have all my life possessed the knack of sitting cross-legged for long periods of time, I sat in comfort among the Indians on the floor of the pewless and chairless nave. I was invited to the annual feast of the men's club attached to the mission, and here too I sat cross-legged on the floor, eating from a big leaf with my fingers and dining on curries so highly spiced that, before the meal was over, I felt as if the roof of my mouth had been completely burned away.

I often drove with one of the Fathers in a tonga to the village of Yerandawana, where they had a missionary outpost. The view as we crossed the river on the way there, with cattle standing in the water or chewing the cud on the bank, was startlingly like an East Anglian landscape by Constable. When we reached Yerandawana we used to lunch with the good Father Elwin and say the office with him in his charming church of St Crispin. It had been designed by Sir Ninian Comper and had achieved his two-fold object of looking as though it belonged to India and yet showing itself to be unmistakably Christian.

From Bombay we made a number of voyages to the Persian Gulf and back. The voyage took five days in each direction. We saw little land, and what little we saw was blurred in the heat-haze, but we were sometimes rewarded with fine sunsets. Once, as we passed through the Strait of Ormuz at sunset on a placid sea, the huge rocks were silhouetted against a blood-red and yellow sky, in which hung a big white crescent moon.

As we drew too much water to get above the Shatt-el-Arab bar at the northern end of the Persian Gulf we had to anchor below it, out of sight of the low-lying coast. Once we lay at the bar in the sultry heat a whole fortnight, and while we were there the Mohammedan members of the crew were given permission to celebrate the festival of Moharrem on the aft well-deck. They were led by the serang who, disguised as an old man, did some acting with two other members of the crew dressed as women. The acting was interspersed with dancing and chanting, to an accompaniment of tom-toms, tins beaten with canes, and loud rhythmical hand-clapping. From time to time twelve men would link arms, advance and retire, and gradually move round in a circle by taking oblique steps. About every third step they would bark like dogs, working themselves to a frenzy and not giving place to other dancers until they were hoarse and exhausted. The whole performance was very much like an amalgam of 'Hokey-Kokey' and the 'Palais Glide' as danced in English ballrooms about 1950.

After several voyages up the Persian Gulf and back we left Bombay for East Africa. We performed the crossing-the-line ceremonies on the way there and, after calling at Dar-es-Salaam, lay a few days at Zanzibar. Here I went with some of my shipmates to Evensong at the beautiful Anglican cathedral, built on the site of the slave market. Next day, guided by African boys from the schools of the Universities' Mission to Central Africa, we walked through groves of coconut palms, orange trees, lemon trees, guavas, and banana trees, and through fields of pineapples, cassavas, and wild tiger-lilies, to Mbweni. Another day we went an hour's journey by train to Bububu and walked back most of the way through woods smelling of cloves, cloves, nothing but cloves.

A few days after our return to Bombay about a dozen of us were transferred from the *Egypt* to the *Nevasa* for one voyage. We went first to Mauritius, and from there to Cape Town. Here we explored the city and the neighbouring parts of the Cape Peninsula. It was spring in South Africa; the oak leaves were a vivid green, and the freesias, which are native there, were in bloom, spreading a white sheet of fragrance over the parkland of Cecil Rhodes's old estate at Groot Schuur and along both sides of Government Avenue at Cape Town. On the way back to Bombay we called at Durban, where we managed to get on shore to explore the city and take a ride in a rickshaw.

We rejoined our old ship at Bombay and were still east of Suez in November 1918, when we received wireless news that an armistice had been signed with Germany two days previously. We went through the Suez Canal towards the end of December and spent the first three months of 1919 cruising about in the Mediterranean, often in very rough seas.

Meanwhile I was negotiating my return to civil life. I had loved my life at sea. I had learned something, not merely of blue seas and skies, but also of 'what the long green seas and the grey clouds say', and would probably have made the sea my career if it had not been for an overmastering ambition. This was to take a degree at Cambridge, the vision of which had never faded from my mind since that visit in 1914. It was now possible for me to think of entering a university, as the State was, for the first time in history, making financial grants to ex-service men for the purpose; and, even if I failed to get a grant, I had received most of my Civil Service pay throughout the war and had saved it, with Cambridge in view.

Our ship's chaplain at the time, the Rev. William Hodges, was a Cambridge man. He had taken his degree from Jesus College, and on his advice I wrote to the Master of the College, Mr Arthur Gray, asking if he could possibly admit me that year, to read for a degree in modern and medieval languages. His reply was so encouraging that I asked to be sent home for early demobilization. Permission was granted, and on April 1st, 1919, when we were lying at Marseilles, I left the *Egypt*, together with two shipmates who had been with me ever since my first day at Chelsea. We spent the night in a camp on the hillside high above Marseilles and next morning saw the old ship put to sea. When she began to turn the headland we instinctively took off our hats and watched her in silence, nor did we speak again for some minutes after she had disappeared from view. We were discharged from the forces at the Crystal Palace on April 8th, 1919, and late that evening I reached home.

My three-and-a-half years at sea had taught me many things. They left me with a lifelong desire to keep everything shipshape and to tidy up as I go along. I have retained all my life a love for the sea, for seafarers, and for ships, and many of the friendships that I formed at sea proved lifelong. One of my first acts on returning to shore life was to form an old shipmates' association, with Commander Montford as President, and we held reunions from time to time at London or Portsmouth down to 1939. Another bond of union between us was the *Egyptonian*, which I continued to produce at irregular intervals from Cambridge throughout the same period of twenty years.

Occasionally, to my great pleasure, an old shipmate would pay me an unexpected visit or I would meet one accidentally in a train or street. Once, years after I had left the sea, when I had gone up to London for a dinner at the Dorchester and was just paying my taxi fare outside that very dignified hotel, with a couple of grave uniformed footmen standing by, I received a tremendous slap on the back and a voice that I had not heard for many years — the voice of a lifelong seafarer — exclaimed loudly, calling me by the nickname that had been mine at sea, 'Well, I'll be ——d and ——d if it ain't —— old Tubby! How the —— hell are you, you —— old ——?' I was delighted at this recognition. My hand disappeared into my old shipmate's huge shoulder-of-mutton fist, and I was very late in arriving at the dinner.

12

A few days after my return to England I went to Cambridge in fear and trembling to be interviewed by the Master of Jesus College. Arthur Gray was nearer 70 than 60. He had entered the College as long ago as 1870 and had been a Fellow since 1875. Utterly devoted to the College, he had been elected to the Mastership in 1912, the first layman to hold the office. He had written histories of both the Town and the University of Cambridge, as well as of his own college, and had made Jesus the setting of a book of ghost stories, *Tedious Brief Tales of Granta and Gramarye* so convincingly written that many of his readers accepted his fictions as facts. One story was called 'The Everlasting Club' in which he gave the characters names of Jesus men who were up in the mid-eighteenth century, which helped to fool some of his more gullible readers. Another was called 'The True History of Anthony Ffryar' and ended

> Whether he really died of 'the sweat' I cannot say. But that the living man was sung to his grave by the dead, who were his sole companions in Jesus College, on the night of August 12th, 1551, is as certain and indisputable as any other of the facts which are here set forth in the history of Anthony Ffryar.

Of all this, however, I knew very little when he received me in the Conference Room of the pleasant Master's Lodge, with its windows looking into the cloister at one end and into the three-sided outer court of the College at the other. He was very kind to me and talked for some time, being apparently always on the point of breaking into a smile. I discovered afterwards that this was a permanent characteristic and did not necessarily mean that he was pleased with the person whom he was interviewing, but was due merely to his possessing unusually high cheek-bones and (I did not notice this until years later) to one of his ears being higher than the other. When he asked me what career I hoped to follow on leaving Cambridge if I was admitted I had to reply that I did not know. I had, it is true, an idea that I might return to the Civil Service (if they would have me), but I was quite vague about it. I had not looked so far ahead as that. All I knew — and of this I was certain — was that I wanted three years at Cambridge. Beyond that, I was content to let the future take care of itself. The Master made some notes in a book, told me that I would be hearing from him later, and dismissed me. I was too timid to explore the college, and even came away wondering whether the parish church of All Saints, just across the road opposite the entrance gate, was the college chapel.

Whatever Cambridge was to have (or was not to have) in store for me, I found South Mimms as delightful as ever. The parish was never dull under Allen Hay because, although he lived to be nearly eighty-eight, in many ways he never grew up. That constituted a great part of his charm. He seemed to be endowed with perpetual youth. He kept the mental resilience of a boy to the end of his life, he had a boy's freshness of outlook, a boy's liking for novelty, and his interests changed as rapidly as a boy's. This liking for novelty was closely allied to his gift, amounting to genius, for making friends immediately with any stranger, without the slightest effort and regardless of age, sex, occupation, interest, or race. Yet this gift had its disadvantages, particularly to his wife. She seldom knew, for instance, when a stranger appeared at the house, whether he was staying for a mere half-hour, or whether he had been invited to stay for a meal, a night, a week, or even a month.

Our Vicar's liking for novelty had other drawbacks. We knew, for instance, that if he went for a seaside holiday he would probably bring back with him some ceremonial or ritual peculiarity of what used to be called the London, Brighton and South Coast religion and plant it among us, whether we liked it or not. Still, we did not get very upset about it, knowing as we did that it would have only a brief reign before it was supplanted by some other peculiarity.

Another effect of his liking for novelty was that it attracted to South Mimms a long stream of oddities from what might be called the ecclesiastical underworld. They probably did not realize that he took most of them much less seriously than they took themselves, and that they appealed strongly to his sense of humour.

An ecclesiastical oddity whom I had met several times before the war began settled at South Mimms at Allen Hay's suggestion in the summer of 1919, boarding at a cottage near the church. He was Arnold Harris Mathew, who might perhaps most easily be described as an ecclesiastical tramp. He had been by turns an Anglican layman, a Roman Catholic priest, a Unitarian (and probably also an agnostic), an Anglican priest, and since 1908 an Old Catholic bishop, having obtained episcopal consecration in Holland. At one time he had called himself Count Povoleri. He now (as until his death) styled himself *de jure* Earl of Landaff of Thomastown. In 1910 he had broken with the Dutch bishops of the Old Catholic church, who afterwards asserted that his episcopal consecration had been obtained from them by fraud. He then began to style himself Archbishop of London of the Ancient Catholic Church – the name of his tiny communion varied from time to time – and showed a readiness to ordain or re-ordain almost anyone to the priesthood and even to the episcopate. Some of his spiritual sons were honest men, some were rogues, others were merely vain. As time went on, he did not seem to know where he stood, and appeared to be negotiating surrender to both Rome and Canterbury almost simultaneously and yet asserting his independence in the same breath.

By the time he settled at South Mimms he had scarcely any followers left and was reduced to penury. This in itself was sufficient to rouse the compassion of Allen Hay, who was in any event always fascinated by any eccentric who came along. Certainly, ecclesiastical vagaries apart, Bishop Mathew possessed great personal charm and was deservedly popular in the village. He was a man of fine presence, with beautifully moulded features and a mass of white hair. He was very kind to me, as indeed he was to everyone who knew him. Now and then the Vicar, who loved to have a kind of prelate-in-waiting, allowed him without authority to pontificate in cope and mitre at services in the parish church. On those occasions he looked as if he had just stepped out of a stained-glass window; but although he was undoubtedly in valid episcopal orders and morally above reproach, the news of his officiating in an Anglican church naturally caused trouble with the Bishop of London and the Archbishop of Canterbury, and his pontifications had to cease.

Towards the end of July that year I received a letter from the Board of Education telling me that I had been awarded a grant of £205 a year to enable me to go to Cambridge. This was followed about a month later by a letter from Arthur Gray to say that I had been accepted for admission at Jesus College and was to begin residence there in the autumn.

My mother thereupon asked me the question that the Master of Jesus had asked earlier in the year – what was I going to do when I left Cambridge? When I answered that I had not the slightest idea she suggested that I was rash in abandoning a Civil Service post with regular income and good prospects for an unknown future, and advised me to think about it. I did so that evening, when I took her to London to a performance of *Aida*. She was delighted with the opera, but my mind was running all the time on what she had said. I was worried, too, by

what a silly misinformed snob had said to me a few days previously —
that if I did not have a car or at least a motor-cycle at Cambridge
(neither of which I have ever wanted or could possibly have afforded at
the time) I would probably be the only undergraduate in the college
without one and would be very much out of things. I had further
misgivings when I reflected that, from what I had heard, the great
majority of the men who went to Jesus College were public-school men,
that most of those who had served in the Forces had probably been
commissioned, some of them having had distinguished war records. I
did not know, either, that there were Cambridge men before my time
who had begun their education in elementary schools, among them
being one of the most distinguished of Jesus men, Sir Harold Spencer-
Jones, afterwards Astronomer Royal. I therefore returned only mechanical absent-minded answers to my mother's enthusiastic comments and
questions about the opera during the intervals, and I hardly slept all
that night. I almost decided to write to the Master of Jesus College to
say that I had changed my mind and would not be going into residence
after all. By the next morning I had regained my composure somewhat
and decided that I must go to Cambridge, whatever happened; but to
this day I never hear the music of *Aida* without recalling the mental
agony — for it was nothing less — from which I suffered at that time.

In September I had to face what I thought would be a further ordeal
— an interview with Mr Edwin Abbott, the senior tutor of Jesus
College, at Hampstead, where he lived with his father and sister during
vacations. I went to see him, as I had gone to see the Master, in fear and
trembling. I was reassured when I found myself facing a gentle, shy,
nervous man with blue eyes and a pointed beard, and I soon realized, to
my astonishment, that he was as frightened of me as I was of him.

When October came, a big railway strike made it impossible for me
to get to Cambridge by train. I managed to send my luggage in advance
in a friendly car, but had to go by cycle myself.

I set off from home at ten o'clock in the morning, reached Cambridge at half past five and went to my lodgings at 56 Cam Road, on
the Chesterton side of the river, with Midsummer Common between me
and Jesus College.

I was surprised to find that someone had already paid me a social
call, for a black-edged visiting card, with two crests on it, was lying on
the table when I arrived. It read: 'Mr R. H. Edleston, 57 Jesus Lane',
and I wondered who he was. My landlady could only say that he was a
middle-aged gentleman, dressed in black, and that he had 'a big

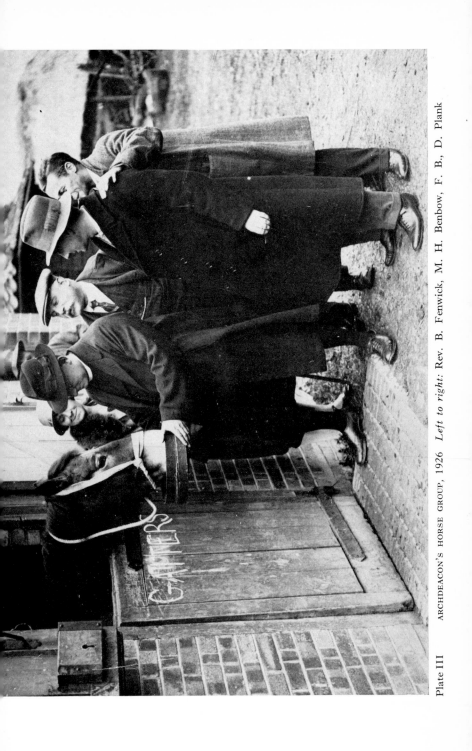

Plate III   ARCHDEACON'S HORSE GROUP, 1926   *Left to right:* Rev. B. Fenwick, M. H. Benbow, F. B, D. Plank

moustache and a funny little beard'. The mystery was solved a day or two later, when I had a letter from Bishop Mathew to say that he had asked his friend and disciple, Mr Edleston, to call on me. I returned his call as soon as I could, and so began a long and delightful friendship, which lasted until his death in 1952. I also enjoyed the friendship of his sister, who kept house for him. She was a woman of considerable learning and devoted to her brother. Although some years older than he, she outlived him, dying in 1956 at the age of ninety-one.

Mr Edleston was indeed a good friend to me, but even those who admired him most could not deny that (unlike his sister) he was an eccentric. I never knew him to wear anything but black, with a black armband on his black jacket and a black crape band round his black hat, but I could never discover for whom he was in mourning. It was either for his wife, who had died some years before I first met him, or for Napoleon III. Devoted as he was to the memory of both of them, he was as likely to be in mourning for the one as for the other. He had never met Napoleon III, but he always referred to him simply as 'the Emperor', and he wrote two books about him, describing him in one of them as 'the greatest Liberal who ever occupied a throne'. His little imperial beard was copied from Napoleon III's. His house in Jesus Lane and his home at Gainford in the County of Durham were full of portraits and mementos of him; and he had a whole collection of relics of the Emperor and the Empress Eugénie at Buckden Palace, near Huntingdon, which he bought a few years later.

Mr Edleston had received the first tonsure from Bishop Mathew. On the strength of that, though he never intended to go any farther with ordination, he sometimes styled himself 'the Reverend' and occasionally wore a clerical collar. He held the title of Baron de Montalbo from the tiny republic of San Marino and was Consul for San Marino in the northern counties of England. Most of the dispossessed or bogus monarchs of Europe appeared to be included in the circle of his friends or at least of his correspondents. One of them called himself 'the lawful King of Poland' – an impossible title, seeing that the Polish monarchy, when it existed, was elective. He took them all very seriously and when talking about them always referred to them by their full titles. He was perhaps the greatest living authority on medieval church brasses, but could never be persuaded to put more than a very little of his vast knowledge of the subject into writing. Once every ten years he travelled all night, so as not to be included in the census, of which he disapproved on principle. Although he never backed a horse in his life, he

F

never missed a race meeting at Newmarket if he could help it. Late in life he took up the breeding of race horses as a hobby and had a horse running in the Derby, though he never won it. With all his peculiarities, he was one of the most charming, urbane, and kind men I have ever known, and one of the most devout.

Although, as I have said, I knew nothing whatever about Mr Edleston when I first arrived at Cambridge, the sight of his visiting-card lying on my table was a tonic to me. It showed that at least one man was interested in my arrival. I sat down and enjoyed the big tea that my excellent landlady had provided and then went to Jesus College to report my arrival. The head porter told me to come back in the morning, and meanwhile to buy an undergraduate's gown, a square cap, and a surplice, which together would cost me £3 13s. 6d. The gown, he told me, was to be worn at dinner in Hall, at lectures, at official calls on dons, and in chapel on ordinary days. The surplice was to be substituted for it in chapel on Sundays, Saturday evenings, saints' days, and the evenings before saints' days. Both cap and gown were to be worn in the streets of the town after dark on week-days and at all times on Sundays. This Sunday rule was, however, already fast becoming a dead letter, and in the spring of 1921 Sundays were officially brought into line with week-days. The compulsory wearing of gowns in the streets on week-days was abolished in 1965.

I went to an outfitter to buy the articles in question; and, as it was now dark, I came out of the shop somewhat self-consciously wearing cap and gown, with a surplice on my arm.

13

Jesus College – or, to give it its full official title, the College of the
Blessed Virgin Mary, Saint John the Evangelist, and the Glorious Virgin
Saint Radegund, commonly called Jesus College – is by general consent
one of the most beautiful and interesting of all the twenty-odd colleges
in the University of Cambridge and differs from all the others in its
plan. It was founded in 1496 by John Alcock, Bishop of Ely, whose
punning device – a cock standing on a ball (the terrestrial globe, or *all*)
– can be seen displayed all over the college, in stone, wood, metal, and
glass; but it has buildings which antedate its foundation as a college by
several centuries, because it incorporates into its present structure a
complete convent. This is the Benedictine nunnery of St Mary and St
Radegund, founded in the early years of the twelfth century, before the
University existed, and suppressed by Alcock.

When the nunnery was converted into a college, its buildings were
not destroyed but adapted to their new uses. Thus the greater part of
the conventual church became the college chapel, most of the rest of it
being added to the Prioress's Lodging to make the Master's Lodge. The
refectory became the college hall, and the dormitories, chapter houses,
and novices' house were converted into sets of rooms for Fellows and
undergraduates. Another reminder of the monastic origin of the college
is that it is the only foundation at Cambridge which possesses a complete cloister. It is unique also in standing well back from any road and
in being completely surrounded by its own beautiful walled gardens and
a big tree-fringed close (likewise inherited from the nunnery) on which
it would be possible to play simultaneously Rugby football, Association
football, hockey, cricket, and a dozen tennis matches, all within sight
of the college windows.

When I went into residence in 1919 the college walls, in accordance
with the fashion of the time (though the fashion was on the point of
changing), were almost completely shrouded in ivy, and there must
have been nearly a thousand laurel bushes scattered round the sides of
the courts or growing in serried masses against the outer walls. The
buildings had naturally been enlarged since the days when they had
housed only a prioress, twelve nuns, a few novices, and the handful of
guests and boarders who were normally to be found in medieval

nunneries. The enlargement had been gradual, beginning soon after the nunnery was converted into a college and continuing until 1885. There were in 1919 about 200 undergraduates, half of whom had to be housed in lodgings, because building had not kept pace with the increase in numbers. A minority of the 200 were Scholars or Exhibitioners on the foundation. The remainder, of whom I was one, were officially styled Pensioners — a title for which the Oxford equivalent is 'Commoners'.

Most of the undergraduates had served in the Forces, and between them they had held every rank up to lieutenant-colonel. A number were married and a few had been in residence before the war. About two-thirds came from public schools, with Marlborough, the Leys, Charterhouse and Rugby predominating. Seventy-five of the 200 ultimately took honours degrees, the favourite subjects being natural sciences, history, law, mathematics, classics, and modern languages.

At Jesus, as at nearly all other colleges at the time, dinner was the only meal normally served in hall and was compulsory for undergraduates on five evenings a week. First-year men dined at 6.30, dons and senior undergraduates at 7.30. Men could either provide their own breakfast and lunch, or (unless their rooms were a long way off) they could have them sent from the college kitchen. These could be either inexpensive table d'hôte meals, or à la carte meals, as elaborate and expensive as they wished. The food, plates, and dishes were taken round to the rooms in big baize-covered wooden trays carried on the heads of kitchen porters. Tea, coffee, groceries, and other small items were delivered by buttery boys aged about fourteen to sixteen. Like all other kitchen and buttery employees at Cambridge until 1939, they worked seven full days a week during term.

My first hall dinner, though simple enough, was a turning point for me psychologically. I went to it full of anxiety, wondering how I would get on with the other undergraduates. To my relief — and, strangely enough, to my surprise — they were all very friendly and no one was in the least inquisitive about who anyone was or where he had come from. In three days I felt completely at home in the college, within a week I felt that I had been there for years, and within a month I knew that I wanted never to leave it.

On my first morning at Cambridge I naturally had to call on the tutor to whom I had been allocated. This was C. A. Elliott, who had gone to Jesus College from Eton via Trinity and was to return to Eton in 1933 to be headmaster and subsequently provost. At Cambridge the

word 'tutor' is used strictly in its etymological sense, so that Claude
Elliott looked after my general interests but gave me no academical
instruction. It had already been agreed that I was to read for an
honours degree in modern, and medieval languages and literature – a
Tripos which had not been introduced into the university curriculum
until late in the nineteenth century. The number of men reading for it
in any one college had hitherto been small; and Jesus, a conservative
college, had never yet elected a Fellow to deal with it. Elliott therefore
sent me to E. G. W. Braunholtz, a member of King's College, who
directed the studies of Jesus men reading modern and medieval languages and whose university office carried with it the delightful title of
Reader in Romance.

Braunholtz was my director of studies for three years. He supervised
me (sometimes alone, sometimes with one other man) for an hour or
sometimes two hours a week at his house on the far side of the Backs in
Adams Road – called Goslar, after his birth-place in Germany. His
linguistic knowledge was unparalleled at Cambridge: there can have
been few European languages that he could not read and enjoy. When
the Medieval and Modern Languages Tripos – the order of the two
adjectives was afterwards reversed – was founded in the eighteen-
eighties, Braunholtz and his brother-in-law, Karl Breul, ran it for many
years unaided. Breul did the German, Braunholtz the rest. His interests
were predominantly philological and he was an enthusiast on his subject. In matters of scholarship, as in his personal relationships with
everyone, he was most gentle and modest. None of his pupils can ever
forget his humility, or the kindness and charming courtesy with which
he treated them.

In reading for an honours degree in Modern and Medieval Languages
a candidate had a wide choice of subjects. He had to offer two languages for Part I, and I chose French and Italian. In Part II a candidate
had to take five subjects. As my interests were now predominantly
medieval I chose four medieval subjects out of five. My choices were
Dante, Italian Literature and History of the Nineteenth Century, Old
Provençal Literature, Old Spanish Literature, and Vulgar Latin and
Romance Philology. Medieval Latin Literature was not included in the
curriculum at the time or I would have chosen it.

My chief lecturers in French were O. H. P. Prior and the Rev. H. F.
Stewart. Oliver Prior, who was the first Professor of French at Cambridge, lectured in the University Arts School in Bene't Street. Undergraduates appeared to give him endless amusement, for his face always

wore a smile when he was with them. No matter at what hour they called on him – and he apparently never went to bed before one o'clock – they were always welcome, whether they came to discuss linguistic problems or were paying a social call. I came to know him much better after I had taken my degree than in my undergraduate days. For no reason at all except his good nature, he was very kind to me, and with many others, I lamented his death in 1934 at a comparatively early age.

H. F. Stewart, who lectured at Trinity (of which college he was Dean) had taken the degree of Doctor of Divinity with a work on Boethius which has never been superseded. He now lectured on French writers of the seventeenth century, laying special emphasis on St Francis of Sales and Pascal, to both of whom he was devoted. His face was most striking and full of character. He came to look more and more like the subjects of his lectures, so that a portrait of him might well have been mistaken for a portrait of a French cleric of the seventeenth century. I had little opportunity of speaking to him during my undergraduate career or for some time afterwards; but I came to know him more and more intimately in later years, and the more I knew him the more I admired him. He lived to be eighty-four, and I visited him regularly at his house opposite Girton College up to the time of his death in 1948. To put it briefly, he was a saint and I loved him.

In Italian, my chief lecturers were Professor Okey and Edward Bullough, both of whom were Fellows of Caius College. Okey was an admirable lecturer, the best I ever heard at Cambridge. Every one of his lectures, which were given at Bene't Street, had obviously been thoroughly prepared, was most logically arranged, well seasoned with humour, and delivered in a very clear voice. Like H. F. Stewart, he looked his part: he might well have been an Italian scholar who had suspended his lectures for a time in order to fight under Garibaldi, yet he was as English as anyone could be. I did not know for some time – he was the first to tell me – that he was one of the eight children of a poor basket-maker in the East End of London, and had had only an elementary school education. He left school at the age of eleven and worked for many years as a basket-maker, teaching himself Italian and other languages during his meal-times or before or after his long working day, which for years began at six o'clock in the morning and lasted until eight o'clock at night. In course of time he became well-known as an Italian scholar, but when he was informed of his election to the chair of Italian at Cambridge he was, he told me, terrified at the prospect, and all but declined the offer. He was a most affable and warm-hearted man, and I was very intimate with him from my first year at Cambridge until his death in 1935. The charming simplicity of his character is reflected in his autobiography, which he appropriately called *A Basketful of Memories.*

Bullough had been a University Lecturer in German but had gone over to Italian — possibly under the influence of his wife, who was a daughter of Eleanora Duse. Tall, slim, and bird-like in his movements, he was always smartly dressed. He smoked incessantly during his classes in his rooms at Caius College, making his cigarettes with his long delicately tapering fingers while he kept on talking, smoking them through a very long holder, and rolling another cigarette as soon as one was finished.

For Old Spanish I attended lectures by the gentle and courteous F. A. Kirkpatrick, who was University Reader in Spanish, and by Braunholtz. I went to Braunholtz also for Old Provençal and for Romance Philology and, during my second year, attended a short course that he gave on Romanian. He appeared to have known that language all his life but afterwards told me that he had taken it up quite recently and was lecturing on it to show that (as he put it) he was still alive. Most of his lectures, on whatever subject, were timed to begin at nine o'clock, but he always left his house too late and ran all the way across the Backs, arriving ten or more minutes late at his lecture room at Bene't Street breathless, purple in the face, and full of embarrassment.

14

At my own college, the dons whom I knew best during my under-graduate career, in addition to the Master, Elliott, and Abbott, were Watt and Nairne. The Master and Elliott were married but both were readily accessible, having houses within the college precincts. Abbott and Watt were bachelors, living in their college rooms throughout term. Nairne was married but, having no house at Cambridge, lived a bachelor life in college during term.

John Campbell Watt, a tough, squat, red-faced Glaswegian, was always referred to as 'Tommy.' He had been one of the Fellows of the college in the days of compulsory celibacy and was the only resident one among them who had remained unmarried when the statutes were relaxed in 1882. He had done no teaching for some years before I went into residence, but was nevertheless a great asset to the college, quite apart from his official duties as Praelector. The alternative title of this office — 'Father of the College' — suited him well, for he was devoted to the college and the undergraduates were his family. His duty was to present them for matriculation, and to present them for their degrees in due course. On such occasions he fussed round them like an old hen with her chickens, and if one of them was late at a meeting-place he would get redder and redder in the face and express his feelings with a broader and broader Scotch accent until the culprit arrived. I met him early in my first term, when he took me with the other freshmen to the Senate House, where we matriculated as members of the University by signing a declaration that we would observe the statutes and ordinances and pay due respect and obedience to the Chancellor and other officers. The ceremony of Matriculation was discontinued in 1962.

I saw Watt very many times after that, as he kept open house and we called at his rooms at any hour of the day. Conversation never flagged there, because he had travelled widely and was an excellent raconteur. He had a remarkable knowledge of literature, too, particularly the English poets, and could recite long passages from Shakespeare and Milton without a book. Although he had been brought up a Presby-terian and still sometimes referred to surplices as 'papistical roobes', he was a most faithful attendant at the college chapel, where the services were of course Anglican, and rarely missed morning chapel from

beginning to end of term. He would often rebuke others for extrava-
gance, even if he were their guest, but was a most generous man
himself. He was so tender-hearted that, if any man failed in an
examination, or did not get as high a class as Watt's patriotic over-
estimate of all Jesus men's abilities led him to expect, he would express
his disapproval of the examiners in language that was always vehement
and often unparliamentary.

Alexander Nairne, who had been brought back to the college in
1917 to be Dean, was a Highlander by race but had been born and bred
in Hertfordshire, where his father was a country parson. A man of wide
learning and experience, he had taken first classes in both classics and
theology, won several University prizes, been vice-principal of the
Clergy Training School (Westcott House) at Cambridge, an assistant
master at Harrow, a country curate, Professor of Hebrew in the
University of London, and for nearly twenty years rector of the rural
parish of Tewin, a Jesus College living in Hertfordshire. During his first
years as Dean of Jesus he was also a canon of Chester, keeping his
residence there while the University was on vacation. In 1922 he moved
from Chester to a canonry at Windsor, and in the same year became
Regius Professor of Divinity at Cambridge.

Unlike most people, Nairne felt that he was overpaid. He therefore
arranged for the stipend of his canonry to be used for buying books for
the library of St George's, Windsor. A deed was drawn up and Nairne
called at his solicitor's office to sign it, with a clerk standing by to witness
his signature. As he was signing, he said to himself aloud, as was his custom,
'Oh dear! I wish they wouldn't make me take all this money.' Next day
he had a letter from the clerk, asking him to lend him fifty pounds.

While he was at Windsor he attended a film show given by King
George V and Queen Mary to entertain the inhabitants of the Castle.
After the performance the Queen stood at the exit to say good-night to
the guests one by one. When Nairne's turn came she said she hoped he
had liked the film. He thanked her and, without thinking, gave the
conventional reply that he had enjoyed it very much; but he had hardly
got outside before he realized that he had not told the truth. He therefore went back into the room and took his place at the end of the
queue. When he reached the Queen she expressed her surprise at seeing
him again so soon. Nairne explained.

'I have come back, ma'am,' he said, 'to apologize for having told you
a lie. When you asked me if I had enjoyed the film I said I had. That
wasn't true. I didn't enjoy it at all. I'm so sorry.'

The Queen smiled and rose to the occasion. 'Neither did the King', she said.

Nairne was a skeleton of a man, nearly all skin and bone, with clothes that always seemed too big for him and a shrunken neck emerging from an abnormally high clerical collar. He was an ascetic, making both his breakfast and his lunch off a stale bun (his favourite food), his tea off a slice of cake, and his dinner (when he went to hall at all) off a very little fish followed by a meagre helping of vegetables – he never took meat – and a tiny piece of sweet. When he gave a lunch or dinner party he provided a generous meal for his guests but most of the time sat talking or watching them eat. His luxuries were a cup of coffee, a pinch of snuff, an Egyptian cigarette, and although he was colour-blind, he was an excellent artist in sepia. He sketched out of doors during the afternoons and at committee meetings at any time of day. The cold Cambridge winters caused him great discomfort. Those who knocked at his door on the top floor of C staircase would hear his high-pitched voice inviting them to come in; but, though audible, he was invisible when they first entered, as he sat behind a high screen. When they went round it they would find him, during the greater part of the year, sitting at his long work-table in cassock, shawl, and mittens, with his feet in a wool-lined muff. He would be either reading or writing in a beautiful hand with a long quill pen. He usually folded and sealed his letters with wax, posting them without envelopes in the old-fashioned way. If it was election time he might be found addressing envelopes for the Labour Party.

Nairne's influence over the undergraduates was far greater than he ever imagined. It was due mainly to his sanctity, but partly also to his learning and the zeal with which he threw himself into the life of the College. He presided over at least four of its societies. Two of these – 'The Clouds', for the study of Plato and his philosophy, and the Theological Society – I did not attend, but I was very regular at two others. One of them, for the study of the Greek Testament, was for beginners. At the other we studied the works of Italian poets, particularly Carducci.

Ecclesiastically, Nairne was a moderate but firm High Churchman, with a great love for liturgies in general and the Book of Common Prayer in particular. His favourite book of devotions was the *Mozarabic Psalter*. When he died, his copy of this, in the Bradshaw Society's edition, was found to be falling to pieces from constant use. He read the chapel services beautifully, intoned well, and was an admirable preacher, lucid and concise. His sermons were models of English prose and could have gone straight into print.

During my second year Nairne instituted altar servers at celebrations of the Holy Communion and I had the privilege of being the first lay server in the chapel for centuries. He also instituted a choral Eucharist every Sunday, at which he appointed me to be cantor, and he instructed me that there was to be at least one Latin hymn each Sunday, two if possible. He made all chapel services voluntary, but a relic of the days of compulsion survived for some time at Mattins and Evensong, when William Meek, the chapel clerk, limped up and down the centre gangway during one of the canticles, armed with a long board on which he pricked the names of those present. He sang as he pricked, and passages from the canticle alternated with undergraduates' names, spoken in an undertone but still audible to those in the front row, like this: 'We praise thee, O God — Allen, Ashwin: all the earth doth worship thee — Meglaughlin, Wyld.' Chapel attendance was good, particularly on surplice nights, which a few jesters profanely called 'shirt nights'. On one of these occasions, my old shipmate 'Chippy' Prior, who was home from sea and was staying a week-end with me, came to chapel and, in order not to appear conspicuous, was swathed in a surplice for the first time in his life, to his great amusement and delight.

It was through Nairne that I joined the Confraternity of the Holy Trinity, of which he was a vice-president. The Confraternity had been founded in 1857 for the furtherance of High Church principles in the University and was usually known simply as 'S.T.C.', these being the initial letters of its Latin title, Sanctae Trinitatis Confraternitas. Among the members whom I came to know well there were three clerics — Eric Milner White, Dean of King's; John How, Precentor of Trinity; and Edward Wynn, who just before the war had been a Scholar and Chaplain of Jesus. He was now Vice-Principal of Westcott House, just opposite the College, and I often went there to his Sunday evening 'squashes' for undergraduates. These three clerics were members of a society of Anglican priests and laymen called the Oratory of the Good Shepherd, some of whom worked in England, others abroad. In 1920 the Oratory acquired a house in Lady Margaret Road, very near the Backs, as a Cambridge centre for its work. John How resigned his office at Trinity in order to be Warden of the Oratory House, as it was called, and I went there occasionally with undergraduate friends to see him.

On my way to Chapel at Jesus one week-day evening I was joined by a boxing Blue, Dick Allum, whom I had seldom, if ever, seen in chapel before, certainly not on a week-day. He explained that he had a big fight to face next day, and that men had been calling on him all day long to talk about it. The subject was getting on his nerves, he said, and he had consequently decided to go to chapel, so as to get right away from all mention of fighting for a little.

As it happened, however, it was the third evening of the month, and so we had the eighteenth psalm, which contained the following verses:

> He teacheth mine hands to fight: and mine arms shall break even a bow of steel.
> Thou hast given me the defence of thy salvation: thy right hand also shall hold me up, and thy loving correction shall make me great.
> Thou shalt make room enough under me for to go: that my footsteps shall not slide.
> I will follow upon mine enemies and overtake them: neither will I turn again till I have destroyed them.
> I will smite them, that they shall not be able to stand: but fall under my feet.
> Thou hast girded me with strength unto the battle: thou shalt throw down mine enemies under me.
> Thou shalt make mine enemies also to turn their backs upon me: and I shall destroy them that hate me.
> They shall cry, but there shall be none to help them: yea, even unto the Lord shall they cry, but he shall not hear them.
> I will beat them as small as the dust before the wind: I will cast them out as the clay in the streets.

I believe he won his fight.

In my first term at Cambridge I took up rowing with enthusiasm. Jesus was one of the leading rowing colleges in the University and the officers of the boat club at the time were those two very distinguished oarsmen, J. A. Campbell and H. B. Playford. As I possessed neither the stamina nor the aptitude to make even a moderate oarsman, my record on the river was completely undistinguished, but my enthusiasm for the sport, as followed from the towing-path, has never waned.

The college had risen to pre-eminence on the river in 1875 and had held the headship from that year until 1886 without a break. After a long period in the doldrums it had regained the headship in 1909 and held it until the outbreak of war in 1914. Its recovery had been largely due to Steve Fairbairn, who had been a rowing Blue and captain of the Jesus boat club in the 1880s. After taking his degree he had gone back to his native Australia to be a grazier. From the early years of the twentieth century he began to spend more and more time in England, living at Cambridge during term and coaching the boats of his old college. At first he used to stay at a hotel near the centre of the town. In later years he stayed at rooms in Maids' Causeway, separated from the college, the river, and the boathouse only by Midsummer Common.

One of the chief points at issue between Steve Fairbairn and the orthodox school at the time was that he wished to abolish fixed-seat rowing altogether, whereas they were determined to retain it in the Lents and certain other races. In the autumn of 1919 no one knew at first what seats would be used in the following spring and all the Jesus eights began hopefully to practise on slides. By the middle of November, however, an adverse decision by the University Boat Club sent us back to fixed seats, and slides were not used in the Lents until 1929, except that they were allowed for first-division boats in 1920 only. I rowed in one of the lower Jesus eights throughout the term, being occasionally coached by the great Steve himself. It was hard work rowing the three miles to Baitsbite and back every afternoon in all weathers, and often to Clayhithe (ten miles there and back), but I thoroughly enjoyed it, even though my account book for that term shows the entries: 'rowing pad 2s. 6d.' and 'rowing ointment 2s.'

To my great disappointment, I was not wanted for the Lent races in my second term, and so I took up sculling instead. Cutting a lecture one very gusty morning in January, I embarked in a 'whiff' for my first outing and narrowly escaped capsizing many times. Steve Fairbairn happened to come down to the river just then and characteristically decided to lend a hand even to such an obscure beginner as myself. This naturally made me all the more determined not to fall in if I could help it, and with Steve's patient coaching from the bank I managed to keep afloat and scull upstream to Jesus Lock and back. A few weeks later I graduated to a 'funny', and from that to a double sculler and a cox-swainless pair. I went out very frequently in one or other of these craft and would occasionally go as far down the river as Upware, ten miles away. Here my companion and I would disembark to lunch at the little *Lord Nelson* inn, appropriately nicknamed *Five Miles from Anywhere – No Hurry*, and enjoy the strange fascination of the limitless fens before returning to Cambridge.

Although I spent many hours on the river I found time for other pursuits, including writing. I contributed a few light articles to *The Granta*, which was a kind of Cambridge *Punch* founded in 1889 by R. C. Lehmann and other undergraduates to annoy Oscar Browning. Among my contributions was a parody of the contemporary demagogue Horatio Bottomley, disguised as Rotatio Blottoley. I also wrote a few articles for the Jesus College magazine, published once a term and appropriately named *Chanticlere*. One of these was a jocular plea for the institution of an eight-day week.

In my first term I joined the Union Society. Although I joined as a life member and often attended debates during my undergraduate years I have spoken at the Union only once in my life, and that was thirty years after I joined. On that occasion I contributed a minor speech to a frivolous debate between the comedian, Gillie Potter, and Admiral Lord Mountbatten. The latter had recently been created a peer and appointed Viceroy of India by a Labour Government. I reminded him that the last time I had heard him speak at the Union was in 1920, when he opposed a motion 'that the time is now ripe for a Labour Government' and accused the Labour Party (according to *The Granta*) of 'diplomacy, ducal and dog-gone incapability.' Winston Churchill had spoken on the same side in that debate and *The Granta* stated: 'We didn't believe all he said; but there is that magnetic, boyish, over-the-hills-and-far-away touch of greatness about him that made us shout for joy.'

The first debate I ever attended at the Union was on the subject of Prohibition, which was supported by T. R. Glover of St John's and opposed by J. T. (afterwards Sir John) Sheppard of King's. An undergraduate audience is a light-hearted one, and it did not seem likely that the Prohibitionists would get more than a handful of votes. Glover, however, made a profound impression on his hearers. As *The Granta* said, his was 'a really wonderful speech. We were charmed, bluffed, cajoled, and thrilled by turns.' As the reporter went on to say, if a vote had been taken as soon as Glover finished speaking there would probably have been a majority for Prohibition. Even at the close of the debate it was defeated by only twenty-three votes in a total of 387.

Another don who made a great impression on me at a Union debate was G. G. Coulton, the medievalist, who spoke in defence of tradition. His conclusion still seems to me very sound:

> Change and tradition are both necessary for progress. You must not exercise one at the expense of the other. The most laudable characteristics of England are due to her steady progress. Loyalty to tradition and courage to dispense with tradition when necessary mark English history. Moderation is the key to success, and the history of the Labour Party will prove this.

At other Union debates I heard such well-known public men as Lord Haldane (opposing Sir Ernest Wild), Oswald Mosley, Josiah Wedgwood,

Philip Snowden, and Hilaire Belloc, who used a good phrase when he described something — I forget what — as 'enough to make a jackass weep.' Speakers whom I heard elsewhere included Sidney Webb at a meeting of the Fabian Society and J. H. Thomas at a Guildhall meeting; and at St Mary the Less I heard Frank Weston, the Bishop of Zanzibar, who had caused an ecclesiastical sensation a few years previously by excommunicating the Bishop of Hereford.

I joined several serious University societies, such as the Italian Society, of which I was later secretary, but did not neglect those that catered for the lighter side of Cambridge life. One of the most entertaining of these was the Pavement Club, which was formed in the May Term of 1921 and laid down its programme in these words:

Cambridge University Pavement Club

The object of this Club is to lend verisimilitude to the rapidly disappearing illusion that University Life is a Life of Leisure. Facilities will be offered to members of the Club at noon on every fine Saturday of the Easter Term for the pursuit of entertainment, quiet conversation, and the reading of newspapers aloud. The Club will meet on some choice and central pavement, and the sole condition of membership is that all members shall sit while meeting.

In fact, the club held only three meetings. The first was on King's Parade. When the clock of Great St Mary's struck twelve we all sat down, about a thousand strong, in a solid mass right across the street, from the houses on one side to the railings of King's College on the other. All traffic had to be diverted for about three-quarters of an hour while we played draughts, snap, old maid, tiddleywinks, and similar games. At the request of the police and proctors the second meeting was held on Parker's Piece, where we all sat on the grass when a bugle was blown, and ate a picnic lunch, cooking it first if necessary. One fat, middle-aged, pompous visitor who had arrived to see the fun refused to sit on the grass when the rest sat, thinking it beneath his dignity to do so. He stood puffing a big cigar in isolated embarrassment until a few well-aimed tomatoes and banana skins induced him to qualify for membership of the club. The third and last meeting took the form of an unheralded tour of the courts of Newnham College by about 500 cyclists, including a few who rode tandems and one a 'penny-farthing.' That was my first visit to Newnham College — or rather, it was a series of visits, because we rode through the college several times before dispersing.

15

My life during vacations, as during term, was a mixture of the light and the serious and was fairly strenuous. On Sundays, of course, and often on week-days as well, I was in my usual seat in the chancel of South Mimms parish church. My week-day mornings and afternoons were mostly given up to reading for my degree. I spent many evenings in the village hall at South Mimms acting in plays, rehearsing for them, performing at concerts, or dancing. During my first vacation Bishop Mathew died suddenly in his cottage at South Mimms. As negotiations for his submission to Canterbury were taking place at the time, he was buried with Anglican rites in our churchyard.

During that same vacation I took part in a Parliamentary by-election campaign in the St Albans division, and we came within a few hundred votes of getting a Labour member elected at the first attempt. In that and some subsequent vacations I addressed a number of political meetings in towns and villages throughout the constituency, but I abandoned active political work soon after the middle 'twenties.

In the summer of 1920 my Long Vacation was occupied by a visit to Italy, sandwiched between two bouts of school teaching. I had to go to Italy to improve my knowledge of the language; and I had to teach in order to earn money to pay for the Italian tour. My Government grant was not large enough to cover my college bills and also my keep at home during vacations, even without any foreign travel. I taught in the village school at South Mimms. It was a mixed school, and so I had girls as pupils for the first time in my life.

I left for Italy towards the end of July. After a couple of days in Paris and Versailles I went on to Milan and so to the village of Mandello, on the banks of Lake Lecco, as the eastern arm of Lake Como is called. Mandello was my headquarters throughout my visit to Italy. I stayed at a little hotel there, made friends with a number of Italians, and went for many walks and expeditions on the lake by steamer and rowing boat with them. I also met an innocent English governess who was looking forward to seeing macaroni trees, of which she had heard much from a friend before she left England.

From Mandello I made two tours of Northern Italy. On the first tour

I went to Bergamo, Brescia, and Lake Garda, where I was anxious to visit Catullus's Sirmio. I was rowed out to it from Desenzano by a boatman who discoursed Communism all the way there and all the way back. From Lake Garda I went on to Verona, Padua, and Venice. There I took a gondola from the railway station to the Piazza of St Mark, where I landed and, like many thousands of travellers before me, was astonished at the sight.

After a few days at Venice I went on to Florence and Fiesole, taking in Bologna on the way. The beauty of the cathedral at Florence was marred for me by the presence of spittoons at each end of the high altar and all round the choir, and by the frequent and loud use that was made of them by the celebrant during High Mass and by the canons during the recitation of the office immediately after it. I then spent a night at Pisa, where I had a room at a little hotel for three lire a day — that is to say, for about ninepence-halfpenny. From Pisa I set out for Parma, but got no farther that day than the little-known walled town of Sarzana, where I lost a railway connection and had to stay the night. I had not intended to stay there but was glad to do so, as it was at Sarzana that Guido Cavalcanti spent his exile from Florence in 1300 and probably there that, thinking that he would die before returning to Tuscany, he wrote his immortal 'Perch'io non spero di tornar giammai', one of the most exquisite of all lyrics. Next morning I got up very early in the dark, caught a train at five o'clock in thunder and lightning and spent the day at Parma. A friendly Parmesan (evidently a prosperous business man) whom I met in a café took pity on the poor foreigner, insisted on showing me all the sights of his native city, and finally conducted me to the railway station, where he bowed me into my train and I returned to Milan and Mandello.

The chief object of my second tour from Mandello was to visit Genoa, of the beauty of which I had heard varying reports in England. I found it delightful and, despite the unutterable filth on the cathedral steps and in other public places, the most beautiful city I had yet seen in Italy, except Venice. I climbed to the top of the dome of Santa Maria di Carignano and enjoyed the magnificent theatre-like view of the city, well named 'La Superba,' with the hills behind it and the Ligurian Alps behind them. I went along the coast to Nervi, with its groves of olives, oranges, and lemons, and back to Genoa to stroll along the quays and look at the ships from many countries lying there. The sight and the sound of them at such close quarters filled me with restlessness for a time and made me want to go to sea again.

G

From Genoa I went to the tomb of Saint Augustine at Pavia, to the wonderful Certosa five miles further on, and back to Milan, where 'Viva Lenin' was scrawled everywhere and red flags were displayed. I took the train to Lecco and from there walked the six miles to Mandello along the lake-side in a fine, fresh, starry early September night.

The chief topic of conversation at the hotel during the next few days was the social revolution that had broken out in many Italian industrial towns, where the workmen had ejected their employers from the factories and established a Soviet system. During dinner we heard people singing in the streets, 'Viva il Bolscevismo e la libertà'. At Lecco one morning I saw numbers of young men in the street with red ribbons in their hats and wearing arm-bands; but they were very orderly, and there was no noise or sign of violence. At Milan on my way home I saw red flags and barbed wire in the streets, and sandbags on chimneys and roofs; but I had seen no violence anywhere when I left Italy next day for England.

In the summer of 1921, when I was at the end of my second year, I sat for the first part of my Tripos and was awarded a second class. Under special University legislation on behalf of ex-service men, this entitled me to the degree of Bachelor of Arts without further examination. I decided to take the degree, intending nevertheless to stay in residence for a third year in order to sit for the second part of the Tripos and so complete the usual course.

Accordingly, on the morning of June 21st Tommy Watt took me with a number of other candidates to the Senate House, where we signed our names and paid the degree fee in cash. This preliminary visit to the Senate House before graduation was abolished a few years later, the fees being thereafter collected by each man's college and passed on to the University.

As black clothes must be worn by a candidate for the B.A. degree I went to the Senate House in the afternoon wearing a dinner-jacket suit (borrowed for the occasion, as I did not possess one), my short undergraduate gown with its distinctive Jesuan pleats and velvet strips on each arm, a pair of bands, and a B.A. hood of black cloth lined and edged with white fur. The Praelector led us to the Vice-Chancellor, who was in the scarlet cope with big ermine hood worn on such occasions. He presented us four at a time, each of us holding one of the fingers of his right hand while he vouched for our morals and our learning in a Latin formula. When our names were called we let go his finger and went up to the Vice-Chancellor one by one. Like a medieval vassal doing homage to his overlord, we knelt in front of him, pressed the palms of our hands together, and put them between his while he pronounced the Latin formula that admitted us to our degrees: 'By the authority committed to me I admit you to the degree of Bachelor of Arts, in the name of the Father and of the Son and of the Holy Ghost.' Technically, we were only Bachelors-designate until December 31st, when we were 'inaugurated' as complete Bachelors without any further attendance at the Senate House. This period of probation, which had survived from the Middle Ages, was abolished in 1926.

I was now styled 'Dominus' in official lists, wore a long gown with two silk streamers in front and no distinctive college marks, and had to take my turn with the other Bachelors at reading the lessons in the college chapel on Sundays, when of course I wore my hood with my surplice. I escaped a few University dues, but there were no other privileges attached to the degree. I was still under the control of my tutor, and if I infringed any University rule I was in fact liable to double the penalty that an undergraduate would incur for the same offence. If, for instance, the Proctor caught me in the streets after dark without a gown, he would fine me 13s. 4d. instead of the usual 6s. 8d.

After taking my degree I went home, and a fortnight later returned to Cambridge for the voluntary period of residence commonly called the Long Vacation Term. It lasts from early July until a little after the middle of August; and, in accordance with custom during that term I had rooms in college, rent free. In some ways, life at Jesus was primitive at the time. There were, for instance, no bathrooms in the College, and never had been throughout the 800 years of its history and pre-history. When a bath was wanted, the bedmaker used to spread a tarpaulin on the floor of the keeping-room (or the bedroom, if it was big enough) and roll in a kind of big metal saucer, about four feet in diameter, in which the bather squatted and poured a couple of cans of tepid water over himself. Yet St Radegund had had bathrooms built in her nunnery at Poitiers as long ago as the sixth century and had insisted that they should be used. When, therefore, the first bathrooms were opened at Jesus in 1922, I suggested that the statue of the saint which already adorned another part of the College should be moved to the new bath building, so as to commemorate the triumph of her principles after the lapse of nearly fourteen centuries in the College named after her.

During that Long Vacation Term I did a considerable amount of reading (mostly in the University Library) and some rowing in pairs and fours. I also did a little excavating with pick and shovel at Buckden

Palace in Huntingdonshire, where Mr Edleston was busy digging up the tennis courts to discover the foundations of the former chapel of the Bishops of Lincoln. When he had done so, he rebuilt the walls with the old material to shoulder height. Inside them he erected the stone altar-tomb, with a high-sounding Latin epitaph, which Allen Hay had hesitated to allow him to place over Bishop Mathew's grave at South Mimms until he had obtained the approval of his bishop. Mr Edleston had taken umbrage at this delay and had chosen to construe it as a refusal. As he never finished anything, the unfinished chapel was crowned with a hideous galvanized-iron roof and left to be a nesting place for birds. It was still like that when he died thirty years later.

In October 1921 I went up to Cambridge to begin my third year of residence. The question of the admission of women to the University came to a head in that Michaelmas Term. At Oxford the women's colleges had been admitted to full membership of the University in 1920 but at Cambridge a year later the vote went against them. It was decided that women should be given titular degrees but could not be members of the University. When the vote approving of this ungenerous compromise was announced, some irresponsible Master of Arts (who was afterwards reprimanded by the Vice-Chancellor) shouted gleefully to the crowd of undergraduates assembled outside the Senate House, 'Now go and tell Newnham all about it,' and the more hot-headed among them took him at his word. Unfortunately, when the authorities at Newnham heard that a crowd was coming they locked the college gates. This was a serious tactical error. If they had left the gates unlocked, it is probable that nothing more than a little shouting would have followed. As it was, when the demonstrators found the gates locked against them they proceeded to burst them open with their hoofs and then, with their ardour cooled, they slunk away. Although this behaviour was the work of a small minority and was publicly denounced by all the leading undergraduate societies in Cambridge, it brought discredit on the University at the time.

When I look back, it seems astonishing that it was not until this term, when I was in my third year, that I joined the Jesus club with which I was to become so completely identified – the Roosters. The club, whose name is an obvious tribute to the founder of the college, was started in 1907 by a New Zealander, J. H. Allen, as a light-hearted debating society. Debating continued to be one of its functions after I joined it, but various others were added in the course of years and it has often been said that the Roosters are unlike any other club anywhere.

It was shyness that kept me from joining earlier; but, once I had been emperched (to use the technical term), I threw myself heart and soul into Roosting.

I rowed hard in a Jesus boat all through that autumn term, stroked the winning 'crock eight', and was selected to row in the fourth Lent boat but transferred to the bow side. Before the end of January 1922 we went into strict training for the Lent Races. The crews breakfasted together in Hall at eight o'clock and anyone who arrived late was fined half-a-crown. There have always been superstitions about training diet. Rowing men had by this time abandoned the old superstition that any meat consumed must be half raw, but we still had to eat a gargantuan breakfast. We began with half a grapefruit, which was followed by a large plateful of porridge thickly sprinkled with brown sugar and covered with cream. Next came a big sole or a pair of kippers or herrings. Then came the main course of several rashers of bacon and two fried eggs, or else a steak (which had to weigh three-quarters of a pound) or a mutton chop. We had nothing more after that, except some marmalade, some more toast, and what was left of a large ball — a sphere, not a mere pat — of butter, about an inch and a half in diameter. The meal was washed down with an unlimited amount of coffee and milk.

The college was most successful in those Lent Races. The first, second, and fourth boats all won their oars — the first by going head, the second and fourth by making four bumps each — and the third boat missed its oars by only one bump. The bump supper in Hall was on the traditional lines, with speeches by the officers of the club, the coaches, and Alf Parsons, the college boatman, who fitted his hands round his mouth like a megaphone, in order to make himself heard above the din. Steve Fairbairn, as usual on such occasions, was absent, but we all stood on the tables to drink his health. At the bonfire on the Close afterwards about half the University seemed to be present. We walked round and round the fire, slapping everyone on the back and shouting through the din, 'Well rowed, sir! Jolly well rowed!' When we were tired of doing that, a number of us went to a friend's rooms to sing and drink. One of the company disgraced himself by vomiting into the grate and putting the fire out, after which he fell asleep. The rest of us thereupon carried him solemnly to his rooms, put him into bed with all his clothes on, and left a note for his bedmaker, 'Please call me at 6.30 sharp'. I was so hoarse next day that I was unable to officiate as cantor at the 11.15 service in chapel. Nairne therefore cancelled the singing of the *Dies irae* which he had included in the service list for that Sunday.

During that term and the May Term, as I was due to leave Cambridge for good that summer, I went several times to the University Appointments Board to be interviewed and to enquire about possible employment, but my enquiries were half-hearted at best. To put it plainly, I had fallen desperately in love with the College during my first term. If that sounds foolishly sentimental, I cannot help it, for I know no other words to express my feelings adequately. Consequently, I could hardly bear even to think of leaving Cambridge, and the words 'going down', which one heard so often at that time of year, sounded like a funeral knell to me when anyone uttered them. It often amazes me that anyone can feel otherwise at the prospect of leaving the University, and the fact that many are apparently quite indifferent about it seems to be a merciful dispensation of Providence.

Others must nevertheless feel every June as I felt in 1922, and I have the greatest compassion for them. When I attended the Footlights revue in May Week in later years I felt quite overcome if it ended (as it often did) with the whole company of undergraduate actors singing a finale of the 'Goodbye, Cambridge' type.

As the May Term wore on, I kept on hoping that a miracle would somehow bring the life of a don within my grasp, but any small chance that I had of an academical career, whether at Cambridge or elsewhere, vanished at the end of the term. More than one of the Fellows had made it clear to me that they would like me to stay at the College and had hinted at a Fellowship if I did well enough in the second part of my Tripos, and Braunholtz had told me that he expected me to get a first class, but I got only a second. When my friend E. J. M. Wyld brought me the news from the Senate House — I did not dare to go to see the results posted up myself — everything went black and I lived in misery for days.

Still clutching at less than a straw, I took no definite steps to find an opening away from Cambridge and even went into residence at Jesus for the latter half of the Long Vacation Term, to taste the unspeakable delights of life at the College for what I felt would be the last time. I had a set of medieval rooms in the Cloister, on the same staircase as Charles Whibley, an Honorary Fellow of the College, and I worked feverishly at a history of Old Provençal literature which has never yet been finished and was never worth finishing. It was a bitter-sweet term for me, and as it drew to an end I woke to the necessity of earning some money, for my Government grant had now come to an end and I possessed nothing.

I was most fortunate in the post which I managed to secure as a vacation tutor at Hove. My pupil was a Harrow schoolboy, C. M. H. Harmsworth, nicknamed 'Joe' after his godfather, Joseph Chamberlain. He had been accepted for admission at Pembroke College, Cambridge, that autumn, provided that at the beginning of October he passed the one part of the Previous Examination from which he had not obtained exemption on school certificates. I spent six enjoyable weeks at Hove. Joe Harmsworth was a most agreeable pupil; his mother was charming; and his father, Sir Hildebrand, a brother of Lord Northcliffe and the first Lord Rothermere, was a wag who liked to annoy his mother-in-law by sitting at the tea-table in his shirt sleeves and drinking his tea from the slop-basin.

One Sunday morning I went to service at St Bartholomew's Church, Brighton, where I noticed John How sitting behind me. He was getting a change from the Oratory House at Cambridge by filling a vacation chaplaincy at Brighton. When we got out of church he asked me where I was going to 'keep' next term, and I replied sadly and almost tearfully that there was no next term for me. He thereupon asked me what I was going to do for a living and I answered that I had not the slightest idea. When he went on to enquire whether I had any idea what I wanted to do, I replied that I certainly knew what I would like to do but there was no possibility of my doing it. By means of further questions he dragged from me the confession that the only thing I wanted to do was to stay at Cambridge, and that I would almost as soon be dead as doing anything else. Upon this he invited me to live at the Oratory House, and said that I could earn my living by coaching and the supervision work that he was confident I would get from colleges. I found it difficult to believe that I should be able to get such work, but starvation at Cambridge seemed bliss in comparison with affluence anywhere else and I therefore accepted his invitation, which seemed to me to have dropped from the clouds.

At the beginning of October Joe Harmsworth went to Cambridge to sit for his Previous Examination and I to take up residence at the Oratory House. I lived there during term for the next eight years.

16

The Oratory House (afterwards St Francis House) stood in a very attractive part of Cambridge — at the beginning of the beautifully timbered Madingley Road, the quietest and pleasantest of all the main roads leading out of the town. On one side of us was the ancient Castle End, with its tiny medieval church of St Peter. On the other side lay the playing fields of St John's College, with the Backs adjoining them. Next to us was Westminster College, a modern foundation for training Presbyterian ministers. We had a pleasant old-fashioned garden, in which stood the chapel, made of wood and consequently very cold in winter and very hot in summer.

The House could accommodate about ten residents. Each man had a bed-sitting room which he cleaned himself. The cooking was done by a married woman who, with her husband, cleaned the common rooms. The residents took turns in calling the house in the morning, putting the meals on the sideboard, and waiting at dinner. At other meals everyone helped himself. Breakfast was eaten in silence, except on Sundays and festivals. This rule seemed a little irritating at first, but I soon came to value and even to like it. There were in fact no irksome rules: John How was too shrewd a man for that. He ruled the House firmly but tactfully, with admirable good humour, sympathy, and common sense.

He presided also over the Cambridge members of the Oratory who, whether living in the House or not, assembled there every Friday afternoon for a chapter meeting. We were accordingly joined at lunch that day by Edward Wynn, who had now left Westcott House to be Dean of Pembroke College, and by Eric Milner-White, whose fine sense of liturgical fitness was to remain clearly stamped on the services in King's College Chapel when he left Cambridge twenty years later to be Dean of York. Another member of the Oratory who occasionally appeared at lunch was an Oxford man, Wilfred Knox, who was at the time engaged on parish work in the East End of London.

There were generally several laymen living in the House but the only one who was a member of the Oratory was Joseph Needham, and he subsequently resigned from membership. A warm-hearted man of unusual character, an original thinker and an omnivorous reader, he soon began to make his mark in the world of science. Elected a Fellow of Caius College in 1924, he later became a Doctor of Science, University Reader in Biochemistry, a Fellow of the Royal Society, a prolific writer and (*inter alia*) an authority on Chinese subjects. He was elected to the Mastership of his college in 1965.

When I began residence at the Oratory House my prospects of making a living were exiguous. I conducted evening classes in elementary French for four hours a week — two hours on Monday and two more on Wednesday — in a town school under the Local Education Authority, and in addition I had one private pupil in French for two hours a week. This was a middle-aged man, Arthur Beales Gray, who was head of the book-binding firm of John P. Gray and Son and the author of a pleasant antiquarian work, *Cambridge Revisited*. I taught him in his private room over his shop at Green Street after business hours for three years.

I had no other source of income at the beginning of October. Fortunately for me, however, Joe Harmsworth passed the Previous Examination a week or two later, went into residence at Pembroke College, and came to me for four hours a week for coaching in French and Spanish. About the same time, Abbott sent an Indian to me to be coached for two hours a week in Latin for the Previous Examination.

Even so, I still had only twelve hours' paid work a week, but fortune favoured me at the right moment. Francesco Nitti, a former Prime Minister of Italy, had written a powerful book, mainly devoted to a severe criticism of the peace treaties of 1919. Recognizing a kindred spirit in John Maynard Keynes, whose *Economic Consequences of the Peace*, published in 1919, had made a great stir, he sent him a copy of his book and asked if he could find an English translator for it. Keynes approached Professor Okey, who recommended me for the work and sent me to see Keynes in his rooms at King's College. I found him supervising an Indian undergraduate, who was reading his weekly essay to him. Keynes stopped the reading for a minute in order to hand Nitti's typescript to me and asked me to submit a specimen translation of a page or two as soon as I could. I did so, and when Keynes had rightly criticized my English in two or three places he commissioned me to translate the whole work.

On Okey's advice, I went to the London firm of Fisher Unwin, and made terms with them to publish the book. As its subject was highly topical I had to translate it at top speed — and it contained nearly 100,000 words. I often worked until two o'clock in the morning, posting each chapter as soon as I had finished it, and before long the proofs of the earlier chapters were waiting for me each morning when I rose from my short night's sleep.

The book was published that winter, under the title *The Decadence of Europe.* Fisher Unwin had asked me whether I would like a small royalty on each copy sold or a lump sum of £40 for my translation. Not knowing how the book would sell, I played for safety and chose the lump sum. It would have paid me to choose the royalty, because the book had a very big sale, being reprinted several times in quick succession and running to a second edition with a new preface. Still, I was well content to get my name on the title-page of a book for the first time: that was something which I had never expected. The reviewers, too, praised my translation, and this helped to break down the serious inferiority complex from which I was suffering at the time.

I needed no translation to help me through the rest of that academical year financially, because in my second term I had several new pupils, so that my hours of teaching rose to thirty-two a week, and in my third term they rose to thirty-seven.

Meanwhile, I naturally saw as much as I could of Jesus College. I dined in Hall there twice a week with the other Bachelors of Arts and undergraduates, and every Sunday evening I attended the meetings of the Roosters. I had not yet held any office in that Parliament of Fowls, and was therefore surprised when, at the beginning of my first term at the Oratory House, I was elected President, thus ascending straight from the floor of the Roost to the Grainsack, as the Rooster language puts it. At the end of the term, when there is normally a new President, I was re-elected for the rest of the academical year, and was moreover awarded 'the Order of the Red Herring, with several bars or fins.' I was to hold this 'as a corporation sole,' but during the vacation I reflected that I ought to share so great an honour with other Roosters.

Accordingly during the following term the Corporation Sole was expanded to allow a maximum of twelve resident members of the Most Loquacious Order (the first letter *r* being omitted in pronunciation) of the Red Herring, which was to form a kind of House of Lords (termed the Upper Perch) of the Roost, and I became its first Grand Marshall. The word has ever since been spelled with a double *l* in order to perpetuate a mistake made by a secretary when writing the minutes ('Scratchings').

It was about this time that I began to get well acquainted with three Jesus dons whom I had known less intimately during my undergraduate years. These were Sir Arthur Quiller-Couch (perhaps better known simply as 'Q'), Charles Whibley, and Bernard Lord Manning.

Q, who was 60 at the time, was King Edward VII Professor of English Literature and drawing large audiences to his lectures. He confessed to being a shy man, particularly with undergraduates, and I found in time that this really was so, despite his social charm and his lavish hospitality. I had hardly known him at all during my first three years at Cambridge and must admit that I was somewhat prejudiced against him, having heard rumours that he was on bad terms with his wife. I found afterwards that nothing could have been farther from the truth – that he and Lady Quiller-Couch were in fact utterly devoted to each other. The rumours no doubt had their origin in the circumstance that Q and his wife had no house at Cambridge. They had had one before my time, but only for a year. Being devoted to their native Cornwall, and not being able to afford one home there and another at Cambridge, they had given the latter up. Q accordingly (like Nairne) lived a bachelor life in his college rooms during term, and hastened to Cornwall at the first opportunity when term ended (or a little earlier) and stayed there until the next term began (or a little later).

Many other silly legends were told and believed about Q, as they always are about any don of outstanding personality. As Charles Whibley says in the preface to his anthology, *In Cap and Gown*, 'The same stories against the dons, which amused our great-grandfathers in their first term, are told to the freshmen of today as entirely modern.' Some of these academic legends seem to be as widespread as folk-tales. Of the numerous stories told about Q, for instance, both during his lifetime and since, one asserts that during the course of a lecture he remarked that in some distant land females were so scarce that even university women could find husbands there. The story continues that, when the women rose in a body to leave the lecture-room at this insult, Q called after them, 'You needn't hurry: the ship doesn't sail for a fortnight.'

Now, apart from the fact that no don would behave so insultingly – least of all Q, who was always most chivalrous in his attitude towards women – the same story is told about numerous other dons at various universities. I have heard it told, for instance, about G. T. Lapsley, who was contemporary with Q at Cambridge; and in 1955 a young Belgian woman, who had recently taken her degree at Louvain, told me that during her time at that university exactly the same story was told about one of the professors there.

Charles Whibley, the friend and disciple of W. E. Henley, was four or five years older than Q. When I first knew him he was a widower and lived in college during term. His stout, thick-set figure, fresh complexion, rather long thin hair and smallish eyes were generally accompanied by a high stiff collar and a monocle. He was distinguished as literary critic, editor, anthologist, political writer, translator, wit, conversationalist, and diner-out. Some of his admirers thought that he, rather than Q, should have been appointed to the Chair of English Literature. Secretly, he did not like Q, possibly because he himself had wanted the Professorship, certainly in part because Q was a Liberal and Whibley a diehard Tory. As his obituarist put it in *The Times* when Whibley died in 1930, 'he had a real hatred of Whiggery and indeed of Liberalism in any form'; and Arthur Gray wrote, on the same occasion:

> to the last he was a Classic of eighteenth century type, and in his political views he belonged to the same era. The Cambridge world in which he breathed was the Cambridge of Gray and Gunning. Outside it, he lived with Swift, Bolingbroke, and Bubb Dodington, surviving into the days of Pitt and Castlereagh. Later he transferred himself to Tudor times.

Bernard Manning, who was less than a year older than myself, came from Caistor, a little market-town in Lincolnshire, and was the son of a Congregational minister and the grandson of a Methodist tradesman there. He had gone up to Jesus from Caistor Grammar School with a Scholarship in History, had taken a very good degree and had been appointed Bursar of the College at an early age. Like his father and grandfather, he was a staunch Nonconformist and Liberal in politics. In spite of the bad health which made him a semi-invalid he played his full part in the life of the College, carried out the exacting duties of Bursar, and was very well-known and popular among the undergraduates, few of whom had any knowledge of his disability. Most faithful to all his roots, he disliked Whibley with his frequently expressed contempt (so at least Manning asserted) for Liberals, Nonconformists, tradesmen, and undergraduates from Grammar Schools. What made Whibley's offence much greater in Manning's eyes was that Whibley himself was the son of a Liberal Nonconformist grocer and had gone up to Cambridge from Bristol Grammar School.

Yet, even if Charles Whibley was a snob, he was always most kind to me, as he was to many others. Mr John Connell, the biographer of W. E. Henley, summarizes Whibley as 'a talented, cold, self-protective and cautious being who hid his real character under a mask of almost countless affectations.' He is wrong in calling him cold; for, to those at least from whom he had nothing to fear, Whibley was a warm-hearted man – provided always that politics were not under discussion. Once he encouraged me to tell him my secret ambitions and advised me to stay at Cambridge. 'One thing leads to another,' he said, and he was convinced that something would turn up for me. Certainly, he added, I need not fear the workhouse if I stayed at Cambridge any more than if I went elsewhere. He encouraged me in a practical way too, by giving me small paid jobs, such as reading the proofs of his edition of the posthumous *Collected Essays* of his Tory hero, W. P. Ker, and compiling an index for the book.

Occasionally when I was with Whibley he would burst into a violent political tirade. I remember his asserting once that we must get rid of 'the foul principle of democracy' and hark back to the golden days before the Reform Bill of 1832. I did not dare to tell him that I had been invited and even pressed to become Labour Party candidate for the St Albans division at the Parliamentary election of 1923, or that a year or two later I was elected president of the newly formed South Mimms branch of the Labour Party and took the chair at meetings in the village hall addressed by such well-known Socialists as the veteran John Hodge and Will Henderson. Yet, even if I had told him, I think he would have taken the news mildly, for in his personal relations he was very different from the vitriolic author of the 'Musings without Method' which he contributed regularly to *Blackwood's Magazine* for a quarter of a century. As Mr Connell says, they were characterized by 'almost equal savagery and brilliance'.

I had rooms on Whibley's staircase for a second time in 1923 when, as in the previous year, I kept part of the Long Vacation Term at Jesus. As usual, I drove from the railway station to the College in the one remaining horse-cab that stood for hire, a sad relic of earlier days, among the motor-taxis in the station yard. I continued to use it each term until it disappeared in (I think) 1925. I do not know whether Whibley used it. If not, I feel he should have done so, seeing that he praised W. P. Ker for refusing to have electric lighting in his rooms at Oxford when it invaded all the rest of his college.

During my residence that term I worked hard again at my abortive history of Old Provençal literature, and I indulged in one frivolity.

There were at the time a number of down-at-heel touts who used to haunt the neighbourhood of the Senate House to accost strangers and conduct them round Cambridge for a fee. I suggested in Hall one night that it would be good fun to pretend to be Americans and get one of these guides to show us round our own college. A friend bet me five shillings that we would be recognized as undergraduates at once, and I took him on. Three undergraduate friends volunteered to go with me — E. C. Robey (afterwards a well-known barrister), L. T. Hilliard, and H. O. J. Henwood.

Next afternoon we strolled along to the Senate House. Robey wore a check suit, Hilliard had a false moustache, Henwood smoked a big cigar, and I chewed gum and carried an attaché case. Taking a guide-book out of it, I began to read its contents aloud in my best American accent. In less than a minute a guide had offered his services and we engaged him. We told him that we particularly wanted to see Jesus College, of which we had heard much at Yale, and he took us there. He showed us round the hall, the chapel, and the courts, and took us on to the Close, where a cricket match was going on. James Hoppett, the head porter, was sitting under the pink chestnuts watching it. Like others whom we had met in the streets and in the college, he naturally recognized us but did not give us away. We stood in a row gazing respectfully at him, and I said, 'Say, guide, I guess that's the Master.' The head porter was not displeased, but the guide got a little anxious and persuaded us to go away. A few minutes later we paid him off. He was surprised when we said that we were staying to tea at the college, but we explained that we had been invited by a man we had known at Yale. Next morning, when going round a street corner, I ran full tilt into him. He recognized me and looked sheepish, but neither of us spoke.

17

A new phase in my life began in that same summer of 1923, when I met for the first time Henry Gordon Comber, Fellow of Pembroke College and Director of Studies in Modern Languages there, whom I must always account one of my chief benefactors. He had first heard about me from Joe Harmsworth, who had belauded me to him as a teacher. On finding that I was living at the Oratory House, he had enquired about me from his colleague, Edward Wynn, who also spoke favourably of me. The result was that I received a letter from Comber, asking me to call on him. I have never forgotten my first view of his rooms at Pembroke when Edward Wynn took me there one August morning to introduce me.

The outer room had a highly polished floor and furniture, and its walls were lined with books, particularly Spanish classics. There was nothing remarkable about that in a don's room; but what was striking was the numerous vases of cut flowers on the tables, the row of minia-ture trees growing in little wooden tubs on the window-ledges, and the shoal of goldfish swimming in an enamelled bath on a chair just inside the door. In the inner room there were more books and flowers, rows and rows of framed photographs of men, a large cage full of whistling canaries, another cage full of love-birds, and a tall cabinet packed with curios, mostly from South America, where Comber had been born. As we entered he was standing at the far end of the room, watering another row of miniature trees from a long-necked watering-can. He was a big stout man, weighing about eighteen stone, I should say, with black, beady eyes, a big black moustache, and a completely bald head except for some black hair at the back, below the crown. I was nervous and stammered when I was introduced to him, but his kindly expres-sion and manner soon put me at my ease.

Edward Wynn left us as soon as he had introduced me, and I spent the next hour-and-a-quarter alone with 'the Old Man', as he was in-variably called at Pembroke. The result of the interview was that from that autumn until his death twelve years later I was his assistant, taking classes several times a week in his outer room and occasionally in the College Library. The modern language group at Pembroke was a big one, and thus I came to know a large number of Pembroke men. As I dined in hall with Comber from time to time I also came to know some of the dons well, particularly J. C. Lawson and Aubrey Atwater, both of whom died before Comber, and Sir Ellis Minns, who survived all three of them by a good many years.

I believe it was on Comber's recommendation that, after one term's work for him at Pembroke, I was appointed a regular supervisor at Jesus. The number of men reading modern languages was smaller there than at Pembroke, but the great attraction of the new work was that it was for my own college and that I did much of my teaching in a small lecture room within its walls, on the staircase where Bernard Manning kept. The room, it is true, was ugly and bare, and was at the top of the 1870 Waterhouse Tower. Its only furniture was a table and some hard chairs, and its fire smoked abominably on windy days, sometimes driving me and my pupils out of the room. Still, it was bliss to be teaching within the walls of Jesus College; to look across Pump Court to the Hall and the triangular chimney-buttresses of the 1640 building; to see the yellow crocuses opening in February and March round the trunks of the lime, the sycamore, the pink chestnut, and the false acacia, which stretched in a row from the Waterhouse Tower to the Hall Staircase; to watch those four trees slowly (the acacia most reluctantly) break into leaf in April and May; and to see the fallen rose-red flowers of the chestnut lying thick on the vivid green grass under the boughs late in May, like a circular pool of rosy blood.

I continued, however, to do most of my individual teaching at the Oratory House, where we had a new Warden from the beginning of 1924, as John How had resigned his membership of the Oratory and left Cambridge soon afterwards for parish work, later becoming Bishop of Glasgow. His place as Warden was taken by Wilfred Knox, whom I had hitherto met only on his occasional visits from the East End of London. He came of a very able family, being a son of E. A. Knox, Bishop of Manchester, and a brother of Ronald Knox and E. V. Knox, Editor of *Punch*, and he possessed his full share of the family brilliance.

Wilfred Knox was not a handsome man, and his complete indifference to his outward appearance did not help to make him look any more so. Slim, and of average height, he had a large head, and hair that curled slightly. He was shy with strangers; and his high-pitched voice, which rattled away like a machine-gun, and his extremely nervous laugh accompanied by a hysterical intake of the breath, were the reverse of attractive. He generally wore a pair of stained grey flannel trousers, very baggy at the knees because they were never pressed, a grey woollen pullover, and a black jacket with the usual clerical collar and stock. Out of doors he wore a somewhat greasy and battered black trilby hat, and if the weather was wet a cheap raincoat. All his clothing indeed was cheap, as it was apparently part of his rule of life not to spend an unnecessary penny on clothes. He used to go into outfitters' shops asking for 'the sort of shirt a workman wears.' We sometimes accused him of robbing the scarecrow in the Oratory House garden, and the jest may have had some justification.

Wilfred was very abstemious about food and drink and the only luxury on which he spent any money was tobacco, which he smoked in moderation. He enjoyed a glass of wine, but it was against his rule to buy any. Occasionally, however, when he came out of St Edward's Church after attending a service or hearing confessions there, he would find in his bicycle-basket an offering of a woollen vest, a pair of pants, or a bottle of Benedictine. These were gifts from a lady who shadowed him for years, though he never spoke to her if he saw her, or acknowledged her existence in any way, beyond mentioning to the rest of us that 'the Looney' had apparently been round again. As he disliked Benedictine, I had standing orders to exchange it at a wine-merchant's for claret or Burgundy; for he had appointed me to the offices of cellarer, tramp-master, and clock-winder almost as soon as he came to the House.

My most important office at the House, however, was as Wilfred's vicar choral. It is true that the title was never formally conferred on me, but I in fact carried out the duties of the office for years, even after I had left the House.

Musically, Wilfred was completely tone deaf. If anyone had struck the top note and then the bottom note of a piano when his back was turned to it and had then asked him which of the two notes was the higher, he would in all probability have answered, 'What do you mean?' When he was preparing for ordination some voice-trainer had tried to teach him to intone at least the simpler inflections of church services; but Wilfred remarked afterwards, with a smile, 'The poor dear had to give me up as hopeless, after a very hard struggle.' Yet he loved choral services and even officiating at them. He was therefore often the celebrant at the Sung Eucharist which the members of the Oratory held at St Edward's Church on Sunday mornings. He thoroughly enjoyed it, but to anyone with a musical ear he sounded like a croaking raven bellowing somewhat mutedly for revenge. At the House chapel, where he insisted on having Solemn Evensong every Sunday and a Sung Eucharist every feast-day, and where all choral services were un-accompanied, Wilfred was always the officiant, even if Alec Vidler or

H

some other cleric with an equally good voice was present. He deputed to me at Evensong any of the priest's part that a layman could possibly be allowed to take — that is to say, practically the whole of it, apart from 'The Lord be with you' and the Collects. When the hymn came at the end of the service he joined in it as lustily as any bull-frog.

Wilfred's chief recreation was gardening. Every day after lunch he took off his cassock and worked in the garden until tea-time. He appeared to enjoy gardening, and certainly produced excellent results in flowers; but he asserted that he did it merely for the sake of exercise and because the House could not afford a professional gardener. His passion was fly-fishing, and the moment the May Term ended he used to rush to Kington in Herefordshire for his annual fishing holiday with E. V. Knox and Edward Wynn. When he came back it was time for him to go to the Isle of Ely for the Cambridge Fruiting Campaign, where he worked among the fruit-pickers from East London for several weeks. He returned to Cambridge tired out and coated with grime, which it took two or three days to eradicate from round his eyes.

Ecclesiastically, he belonged to the Liberal Catholic group. There was a good deal of the 'naughty boy' spirit in him, and in his earlier years he loved to be considered an extremist in ceremonial and liturgical matters. In his later years he liked to be considered an extreme Modernist. Yet all the time he was an orthodox Anglican; and at all times he was vivacious, witty, humble, shrewd in his judgement of men and affairs, charitable, compassionate, and saintly.

Owing to my new work at Pembroke and Jesus, my income for the academical year 1923-4 rose considerably, and I decided that I could afford to spend the Long Vacation on the Continent. Accordingly, at the end of June 1924 I set out for Spain, to take a summer course at the University of Madrid. I stopped on the way at Poitiers, where I joined a number of pilgrims to the tomb of St Radegund. I was struck by the sugary hymn-tune, of the Sankey and Moody type, which they sang, and by the number of small mural tablets all round the shrine, recording their donors' thanks to St Radegund for helping them through examinations. Most of the inscriptions were naturally in French, with the names or initials of the beneficiaries attached, but a few were in other languages. One was in English, and as the initials 'S. F.' were appended to it I accused Steve Fairbairn, when I next saw him, of being the author of it; but he replied that he had never had any trouble with examinations.

From Poitiers I went on to Burgos, where I inspected the beautiful cathedral and felt, as I felt when visiting other Spanish cathedrals during the dog-days, that the so-called lazy and dilatory Spaniards were deserving of great admiration for ever having built such a masterpiece in such a climate. I read the notices hanging from each pillar of the nave, 'For the love of God and the sake of hygiene, do not spit on the floor of this cathedral,' and then fled hurriedly from the nasal bellow with which the choirboys sang their verses of the office hymn.

At Madrid I was comfortably housed and well fed in a university hostel. I went to lectures on the Spanish language by Novarro Tomás and on early Spanish poetry by the celebrated medievalist Ramón Menendez Pidal, who also arranged a delightful concert of Spanish ballads. I attended practical classes given by Dámaso Alonso, whom I was to meet again later in Cambridge, and by Amado Alonso, whom I came to know fairly well, and I exchanged conversation in English and Spanish with a young graduate named Laso de la Vega. Sometimes I went out to dine in a hotel garden at nine o'clock (the usual hour for dinner) and on to one of the cinemas, which in the summer opened at half past ten and closed about one o'clock.

On the feast-day of St James, the national patron, I attended High Mass at the Church of the Calatravas, where the singing was good and the organ and orchestra excellent. The church door was opened for worshippers by one of the company of blind beggars who habitually stood in the porch during service time. In some churches the beggars seemed to take turns in occupying the place of vantage nearest the door; but at this church one burly beggar always occupied that position, the others being apparently too decrepit or too cowed to dispute it with him. He seemed to do good business for he was corpulent and out-swelling his clothes. Perhaps half his sustenance was derived from the lottery-tickets that he offered for sale, one of them being stuck in his hat-band to remind the devout of their opportunity of making a fortune as they went past him into church.

In the evening of St James's Day I went to my first bull-fight. I admired the skill of the bull-fighters, but when I witnessed the barbaric cruelty to the horses I felt that I would like to shoot everyone connected with it. Yet I must confess that I went to at least two other bull-fights during subsequent visits to Spain.

From Madrid I made an expedition by train to Toledo, travelling through a blinding heat over what looks like an African desert at that time of year. I reached my destination at dusk, hungry, weary, and with my eyes and nose full of sand. A fried steak and olives, with a bottle of

Rioja, made me feel a new man, and after dinner I strolled on the Miradero, where a large crowd was promenading and enjoying the breeze from the Tagus gorge. Next day I went to the Mozarabic Mass at the cathedral and explored the city which, with its narrow streets, small iron-grilled windows, Moorish arches, and strings of donkeys and mules, reminded me very much of Egypt. I then went back to finish my course of lectures at Madrid and a few days later turned north, as the money which I had set aside for my continental tour was running out.

My departure from Madrid by taxi-cab was not without incident. The driver, on drawing near the railway station, found his progress slowed down by a horse-cab which, after causing several irritating delays, finally stopped in such a position that it was impossible for the taxi to draw up to the pavement, and at the same time caused the front mudguard of the car to get entangled in the spokes of the back wheel of the cab. Both the cabman and the taxi-driver got down. The cabman and I thought that the taxi-driver was going to help him to disentangle the mudguard from the spokes; but, to my surprise, and still more, no doubt, to the cabman's, he suddenly hit the latter violently under the jaw and then in the ribs. Within ten seconds the deserted sun-stricken station yard was swarming with people, who crowded round the combatants and eagerly watched the development of the fight. Men, women and children came running up as if from nowhere and formed a ring. The men lit cigarettes and watched solemnly. The women fanned themselves, craned their necks over the men's shoulders, and fanned themselves again. The children stood on tiptoe or wormed themselves through the crowd to get a better view.

When we arrived at the station I had only a few minutes in which to get my luggage out of the taxi and registered for transmission to Segovia before the train left. The taxi-driver ignored my existence, being busy attacking his opponent, who was now bleeding freely. The car engine was still running. I glanced at the taximeter, stepped into the ring, thrust some money into the driver's right hand, and withdrew to the edge of the ring for fear of accidents. He parried a thrust from his opponent with his left, glanced at the money in his right hand, shouted that it was half a peseta short, and delivered a blow to the enemy's left eye. Rushing to me at the edge of the ring, he pocketed another peseta which I gave him, raised his hat, bowed, wished me 'adiós,' and bent his arms for the next round. I pushed my way through the crowd to find a porter. The last glimpse I caught of the fray showed that each combatant was struggling with two civil guards. The luggage office, as was the rule during the last five minutes before a train left, was now closed; but an extra peseta caused the closure to be suspended for a few minutes, and I and all my luggage caught the train.

On arriving at Segovia I was conveyed from the railway station to the town in an ancient leather-covered vehicle drawn by mules decorated with strings of loud jingling bells. After dinner that evening I sat in the plaza listening to the band, which played until after midnight. Next morning, after visiting the Roman aqueduct, I took the train to the beautiful and relatively cool San Sebastian, which I left with great reluctance two days later.

On arriving back in England I went straight to Hove, to coach Joe Harmsworth for his next Cambridge examination and to give Lady Harmsworth some lessons in Italian. Her desire to learn the language was prophetic, because the three of us left suddenly for Italy shortly afterwards, her eldest son having been taken ill at Stresa on Lake Maggiore. We stayed at Stresa for some weeks. While we were there, I received a letter one day from Signor Nitti, who was now living at Zurich as an exile from Fascism. He asked me to translate a second book into English for him, and I decided to go to Zurich to see him.

He was living at a boarding-house with his wife, two daughters, and two sons, one of whom afterwards made a daring escape from a Fascist prison. For no particular reason, I had pictured Nitti as a tall man, but I found someone considerably shorter than myself and so broad in the shoulders that he seemed even shorter than he was. He was a chain-smoker and a non-smoker in alternate years: this was one of his non-smoking years. A genial man and a very interesting talker, he had an obvious liking for everything English, and I felt at ease with him at once. Before I left the house he handed his manuscript to me and gave me a free hand in choosing a publisher, except that he expressed a wish for a change from Fisher Unwin.

When I returned to England with the Harmsworths I took the manuscript (once more on the advice of Professor Okey) to the firm of J. M. Dent and Sons. The head and founder of the firm, the great Joseph Mallaby Dent, himself interviewed me, frowning at me all down his white beard and making me feel very small. Like Fisher Unwin, he offered me a choice between a lump sum and a small royalty for my translation; and I, with my former experience in mind, confidently chose the royalty.

It was September 27th when the details of publication were settled; and as the book, like its predecessor, dealt with current international affairs, both Nitti and the publisher wanted it to appear as early as possible — by the middle of November if that could be done. Further, the book was estimated to run to 300 large pages, and I therefore set to work at top speed. There was a difficulty about the title. A literal translation of the Italian would have been *The Tragedy of Europe*; but that would have looked depressing and was also liable to be confused with the title of the previous book. I therefore, with the *Solitudinem faciunt, pacem appellant* of Tacitus in mind, suggested *They Make a Desert*, and this was accepted by both Nitti and the publishers.

After a great effort on the part of the printers and the translator, the book appeared on November 12th. As with *The Decadence of Europe*, I had reason to be pleased with the reviewers' remarks about the translation. On the other hand, in choosing a royalty rather than a lump sum I had backed the wrong horse a second time; for *They Make a Desert* dealt with the same subjects as *The Decadence of Europe* and appeared too soon after it. It therefore sold badly, and I would have done much better by accepting a lump sum. My total payment was no more than £11 7s. 3d., which worked out at about ninepence a page for translating, proof-reading, and indexing.

18

In the autumn of 1924 I took my Master of Arts degree, being presented to the Vice-Chancellor this time by L. A. Pars, who had succeeded Watt as Praelector. I now wore the well-known gown with long and curiously shaped 'glove' sleeves and a hood of black and white silk. My new degree made me a senior member of the University, free from the disciplinary control of Proctors and college tutors alike, and I could borrow ten books at a time from the University Library — a privilege of which non-resident M.A.s are often unaware and one of which graduates of Oxford and apparently all other universities (where they cannot borrow books or even have access to them on the shelves) must be most envious. Apart from that, I had few or no privileges, except that I could dine at the Fellows' table at Jesus three times a term. This scanty allowance was, however, in proportion as I became more and more useful to the College, gradually increased to three times a week. I dined, of course, at my own expense.

Strictly speaking, I did not become a complete Master of Arts until the end of the academical year in which I went through the Senate House ceremony. Until then, I was only what was called an Inceptor. This medieval period of probation, which had long ceased to have any meaning, was abolished by the new University Statutes of 1926, when the distinction between a Bachelor-designate and a complete Bachelor was also dropped.

I became a member of high table in time to get to know Charles Hose, one of the Honorary Fellows, who died in 1929. He was the most enormous man I have ever known. He must have weighed from twenty-five to thirty stone, and when he sat at high table the back of his chair seemed to project about a foot beyond all the others, to make room for his huge paunch. He was a very able man and had been made an honorary Doctor of Science by the University for his valuable researches into the anthropology and natural history of Borneo and into the causes of beriberi. In his earlier years in Borneo he had contributed to the advance of civilization by inducing the natives to abandon head-hunting and settle their disputes by boat-racing instead. His great success with the savage tribes was no doubt partly due to his size. A story (founded on fact, though exaggerated) used to relate that once,

when Hose set out to prevent a threatened tribal war, he sent a mes-
senger in advance, displaying a pair of Hose's enormous trousers, which
he hoisted on a pole in the no-man's-land between the rival forces.
'Gentlemen,' he said (or words to that effect), 'those are worn by the
man who is coming to enquire into this dispute and he will be here at
any moment.' When Hose arrived (the story says) there was not a man
to be seen.

A former Fellow who was occasionally (though rarely) seen in the
College about this time was Sydney Cockerell, who was Director of the
Fitzwilliam Museum for nearly thirty years. He claimed to have transformed the Fitzwilliam from a pigsty into a palace; and of this his
biographer says, 'Undue modesty was never one of Cockerell's faults,
but what he says here is no more than the truth.' Cockerell was famous
for his skill in extracting large sums of money from the wealthy for the
benefit of the Fitzwilliam. It was said that if a rich man received a visit
from him he feared that his end was near.

The first words I ever heard Cockerell utter – it was at a College
feast – were: 'So I went to see the duke. He was a dying man then. He
said to me, "How much do you want, Cockerell?" – "I must have
twenty thousand," I answered. – "I can't give you more than ten
thousand," the duke said. However, he left us thirty thousand.'

Cockerell was bitter because his six-year Fellowship at Jesus had not
been renewed in 1916. According to his biographer, 'had Cockerell
been given a free choice, it is unlikely that he would have chosen Jesus
– an athletic college with a frivolous and hearty element among the
younger dons'; but the biographer is wrong on every point. First of all,
Cockerell *had* a free choice. His biographer is an Oxford man, and at
Oxford each professorial Fellowship – which was the kind of Fellowship that Cockerell held – is linked to a particular college; but at
Cambridge it is not so. Further, the junior Fellows at Jesus at the time
of Cockerell's election were W. R. Hughes, a mathematician, Quaker,
and lifelong social worker; the gentle H. G. Wood (afterwards Professor
of Theology at Birmingham), and W. R. Inge, who left Jesus to become
Dean of St Paul's. None of these could be called either frivolous or
hearty. Neither could any of those who had joined or succeeded them
before Cockerell's Fellowship expired, among them being C. A. Elliott
(afterwards Provost of Eton); W. H. Mills, F.R.S.; W. H. Duke, a quiet
classical scholar; J. M. Edmonds, the laborious editor of Greek comic
fragments; 'Q', and Harold Spencer-Jones, who became Astronomer
Royal. It is significant, too, that Inge, who came to the college as a

stranger three years before Cockerell, was most happy in it, describes it
in his memoirs as 'a friendly college', and revisited it frequently up to
his death in 1954.

The cause of Cockerell's failure to be re-elected at Jesus, or to be
elected at any other college for sixteen years, lay in himself. One of his
colleagues said, 'I don't think he had much sense of humour; and he
was always so sure he was right.' Cockerell asserted that Q and he had
the same sense of humour; but, in comparison with Q, he had no sense
of humour at all.

His biographer quotes a long letter of sympathy written to Cockerell
from America by Foakes Jackson, one of the Senior Fellows of Jesus,
who, he says, 'had just emigrated in disillusionment and despair'. How
was it, then, that Foakes Jackson took advantage of his life Fellowship
to come over from America and stay in the College for long periods
whenever he could, until he died, and that he obviously revelled in
doing so? His letter to Cockerell was perhaps inspired by a wish to
soothe the feelings of a disappointed man.

With all his defects, Cockerell will nevertheless be remembered for
his utter devotion to the Fitzwilliam, for the great courtesy with which
he treated the humblest visitors and enquirers, and for the unstinted
amount of his time which he gave them. He must moreover be almost
unique in having instructed his biographer to tell the whole truth about
him and to emphasize his faults and shortcomings.

In 1929 the College inaugurated a daily lunch in Hall for those who
wished it, as an alternative to lunching in their rooms or elsewhere, and
I was given the privilege of lunching at high table as often as I liked.
The meal was much less formal than dinner. Gowns were not worn and
one began lunch and left the table when one liked. Only a few of the
Fellows lunched regularly, but among the few was Q, who disliked
solitary lunches in his rooms. My intimacy with him dated from that
time, because I attended Hall lunch very frequently, and often the two
of us were alone. He soon took it for granted that after lunch I would
drink a glass of wine with him in his rooms, where decanters of port,
sherry, and Madeira stood in a row on a side-table, together with a
bottle of whisky and a syphon of soda-water.

Q detested teetotalism, and I think he had doubts about the morals
of any teetotaller until he knew him to be trustworthy. He also strongly
disliked Nonconformity, even though some of his closest friends were
Nonconformists. One day when we were adjourning to his rooms after
lunching in Hall he invited my friend Conrad Skinner, an old Jesuan

who was an assistant master at the Leys School and was lunching that day at high table, to join us; and Conrad, though Q did not know it, was a lifelong teetotaller and a Methodist. I had no chance to warn him what to do; and consequently, when Q invited him to help himself to port, he replied that he did not drink port. He was thereupon invited to take a glass of sherry, to which he replied that he did not drink sherry either. The same thing happened with the Madeira and the whisky. Q looked more and more puzzled, and when Conrad finally confessed that he was a teetotaller I saw a look of horror spread over Q's face. As soon as Conrad and I got out of the room I advised him, when Q next invited him to help himself, not to refuse, but to tinkle with the glasses and take some soda-water. I assured him that Q would then be quite happy, since he never noticed what his guests took when helping themselves and would have forgotten the previous incident. He did as I suggested, with the pleasing result that Q was soon telling me what an excellent man Conrad Skinner was.

One of the most regular of all lunchers at high table for nearly thirty years was J. M. Edmonds, the classical scholar, who had entered the college in 1894. Between his graduation and his returning to Cambridge he had been a master at King's School, Canterbury. His kindness of heart was shown there in his class lists, which were notorious for the large number of names bracketed together in them as equals. This feature was particularly helpful to the boys in the lower part of the list. If, for instance, there were thirty boys in the class and the last six of them were bracketed equal, each of them could write home saying that he was twenty-fifth among 30. Some members of the school used to hope eagerly that in one of the end-of-term lists the headmaster would read out: 'All the boys in Mr Edmonds' class are bracketed equal first.'

During the war of 1914-18 Edmonds contributed a number of striking epitaphs to the columns of *The Times* and *The Times Literary Supplement*. One of them, for a British graveyard in France, has achieved world-wide fame, being frequently quoted in books, painted in memorial windows throughout the English-speaking world, and carved on innumerable war-memorials — seldom with any acknowledgement of its authorship or request for permission to use it. Perhaps this neglect of the usual courtesies was sometimes due to its air of timelessness, which led many borrowers to imagine it to be a translation from the Greek Anthology. Others ascribed it to A. E. Housman or some other modern writer. Field Marshal Lord Wavell misattributed it in print to General Edmonds, who was a member of his staff during the

Second World War. J. M. Edmonds, always courteous, used to say that he would not have minded the misattributions of authorship or the breaches of his copyright, if only the text had not been commonly misquoted, as it is (for instance) on the Kohima Memorial and even in the Ashendene Press edition of his epitaphs.

The correct version runs:

When you go home, tell them of us, and say
'For your tomorrows these gave their today.'

From about the time when I took my M.A. degree I began to do more and more teaching for the College. I also became a French tutor for the Cambridge branch of the Workers' Educational Association, to which I gave up an evening a week for four years. A little later I began to conduct University classes in French translation for the Faculty of Modern and Medieval Languages, being paid so much a head. This work started (at Professor Prior's instigation) in 1927 and continued for twenty years. I held the classes at Jesus College, sometimes in the Hall, because the class was often too large for a lecture-room. One of my first pupils was Lewis Harmer of Fitzwilliam House, who soon became one of my best friends. It gave me great pleasure when he was elected a Fellow of Trinity in 1944 and Professor of French six years later.

My Jesus pupils during the time when I was living at the Oratory House included a sturdy American, A. P. Bryant, who became a lifelong friend. He was a keen oarsman, overflowing with high spirits which sometimes brought him into conflict with authority. After several minor incidents he stood at the entrance to the College hall one evening while dinner was going on, levelled a pistol at the high table – as the result of a wager, I imagine – and fired it. It did no harm, but it made a tremendous noise; which I believe he expected no more than anyone else. Consternation ensued; and after a tutorial conference it was decreed that 'Buddy' Bryant was to go down.

Knowing him to be (to use a phrase of Duckworth's*) 'not positively evil, don't you know' – far from it, indeed – I interceded for him. After some consideration it was decided that he was to be allowed to stay up, provided I accepted responsibility for him. He was to live with me at the Oratory House, to attend at least one Chapel every day there, to be regular at lectures and supervisions, and to report to me every night at ten o'clock to prove that he was in. He carried out the conditions faithfully. All the tougher members of the boat club dined with

* W. L. H. Duckworth, Master of Jesus College 1940-45.

him in turn at the House, two at a time; and it was noticeable that they seemed to be under the impression that it was a case of 'No chapel, no dinner'.

At the end of his three years at Cambridge he went back to the United States and during the war of 1939-45 had a distinguished career in the American Navy. One day soon after the war he reappeared at the College and I took him — he was feeling rather shy — to dine at high table. Duckworth, who happened to be presiding that evening, said to him, when I introduced him, 'I do not recollect, Mr Bryant, having seen you at this table before this evening's repast.' 'No, sir,' Buddy answered, 'I've never dined at high table before. I've only shot at it.' 'Indeed,' said Duckworth, 'then I conjecture that you must be unique among the members of this college, don't you know.'

When Buddy last called to see me I found that he had become a vestryman of his church in Miami — what we in England term a parochial church councillor. I wonder whether all his dinner-guests at the Oratory House have followed his example.

19

It was not until the year when I became a Master of Arts that I went to my first May Week ball. At the time I had a private pupil living with me at the Oratory House – a middle-aged Dane, who was anxious to improve his English. He naturally wanted to see as much of Cambridge life as possible, and when I asked him whether he would like to go to a May Week ball with me he answered that he would like it very much. I had never been able to afford such a luxury in my undergraduate days, but I could manage it now. I also possessed by this time full evening dress with tails, which were a necessity then: no one would have dared to appear at a May Week ball in a dinner-jacket suit in those days. As there was no ball at Jesus that year, we decided to go to the ball at the Guildhall organized by the Hawks Club, of which Joe Harmsworth and some other pupils of mine were members.

I had of course to find a dancing partner for the Dane as well as for myself. It so happened that Dorothy Lattimer, the daughter of my old headmaster, was an undergraduate at Newnham at the time. I went to tea with her one Sunday and she agreed to come to the ball with the Dane and myself and to find another Newnhamite to complete the quartet. As I was coming down the stairs after tea I met a Newnhamite whom I had never seen before but whose appearance struck me very much. Next day, I wrote to Dorothy Lattimer, giving a description of the girl and asking her to track her down and find out whether she would be willing to come to the ball. The girl was traced with some difficulty and, when all four of us had met for tea at a café, she accepted the invitation. Dorothy found later that she herself could not come, but a Newnham friend of hers agreed to deputize for her.

I was glad when everything was arranged, and yet I felt some trepidation. I imagined that all Newnhamites were expert dancers, and I felt convinced that so handsome and accomplished a man as the Dane must be the same. My own experience of dancing had been limited, with few exceptions, to dances in the village hall at South Mimms, and those were hardly up to ballroom standard. Being determined not to show up my shortcomings, I arranged to take private lessons at a School of Dancing over a Cambridge music-shop. There, every afternoon for about a fortnight, I pushed a big stout woman round the dance floor to

the strains of a gramophone. The weather was unusually hot for early
June, too. If I remember rightly, there was a heat-wave at the time.

At the end of the course I was declared 'quite good' by my instruct-
ress. In spite of that, my knees were knocking together when we
entered the Guildhall. I was delighted to see Joe Harmsworth already
there, because I knew that, on account of his weight, he intended to do
very little dancing and much sitting out. Drawing him aside on some
excuse or other, I rapidly explained the situation and begged him to
help me in keeping my party away from the dance floor as long as
possible. He rose to the occasion magnificently, keeping the party in
fits of laughter with one story after another. All the time that he was
talking I was racking my brains to think of a cue for yet another story
in case of need. At last, however − I knew it must happen sooner or
later − one of the girls said, 'Come on. We must dance'. I followed
reluctantly, feeling like an ox going to be slaughtered. Then the unexpected happened. To my astonishment and relief, the other three
were such poor dancers that I was the best of the four and felt embarrassed on their account rather than on my own. I was further
embarrassed by my partner's trick of flinging first one shoulder and
then the other up and down. That had been all the rage a year or two
previously but was now taboo, as was obvious to me from the glances
that everyone threw in our direction. I did my best to restrain her, by
clutching her hard and letting my weight drag on her shoulders. I was
not, however, entirely successful and was therefore glad to avail myself
of Joe Harmsworth's services as an entertainer as frequently as possible
during what was left of the night. So ended my first May Week ball.

Although I had to teach many hours a week at this time in order to
make a living and was also doing a considerable amount of research and
writing, I managed to take some recreation each day.

On Sundays, after carrying out my duties at Evensong in the Oratory
House chapel, I went off to Jesus College to attend the Roost, the
meetings of which I never missed unless I was ill. I very soon became a
kind of Pope of the Roosters, with the title of Dean and Archdean, and
we evolved some new frivolity almost every term. In 1926, for instance,
we demanded the return of the eleven days stolen from the country by
the so-called reform of the calendar in 1752. As a practical step, we
founded a Union for Getting Back the Eleven Days, called 'Ugbed' for
short, from its initial letters. An inaugural dinner was held at the *Lion*,
where so many good causes have been launched. Among the speakers
was E. V. Knox, whose impassioned appeal on behalf of the Ugbed

appeared as an article in *Punch* on the following Wednesday. At the
dinner, I distributed printed copies of an Ugbed proclamation to the
nation. In it I suggested methods of regaining the eleven days and
pointed out the iniquity of a calendar in which next Wednesday is
really last Sunday week. A clerical friend who asked to see the proclamation remarked, after reading solemnly through it, 'It seems all
right to me, but you'll never be able to get back those eleven days.'

In course of time the Roost became what I wanted it to be – a
blending of a social club, a light-hearted debating society, and a light
dramatic society. It called itself a Parliament of Fowls; and its con-
stitution, rites, ceremonies, and vocabulary, which had their source
partly in Parliamentary ceremonial, partly in Senate House procedure,
and partly (it must be confessed) in the liturgy, all centred on the
cockerel as the symbol of John Alcock and the college that he founded.
I soon persuaded Q to join and become our first High Steward; also
Bernard Manning, who became Lord Chamberlain and Chamberlain.
Other dons followed them from time to time, so that the Roost became
a pleasant meeting-ground for senior and junior members of the
College, while remaining predominantly an undergraduate club.

Some idea of our peculiarities can be gained from a study of the
title-page of our book of forms and ceremonies, 'copyright in all
countries and in the town of Berwick-upon-Tweed' (*see following page*).

I had little time for recreation on week-days, but I generally
managed to arrange my teaching programme so that I could get down
to the river when the boats were out – after lunch during the winter
terms, after tea in the summer. From the end of the First World War
until his death in 1938 Steve Fairbairn spent most of his time at
Cambridge during term, and his genius as a coach kept the College at
the head of the river more often than all the other colleges put together. Despite my insignificance as an oarsman, he realized my
enthusiasm for rowing and, to my great pleasure, made all the use he
could of my services. Occasionally, despite my weight, he made me cox
an eight all the way to Ely, when crews from a number of colleges
rowed down from Cambridge in December to see the University Trial
Eights race. I am afraid that in that course of eighteen miles I called
'like a penny steamer at each shore with stolid alternation', as Sir Owen
Seaman, who had coxed when at Cambridge, says in one of his poems.

From time to time I coached the Newnham eight, for Steve was a
strong advocate of women's rowing and in fact of rowing for everybody, almost regardless of age. Girton, however, did not take up serious

CODEX GALLORUM

wherein are contain'd all the ℞*egulations & Ordinances*
*to be obferv'd in the holding & condu*ᶜ*ting of Roofts,*

as alfo Ordinances touching *Eggs, Chickens, & Perches,*
the payment of *Eggage, Perchage, Quillage, Coopage, ffowlage,*
Beakage, & Chuckage,

the obtaining of *Degrees* in Cockerellty & Roofter Lore,
& the Working of the *Court of Twerpery*;
together with the fform & Manner of
Opening & Clofing a Rooft,
returning *Thanks* upon any Occafion,
Emperching Cockerells,
Orderizing Companions of the
Moft Loquacious Order of the Red Herring,
& *Elevating* a Prefident to the Grainfack;

to which is annex'd a Table of Times & Occafions on which *Gallage* is
proper to be done, & the Method of performing the fame;

all which ℞*ites & Ceremonies* are point'd
as they are to be cluck'd or crow'd in Roofts.

¶ *Tables* to find the ℞*oofter & Pifcal Year,* the time of *Cockcrow,* & the
time of *Pifcal Moonrife* have been infert'd for the greater Convenience of
Roofters, whether of the Upper Perch or the Lower, together with an
Outline of Hiftory for the guidance of candidates for Roofterfhip, & divers
other curious Matters.

The title-page of the Roosters' book of forms and ceremonies.

rowing until some years later. I remember that once, when I was to
umpire a race at Ely between Newnham College and a London women's
eight, the Newnham bow oar, a girl named Eveline Furtado, hit a
floating log as they were paddling down to the start and was knocked
clean out of the boat into the water. I much admired the way in which
she climbed back into the boat and rowed on as though nothing had
happened.

Those were the early days of serious rowing for women at Cambridge. The first time I took the Newnham eight out, and was coming

back from Baitsbite with them, I felt quite embarrassed when I saw that five Jesus boats were coming downstream towards us, with five coaches cycling alongside them. Each of the five coaches grinned broadly at me as he cycled past. Sartorially, Cambridge rowing women were not yet emancipated. Until the middle twenties the authorities at Newnham required them to wear skirts and stockings when in the boat. In 1925 they were allowed to wear shorts instead of skirts but were still required to wear stockings, and it was not until some years later that they were permitted to wear socks instead.

Generally, however, I acted as a kind of adjutant to Steve. He liked company when he was coaching, and I cycled with him along the towpath almost every afternoon from 1926 until he gave up cycling through ill health. Occasionally he would turn to me and say, 'What do you think of them, Freddy?' and I would truthfully answer, 'I don't know, Steve. What do you think?' which was just the answer that he wanted. He would then give me a detailed criticism of each man's rowing, coupled often with some comments on his character, which afterwards proved to be surprisingly near the mark.

Unlike many coaches, Steve did not spoil an outing for his crews by keeping up a continuous chatter through a megaphone from the bank, or by long chilly halts while he lectured to them. He enjoyed every minute of the outing himself, and he wanted his crews to enjoy it too. 'Every good outing is a joy, and every good stroke rowed is a joy in itself,' he used to say. He therefore contented himself with terse remarks addressed to the crew as a whole, punctuating them now and then with a few words of encouragement to an individual whose rowing was showing signs of improvement, and with occasional asides to anyone who was cycling with him: 'Lean her along. Le-e-ean her along. (Jimmy's a lot better today.) Le-e-e-ean her along. (Just look at Jimmy!) Feather high. Le-e-ean her along. (My word, Jimmy has improved.) Well rowed, Jimmy! Easy, cox. Jimmy, you're rowing a lot better today. You're rowing better than you've rowed since Christmas. Right away, cox. Watch y'r blades. Hoo-oo-ook her along with y'r toes. (I've never gone for this before, Freddy.) Hoo-oo-ook her along with y'r toes. Hoo-oo-ook her along.'

On returning to the boat-house he would take each member of the crew aside in turn and talk to him about his individual faults, while the others waited at a little distance. (On these occasions I was always reminded of Orchardson's picture of Napoleon on board the *Bellerophon*, with his subordinates standing respectfully aloof, each

I

waiting for a signal to step forward for a consultation with the Emperor.) When the interviews were over, Steve would indulge in a little banter with the crew as a whole and return to his rooms at Maids' Causeway, where he spent the rest of the day. He would fill up the interval until dinner by answering some of the letters that arrived every day from all over the world, asking for his advice on rowing matters; or he would write a controversial rowing letter to a newspaper, occasionally enclosing a note to the editor with some such postscript as: 'Punctuate to taste, and correct to fact.' After his very frugal dinner he would play bridge with undergraduates – a different relay of men each evening – the play being interspersed with a good deal of Steve's chaff and ever-ready humour, or with his serious reflections on life in general and the University in particular. The opinions that he uttered at these gatherings were at times somewhat surprising. More than once, for instance, he expressed his conviction that all dons ought to be in Holy Orders. After bridge there would be a little more rowing talk, and the company would disperse for the night.

The secret of Steve's great success as a rowing coach was that he was a born teacher with a boundless enthusiasm for rowing and a most remarkable gift for communicating his enthusiasm to others. As an educationist, he was years in advance of his time, particularly in his insistence that the individual members of a crew should have as much freedom of expression as possible and that learners should enjoy their learning. It is a pity that he was never invited to lecture to embryo schoolmasters, who would have profited greatly from his originality of mind. Many of his phrases have stuck in my memory ever since – such phrases as 'Enjoy your rowing, win or lose', 'Coach a man to coach himself'. 'Never criticize one man in the hearing of the others', 'If a man is improving, always tell him so', and 'Never tell a man that he is improving if he isn't'.

The effect of Steve's personality on his immediate pupils was almost magical, and his mere presence among them was more than once responsible for turning defeat into victory. Once, when the Jesus first boat failed to make a bump during the first three days of the May Races, he came down from London – he nearly always kept away from Cambridge during races – to enquire into the matter. On glancing at the oars that the crew had been using he said that of course they could not make a bump with them, and ordered them to use a different set, which he selected. They did so, and made a bump that evening. They were convinced that their success was due to Steve's wonderful skill in

detecting some small defect in the oars that they had used in the first
three races. It is nevertheless probable that if he had ordered a change
of socks, rather than a change of oars, they would have made their
bump just the same.

Steve's greatest memorial is the race for the headship of the Thames
— an unparalleled race, in which nearly 3,000 men have taken part in a
single year and which has been imitated in many other places. He
founded it in 1926 and a few years later founded a similar race at
Cambridge. Until then, the only races for eights during the Michaelmas
Term were organized by each college solely for its own boats and rowed
over a short course in heats. In the autumn of 1927 Steve made the five
Jesus boats row a time-race over the three-mile lock-to-lock course
instead. In the following year he opened the race to boats of other
colleges coached by Jesus men, and thirteen eights took part. In 1929 it
was opened to all boats in the University and became the Fairbairn Cup
race — one of the biggest events in the Cambridge rowing calendar, and
the only one rowed downstream. The same year saw the triumph of
Steve's campaign for the use of sliding seats in the Lent Races — a
campaign which he had carried on for years in the teeth of strong
opposition from the orthodox.

It is difficult enough to organize boat-races at Cambridge even now,
but not nearly as difficult as when I first entered the University. Except
for a railway bridge, there was no bridge across the Cam between
Victoria Avenue (Jesus Green) and Baitsbite lock, three-and-a-half miles
away. As a consequence there were numerous ferries (called by the now
almost forgotten name of 'grinds') of which coxswains had to beware.
There were four public ferries, and in addition almost every college
boathouse had its own private grind.

The ferry at the *Pike and Eel* at Old Chesterton was, to rowing men,
the most important of all, because it was there that all coaches perforce
crossed the river. The grind was for a long time worked by the landlord
of the *Pike and Eel*, named Brown — a quiet, thoughtful man, who,
except for passing the time of day with his passengers, seldom spoke.

D. N. Thorne, a Jesus undergraduate who frequently coached the
lower boats, was equally taciturn. He was commonly called 'The
Dragon,' presumably from his initials, for nobody could be less dragon-
like than he. One day, however, when coaching a boat from his cycle
upstream from Baitsbite, he was roused from his usual quiet meditation
by the sound of his eight crashing into Brown's ferry in mid-stream.
Spurred to anger by the negligence of his cox, he roared to him, at the

top of his voice: 'YOU BLOODY FOOL!' The ferryman, unfortunately, thought that this vote of censure was directed at himself. He therefore roared back, 'BLOODY FOOL? WHO'S A BLOODY FOOL? BLOODY FOOL YOURSELF.' Upon this the Dragon, waving his arms deprecatingly, shouted back, 'NOT *YOU*, YOU BLOODY FOOL. I MEANT *HIM*, YOU BLOODY FOOL.

Honour was satisfied. Brown realized that it was not he who had been publicly stigmatized as a bloody fool, and he and the Dragon relapsed into their habitual calm.

20

During the years 1925-30 my zest for authorship developed and I wrote several books and a good many articles for various periodicals. The first article for which I was ever paid was a short study of John Mason Neale, published in *T.P.'s Weekly.* T. P. O'Connor, the founder and editor of the paper, paid me a guinea for it, and I was as pleased as if it had been ten guineas. I also wrote numerous letters to newspapers on behalf of the Society for the Protection of Wild Flowers, of which I was a keen member and honorary Press secretary.

In 1925 Bowes and Bowes of Cambridge published my first original work, *Saint Radegund, Patroness of Jesus College.* This brief study of her life and cultus was the outcome of my visit to Poitiers in the previous year and of previous and subsequent research. Its publication served at least one practical purpose. Saint Radegund died on August 13th, a day which the College had always found difficulty in observing, as it falls towards the end of the Long Vacation Term, when the number of residents is small and dwindling daily. I discovered that during the Middle Ages St Radegund's Day was observed in England on February 11th. As this date has the advantage of always falling during Full Term, it was adopted by the College and is now observed with an 'Exceeding'.

When, twenty years later, I became Steward of the College, I succeeded in getting Exceedings established on St Radegund's Day, on All Saints' Day, and on the title feast of the College — the Name of Jesus, August 7th. The word 'Exceeding' sometimes shocks people who do not know the Cambridge language. When they first hear it, they picture an Exceeding as a drunken orgy, but it is nothing of the kind. 'Exceeding' is an ancient word for a feast or any kind of meal exceeding the ordinary daily fare. It had been used at Cambridge well into the nineteenth century, when it fell into disuse until I revived it. Whether it has been revived at other colleges I do not know.

In the following year the Cambridge University Press published my critical edition of a rugged Middle English poem, *The Lyfe of Saynt Radegunde*, which had been printed by Richard Pynson at some time between 1508 and 1527. I worked at the copy in our Old Library, which the College believed to be unique; but I found that a second copy existed in America, the owner of which imagined it also to be unique when he bought it in England. I deduced that the poem was written by Henry Bradshaw, a monk of Chester who died in 1513, and discovered that his chief source was the indefatigable thirteenth century encyclopaedist, Vincent of Beauvais, through the medium of a fifteenth century chronicler, Antoninus of Florence. One of the most charming incidents in the poem, telling how St Radegund was saved from her pursuers by a miraculous crop of oats, was a later addition, drawn from medieval folk-lore.

By this time I had become deeply interested in the medieval legends of the saints, in which I read fairly widely. I was struck by the wealth of scientific hagiography produced in France and Belgium and the paucity of it in England, where the same old romantic legends were (and still are) churned out in religious books and periodicals time after time, with little or no attempt at reasoned criticism by either Anglican or Roman Catholic writers. Stimulated and cautioned by the writings of Hippolyte Delehaye and other learned Bollandists, I investigated the legend of Saint Giles, the patron saint of South Mimms, and produced a small book about him, which was published by Heffer in 1928. In it I tried to present the result of a critical but sympathetic enquiry into the legend and cult of one of the most popular saints of the Middle Ages in England. I tried to sift fact from fiction, to discover the reasons for St Giles's great popularity in a land which was not his own, to account for the geographical distribution of dedications to him in this country, and to reconstruct some tiny fraction of the medieval outlook on life from a study of the saint's legend.

One pleasing outcome of the publication of the book was that it brought me into touch with the learned Bollandist Paul Grosjean. We became regular correspondents, even if the intervals between our letters were long, and from time to time he sent me offprints of his numerous contributions to *Analecta Bollandiana*, in which he had published a warm appreciation of my *Saint Giles*. An Anglo-Catholic curate of my acquaintance was less appreciative of the book. In fact, he took me severely to task one Sunday when we emerged from South Mimms parish church side by side after the morning service. He would like to point out, he said, that some of my statements about Saint Giles were clean contrary to those contained in the Lessons for Nocturns on St Giles's Day in the Roman Breviary and must therefore be wrong. He evidently had not heard that, even during the Middle Ages, a person suspected of telling a very tall story was said to lie like the Nocturns.

My next three books (1928-30) were of a very different kind, being all connected with rowing.

The first and most substantial of the three was a history of the Jesus College Boat Club, in which I had the collaboration of Humphrey Playford, who was now an assistant master and chaplain at Stowe. A good deal of research was entailed by it, particularly as the club minute-books for a number of years had been lost. We brought out a second volume of it many years later – in 1962.

My second rowing book was a selection of brief sayings by Steve Fairbairn – one for each day of the year – drawn from his published rowing notes and from his letters to me, of which I had by this time a large number. The book was intended to provide a daily thought for oarsmen, coxswains, and coaches; and in order to avoid monotony and introduce a little light relief I fitted a number of the quotations to appropriate saints' days, like this:

February 14th (*St Valentine*). Orthodoxy is particularly severe on keeping the eyes in the boat. This not only turns the body into cast-iron, but also paralyses the mind.

March 25th (*St Dismas, Protector against Thieves*). Pick the weak point of a crew rather than of an individual.

April 27th (*St Zita, Patroness of Housemaids*). Let the knees rise easily and naturally, just before they feel constrained.

August 16th (*St Roch, Protector against Sores*). Fixed seats are an abomination and should be done away with.

August 25th (*St Louis, Patron of Barbers*). One can tell instinctively by sound and feel whether the blade is being brought through at the right depth.

As I have said previously, Steve could not tolerate levity in con-nexion with rowing; yet, curiously enough, he approved of my saints' days. I think he looked on them merely as useful aids to memory. He was indignant when Claude Elliott told him he thought the book funny.

I called the book *Slowly Forward.* When Steve asked the reason for the title I answered that 'Slowly Forward!' was one of his favourite admonitions to crews when coaching them. He denied this, asserting that he always said 'Slow Forward!' When I retorted that in any event an adverb was necessary in that position he was much amused and somewhat contemptuous. 'Adverbs!' he burst out. 'Adverbs! You're like the rest of the bloody dons – specialized idiots.' I never heard the last of it. From that time onward, whenever he introduced me to anyone — in the Stewards' Enclosure at Henley, or anywhere else — he used to add solemnly, 'He knows a lot about adverbs, he does'; and when he wrote to me he often ended his letter with

'Yoursly everly,
Stevely'.

My third rowing book was a descriptive bibliography of rowing literature in various languages, called *Oar, Scull, and Rudder.* It was based on my own collection of rowing books and pamphlets, reputed to be one of the largest anywhere and now the property of the Stewards of Henley Regatta. I offered the book first to the Cambridge University Press. As they required a subsidy in order to publish so specialized a work and I had no money to spare, I sent it, on Q's advice, to the Oxford University Press, who published it at their own risk. Steve Fairbairn offered to write an Introduction to it. I knew that his style of writing, influenced as it inevitably was by years spent in the backwoods of Australia out of touch with books or educated men, was hardly in keeping with a staid University Press, but I could not refuse his offer. A few days later he handed his Introduction to me and made me read it there and then. It was full of towpath colloquialisms and strange syntax; and Steve, who sat watching me, evidently saw my face drop, because he quickly said, 'You don't like my Introduction.'

'Well, Steve,' I stammered, 'these University Presses are rather a highbrow lot, you know.'

'All right,' he said. 'I'll tell you what to do. Q knows something about English. Get him to knock it into shape.'

So I went to Q and said, 'Steve says you know something about English.'

'That's decent of him,' Q answered. 'What can I do for him?'

'He wants you to knock this into shape,' I said, handing the manuscript to him.

Q put on his pince-nez, and I saw *his* face drop as he read.

'My God!' he said. 'You can't do it. Hang it all, you can't do it. No, you can't do it.' Then, after a pause, he set his jaw firmly and added, 'All right. Tell Steve I'll knock it into shape.'

When the book was published, the title-page asserted that it had an Introduction by Steve Fairbairn. It is true that Q had used the same twenty-six letters of the alphabet as Steve, but he had re-arranged them in his own inimitable style. The opening sentence, for instance, which had been something like 'Me and Freddy have had a lot of talks about

rowing,' was transformed into 'In our discussions "frequent and full"
on the principles of rowing . . . .'

I have heard it stated that I rewrote Steve's reminiscences before
they were published in 1931 under the title *Fairbairn of Jesus*, but I did
not. Rewriting would have taken all the tang out of a book which
overflows with Steve's unique personality. I merely read the manuscript, cutting out the major repetitions, re-arranging the order here and
there, and surreptitiously omitting a few passages which I thought
would be better left out and were short enough not to be missed by the
author. I also, at Steve's request, tried to find a publisher for the book.
The first publisher whom I approached rejected it, on the ground (*inter
alia*) that no one could publish a book which opened like this:

> My grandfather weighed twenty-two stone in good condition, and at
> the Scotch Games he did not go in for the wrestling competition but
> took on the two best together — one in each hand, so to speak.

Yet Hodder and Stoughton rightly published *Fairbairn of Jesus* with
that sentence unaltered. It makes the book open like an epic; and Steve
was cast in the epical mould, both physically and mentally.

21

During the University vacations I travelled a good deal in Latin Europe. I spent one spring vacation in Belgium with a Jesus friend, J. G. Sikes, who was some years younger than myself. From his birth he had been handicapped by a severe nervous affliction that made it difficult for him to control his limbs, so that he could not lift a cup to his lips and had to type every letter he sent. He must have been one of the first spastics (though the term was not used then) to enter the University. The gallant, cheerful and uncomplaining fight that he put up against all his disabilities won him the admiration and affection of all who knew him. He gave promise of becoming a medieval historian of some standing, but unfortunately went out of his mind some years later and came to a tragic end.

One year I conducted a tour of Italy during the dog days for the Workers' Travel Association, an offshoot of the W.E.A. Both men and women were included, a number of them (probably the majority) being teachers. The party needed some handling, as we were twenty-five in all, and the tour was a strenuous one, with a good deal of night travelling.

The itinerary, which had of course been settled in advance, was very comprehensive. After a few hours in Paris we travelled all night to Turin. We stayed a night there, the next night at Pisa, and then three nights at a boarding house in Rome, where our host's private comments on the Fascists were caustic and entertaining. Some hours spent among the ruins of the Forum under a boiling sun nearly made us collapse with thirst. We were saved by the discovery of a running fountain of water and by using my Panama hat as a drinking-vessel, no other being available. Going on to the Vatican, we nearly fell asleep there with the heat. Numerous visitors were inspecting the famous art galleries, but all were too sleepy, or too impressed by the works of Michelangelo and other great artists, to speak. Only once was the silence broken by a voice which came booming along a gallery seemingly a quarter of a mile long: 'Well, I guess this yer Michelangelo must have bin a vurry busy ol' feller', after which very true comment silence fell again.

At St Peter's, admission was refused (on a plea of reverence) to women who were either bare-headed or bare-armed, and most of the women in our party were barred on both grounds. The difficulty was solved by dressing them in the men's hats and jackets, though the resulting effect was decidedly comic and much more irreverent than their former appearance. Men with bare knees were also refused admission; and as we had no spare trousers with us some members of our party had to stay outside.

From Rome we went on to spend three days among the beauty, the filth, and the grinding poverty of Naples and to visit Pompeii and Capri, where my only pair of spectacles was accidentally knocked off my nose by a boatman when rowing us through the Blue Grottoes. After Naples we stayed at Florence, Venice, Milan, and finally Paris on our way home.

In the following spring vacation I toured Spain by car from north to south, and back up the east coast, with two undergraduate pupils. It was a delightful tour, in which we crossed almost every mountain range in the Peninsula; and it was the ideal time of year for touring Spain, when the sun is brilliant but the days are not too hot and the nights are not too cool, when all the flowers of spring and summer seem to be in bloom at once, when the orange trees are loaded with fruit, when the fields are green and one does not feel (as one does in July and August) that Africa begins at the Pyrenees.

We went into Spain by Irun, and ran south-west to Burgos, Valladolid, and Salamanca, thence south-east to Avila and Madrid, and south to Toledo, Jaen, and Granada, where we spent Palm Sunday. After a night at Cordova we went on to Seville, where we stayed for the rest of Holy Week. I spent many hours in the vast and beautiful Gothic cathedral, somewhat perturbed at times by the spitting, the sight of priests smoking cigarettes, and the foul reek of tobacco whenever I passed the open door of the great sacristy where the vestments were kept. I was glad to go outside now and then, to sit or stroll in the sunlight and the purer air of the Court of Oranges.

I attended most of the Holy Week services at the cathedral, and I nearly always went alone. Somewhat to my surprise, however, my two pupils insisted on going with me on Maundy Thursday afternoon to see the Archbishop of Seville ceremonially wash the feet of twelve poor men. The washing was followed by a sermon preached by one of the canons. To judge by his style, he had studied Bossuet closely. His text — 'A new commandment I give unto you, that ye love one another' — was most appropriate to the day, but the sermon soon developed into a criticism of countries that had broken away from the Papacy. 'Take England', he said; and at this point a foreign lady sitting behind us leaned forward and whispered, 'Guess he's going to have a crack at your old country now.' One of my companions thereupon began to bristle with indignation at the preacher and to mutter half-aloud. I managed to restrain him, but that became increasingly difficult because my friend knew enough Spanish to understand that the preacher was charging England with such crimes as civil war and murder as a result of the breach with Rome. He surpassed himself when he asserted that King Charles I was beheaded for trying to force Presbyterianism on the Scotch. When we came out of the cathedral my companions urged me to take them to the archiepiscopal palace to demand an apology for the sermon. I persuaded them to visit a café first to talk things over, and before we had been there long I managed to divert their interest from the sermon to the urgency of getting tickets for the Easter Day bull-fight before it was too late.

On the Wednesday, Thursday, and Friday evenings we sat at an upstairs window of our hotel in the Calle Sierpes to watch the celebrated processions of the confraternities. They began about dusk and continued until long after dark. Each procession had its own life-size model of a scene from the Passion of Christ, displayed on a big platform. This was edged with scores of lighted candles and carried slowly through the streets on the bent backs of a dozen or more bearers, who were paid by the hour and concealed by a valance. Some members of the confraternity walked in front of the platform, dressed as Roman soldiers. Others walked behind, some of them in military or other uniform, the rest in the tall weird-looking conical hats coming down to the shoulders and with slits for the eyes that are commonly associated with members of the Inquisition. All of them carried long lighted candles. Behind them came a military band and a squad of buglers.

Almost immediately under our windows there was a tavern where the procession would stop, the platform would be lowered, and the bearers would emerge for a traditional drink and rest. Occasionally a heated argument, with some shouting, would ensue between the members of the confraternity and the bearers, who were accused of taking more than the traditional amount of time over their drink. Sometimes, even when the wrangling was at its height, a woman, stirred with emotion, would step forward from the crowd, fix her eyes on the statuary, and sing an apparently improvised canticle in praise of Our Lady of Sorrows. At length the procession would move on, with its band incongruously playing selections from Verdi's *Aida* or some other opera, alternating with loud and prolonged passages by the bugle-band. It made its way through the streets to the cathedral, which it entered by the north door and left by the south, having gone through the building in complete silence, in accordance with the rules of the cathedral.

The processions on Good Friday evening continued far into the night. After *Tenebrae*, which reached its climax with a long and beautiful setting of the Miserere, I stayed late in the cathedral. Outside the choir screen a great array of candles rose in a pyramid round the Altar of Repose, but otherwise the vast interior was in darkness, and the stillness was broken only by the muted sound of the bands and bugles outside. Then the transept door would open and a moving platform of statuary, lighted by two or three hundred flickering candles, would enter and move slowly forward through the darkness in dead silence, followed by the brethren in their tall horrifying hood-masks and the now silent bandsmen and buglers. On arriving in front of the high altar the whole procession would turn east and bow, led by the candle-lit platform, which sank and rose again slowly, like a great elephant.

We left Seville on Easter Day, after attending High Mass in the morning and seeing the usual six bulls killed in the arena during the afternoon. Having revisited Cordova and Granada, we made our way over the Sierra Nevada to the east coast. Alicante, Valencia, Sagunto, Tarragona, and Barcelona were all fascinating with their blue seas and wealth of flowers, but the most striking town of all was Elche. Surrounded by a forest of date palms and with palm trees lining its streets of heavy stone-built houses, it looked and felt like an oriental city translated to Spain. At Barcelona we were mistaken for three foreigners who had stolen some pictures from Madrid. Our car was searched by a solemn detective at the hotel garage, where a small crowd (entirely sympathetic to us) gathered to watch the fun and, with their gestures, comments, and laughter, converted the scene into a small comic opera. The climax of the opera was reached when I made the detective ransack a trunkful of our dirty linen which he had over-looked. At the end of the opera he apologized handsomely for the trouble he had caused, accepted a cigarette, and parted from us with the usual Spanish courtesy.

Having re-entered France next day at the Mediterranean end of the Pyrenees, we walked round the over-restored medieval walls of Car-cassonne, visited Toulouse and its grand church of St Sernin, called once more at Poitiers, and made our way home.

The next time I went to Spain was in a sweltering August, when I conducted a strenuous tour of the south for the Workers' Travel Association. I went again a good many times in later years, in less exacting conditions and at various seasons. To this day I can never decide which I like better — Italy or Spain, the Italian language or the Spanish language. I have a great affection for both and do not think I could ever like any other country more, except my own.

22

Greatly though I enjoyed continental travel, I enjoyed exploring England just as much. One spring vacation I stayed at Ravenstonedale in Westmorland, Bernard Manning's home, and saw something of the fell country which he loved so much and a little of the Lake District. Another spring I was Mr Edleston's guest at his house at Gainford in the county of Durham. From there I explored Teesdale, the River Greta, Brignall, and other landmarks of Scott's beautiful *Rokeby* country. Armed with a letter of introduction from my host, I called one day on the Dean of Durham, Bishop Welldon. When I was shown into his room at the Deanery I found myself in the presence of a fair-haired giant. He stretched out to me an enormous hand in which my own disappeared, and in the most hospitable way showed me round the cathedral and entertained me to lunch.

In the afternoon I went on to Auckland Castle, where I presented a second letter of introduction to the diminutive Bishop of Durham, Hensley Henson, whose ecclesiastical opinions were making him obnoxious at the time to the Anglo-Catholic party in the church. With a kindness equal to the Dean's, he entertained me to tea and showed me over his beautiful private chapel, where one of the objects of interest was a large palm-branch. He explained that it had been sent to Bishop Westcott, one of his predecessors in the see, by Lord Halifax, the distinguished Anglo-Catholic layman, and that it had been blessed by the Pope. 'I don't suppose one will be sent to me', he added.

In the summer of the same year I spent several enjoyable days at the other end of England as the guest of a very different kind of ecclesiastic — Walter Howard Frere, Bishop of Truro, the first monk to be raised to the Anglican episcopate since the Reformation. During his twelve years at Truro the bishop's residence, Lis Escop, was run on monastic lines so that he could continue to observe the rule of life of the Mirfield community to which he belonged. Lis Escop was ideally situated for a bishop's palace or a community house, being in a quiet village a mile or two out of Truro and commanding a charming view of the distant cathedral.

I often stayed with my father's first cousin, William Brittain, who farmed at Flitwick in South Bedfordshire, and it was there that I learnt to ride a horse. William always reminded me of the conventional pictures of John Bull and Farmer Giles, being a big stout man, with firm features and ruddy complexion, and as tough as nails. He was as loquacious as his father and his uncle Mark and, like them, had great social gifts. One of the best known and most popular men in South Bedfordshire, he possessed a tremendous voice in both talking and singing, and was a great wag. A shrewd man of business, a highly successful farmer, and a first-class judge of horseflesh, he could ride any horse that had four legs, and my amateurish attempts at horsemanship gave him endless amusement. One day when I had tumbled off a horse and William came home to find me lying on a sofa, looking and feeling very pale, he thought my fall one of the funniest things that he had ever known. He slapped his great thighs, roared with laughter, and kept the incident alive for years by recounting it time after time whenever he introduced me to his friends.

William Brittain was the quickest eater I have ever known. I am a quick eater myself, too quick for good manners, as I often find to my embarrassment when dining out; but, compared with him, I am a slow eater. The rapidity with which he demolished a huge meal was astonishing: it seemed to vanish like smoke. Within a few seconds of finishing his midday meal he was sound asleep in his armchair, with his dog dozing on the rug in front of him. Fifteen minutes later he was wide awake and setting off with his dog at top speed across the farm.

Having, like myself, a desire to discover something of the past history of our completely undistinguished family, he took me round the county from time to time in his car, calling on the clergy and studying parish registers. As a result of these researches, I managed to reconstruct the family tree for some generations back. The same Christian names inevitably recurred time after time. As far as we could discover, William was the eighth of his name in the family and I the fourth of mine. We therefore started a jocular practice of addressing each other as William VIII and Frederick IV, and we went on doing that until he died in 1951.

I often visited Thaxted Church in Essex, to which I was attracted by its beautiful services, its music directed by Gustav Holst, and the unique personality of its Socialist vicar, Conrad Noel. I got to know him fairly well one summer when my mother and I spent a pleasant holiday at Thaxted in an old house called Dick Turpin's Cottage which had been lent to us. He was a much greater man than he shows himself in his unfinished autobiography. All who knew him were charmed by him —

Plate V   THE ROOMS ON C STAIRCASE

Above: View from the window

Below: The Keeping Room

Plate VI

'Q' by Nicholson

FREDERIC RABY by Narraway, 1965

STEVE FAIRBAIRN by James Quinn

ARTHUR GRAY by Nicholson

even the undergraduates who drove over from Cambridge more than once in the early 'twenties to remove the red flag from his church. I remember going by car from Cambridge one Sunday morning with a retired parson who was paying his first visit to Thaxted. Knowing him to be a die-hard Tory, I thought he might well walk out of church in indignation in the middle of Conrad Noel's sermon, but he was completely won over. After that, he attended Thaxted Church almost every Sunday until he died. As far as I know, his politics were unchanged, though they may perhaps have been undermined.

I often cycled home from Cambridge at the end of term, by various routes. A favourite way was one that I discovered for myself. Leaving Cambridge by the quiet Barton road, I went over Orwell Hill and cut across the three-mile-long avenue of elms at Wimpole Hall. Crossing the Old North Road and the infant river Cam, I cycled on by the unfrequented winding road through the tiny village of Wendy and straggling, rose-clad Guilden Morden, the last Cambridgeshire village on that route. Next, visible from miles away, came Ashwell, with its lofty church tower, topped by a Hertfordshire spike, rising grandly above the giant elms which cordon one of the loveliest villages in England. I liked to linger there, by the beautiful source of the Cam, with its clear springs bubbling up from the ground in a little dell shaded by ash-trees, hard by the village street; to inspect the great church with its medieval lych-gate, its Black Death *graffiti*, and its big clear unstained windows; to toil up Claybush Hill and enjoy the broad view over parts of Cambridgeshire, Essex, Hertfordshire, and Bedfordshire, picking out Sharpenhoe Beacon ('the Clappers') in the Barton Hills and other landmarks in the four counties. From Ashwell I would cycle along the switchback road between huge open corn-fields reminiscent of the Middle Ages, to Bygrave and Baldock, and on to Clothall, to call on my relations, the Knights. Then, after making a detour to include remote and delightful Ardeley and its beautiful little church (so like South Mimms), which my mother had often attended during her girlhood at Clothall, I would ride down the valley of the little River Beane — all Hertfordshire river-valleys are beautiful — to Walkern, Watton, Stapleford, Waterford, and Hertford, and so home.

Another and a longer way home from Cambridge was to cycle through Royston to Reed and Buntingford, loiter in beautiful Aspenden and Westmill on the tiny, tortuous River Rib, and go on to Puckeridge, past the Clarkson monument outside Wadesmill, and on through Hertford and Essendon. A longer way still was to go from

K

Cambridge to Chrishall in Essex (from which and from Reed in Hert-
fordshire I have seen Ely Cathedral in the same afternoon), back into
Hertfordshire, and through the remote villages of Meesden, Brent
Pelham, Furneux Pelham, Stocking Pelham, Little Hadham, and Much
Hadham, where one seemed to be turning page after page of a picture-
book of 'Beautiful Britain', and on to Ware and Hertford through
Charles Lamb's Widford, where, as he wrote,

> On the green hill top,
> Hard by the house of prayer (a modest roof,
> And not distinguish'd from its neighbour barn
> Save by a slender-tapering length of spire)
> The Grandame sleeps,

and where he fell in love with Alice Wain. This was perhaps the most
attractive route of all, as it included the whole of the beautiful winding
valley of the diminutive River Ash. The valley reached the zenith of its
loveliness in March, when the numerous budding weeping-willows, with
their sensitive branches bowed down to the water's edge, were caught
by the rays of the sun and converted into brilliant fountains pouring
out streams of living emeralds instead of water.

Almost every peace-time summer from 1929 onwards I have stayed
in or near Henley-on-Thames for about a week at the end of June and
the beginning of July, so as to be with the Jesus College crews competing in the Royal Regatta, which falls during the interval between the
May Term and the Long Vacation Term.

There is nothing like Henley in regatta time. The tree-fringed
Thames, with swans drifting slowly and sedately under the weeping
willows, the wooded hills rising above Temple Island at one end of the
regatta course, and the eighteenth-century bridge and high flint tower
of Henley parish church at the other end, give the regatta a setting of
great beauty. No doubt there are scenes just as beautiful elsewhere; but
what gives Henley its unique distinction in regatta time is that for
nearly a week the town is given up entirely to rowing. Nothing else
seems to count, and nothing else seems to be talked about. Club flags
float from the top windows of the hotels and houses where the competing crews are staying. Shops display whole rows and sheaves of
photographs of the previous day's racing, and every few yards along the
kerb someone stands offering regatta programmes for sale. The flag-
decked streets are thronged with oarsmen from all over the British Isles
and abroad, wearing blazers of every colour and design, their breast-
pockets embroidered with coats of arms, crossed oars, or other rowing
insignia.

The Stewards' Enclosure is packed with veteran oarsmen of all ages, mingled with their wives, sisters, cousins, aunts, and fiancées. The brilliant dresses of the women, of almost every conceivable colour and design, are one of the great features of the regatta. The men's costumes, less elegant and artistic than the women's, are equally varied in colour, though worn in a somewhat bizarre fashion – so, at least, it must seem to anyone unfamiliar with Henley. A man, for instance, may be wearing the scarf of his old college boat club, the cap of his old school boat club, an Oxford or Cambridge rowing Blue's blazer, a pair of salmon-pink Leander socks, and a London or Thames Rowing Club tie. Instead of a tie, he may be wearing the purple stock of a bishop, or the black stock of one of the inferior clergy. Some of the clerics are apparently octogenarians, their club caps faded with age; and the spectator wonders whether the wearers put them on before leaving their parishes, on arrival at Henley, or somewhere between.

The only rule (and that an unwritten one) about dress at Henley seems to be that men must wear ties in the Enclosure and that women must wear hats, no matter how extraordinary. A few women have in recent years been seen (most regrettably) without hats, but I have seen only one man without a tie in the Enclosure at any time. He was a friend of mine, paying his first visit to the regatta, and I had forgotten to warn him. Since a regatta is an aquatic event, he imagined that he would be correct in wearing a jacket and tennis shirt open at the neck, as though he were on holiday at some popular seaside resort. He came dressed accordingly, and I was most embarrassed as we strolled up and down the Enclosure. I felt – I hope he was unconscious of it – that everyone was looking at him as the possible subject of a drawing by H. M. Bateman – 'The Man Who Went to Henley Without a Tie.'

Those who imagine (as some foolishly do) that rowing men are unbusinesslike and deficient in everything but physical strength should pay a visit to Henley and see how the regatta is run by its committee of distinguished oarsmen. They would soon find how mistaken they were, for the regatta is a triumph of organization. Everything is in its place before the first race – the huge car-park; the boat-tents with their racks for eights, fours, pairs, and scullers; the booms which fence the race-course and keep pleasure-boats out of the way; the umpires' launches; the judge's box perched on stilts in mid-stream; the mobile Post and Telegraph office; the lost property office; the rows and rows of deck-chairs along the riverside in the Stewards' Enclosure; the rows and rows of folding seats in the big covered stand; the bar, the huge dining-marquee; the loudspeakers for broadcasting a commentary on each race from the moment of starting; the closed-circuit television; and the brilliant flowerbeds of massed pink geraniums, blue hydrangeas, golden calceolarias, and scarlet salvias, all of which seem to spring up overnight in exactly the right places year after year. Every race starts punctually at the advertised minute, and the winning crew has hardly passed the judge's box before the military band is playing the appropriate national anthem, club song, or other tune suited to the occasion.

For my first ten Henleys I stayed with the Jesus crews, who took a house sometimes in the town and sometimes a few miles out. After the war of 1939-45 I booked a room at the *Red Lion*, at the end of Henley Bridge. I had, however, made the acquaintance of the *Lion* from the time of my first visit to Henley, because Steve Fairbairn used to stay there during the regatta and held his court there every evening, both before and after dinner. He sat enthroned in a chair on the narrow strip of riverside lawn that belongs to the hotel, and was always attended by his intimate friend, A. M. Hutchinson, who acted as a kind of Lord Chamberlain. 'Old Hutch', as he was called, had been captain of the Jesus Boat Club when Steve was a freshman, and he made an excellent foil to him. Steve was stout and weighed about three stone more than Hutch. He had a cheerful expression and a powerful voice. Hutch was slim, with a long, drooping moustache, a sorrowful countenance, and a quiet voice. He was as taciturn as Steve was loquacious. He seldom spoke, except when Steve put a question to him. Even then, he answered in as few words as possible. Steve, for his part, seldom ventured on an assertion without afterwards appealing to Hutch for his opinion before he considered the matter closed. It must be confessed, however, that the dialogue usually went like this:

STEVE: 'That's right, ain't it, Hutch?'

HUTCH: 'Yes, Steve.'

STEVE: 'There you are: Hutch says it's right, so it must be'.

One evening during my second Henley I was commanded to dine at the *Red Lion* with Steve and Hutch. The meat course was roast mutton; and Steve, after remarking that he never could understand why mint sauce was not served with mutton as well as with lamb, asked the waiter to bring some. When it came, Steve and I helped ourselves to it. Poor Hutch, who was very deaf and had not gathered much of what Steve had said, looked very suspiciously at the mint sauce. 'Help yourself, Hutch,' said Steve. Hutch did so, with obvious reluctance, and Steve went on talking. A few minutes later he asked Hutch how he liked the mint sauce.

'Very good, Steve,' Hutch answered. 'I had no idea it went so well with beef.'

'It goes even better with mutton,' said Steve, winking at me. 'You'd better try it some time.'

'I will, Steve,' said Hutch, and went on eating his mutton.

23

Since Henley regatta always ends on a Saturday, I almost invariably left the town that evening, so as to be in South Mimms for the Dedication Festival, which in Allen Hay's time we used to keep early in July and which I would not willingly have missed. My growing absorption in Cambridge life during term did not make me any less 'Mimms mad' than I had been ever since boyhood, neither would I have become so even if Allen Hay had not continued to be Vicar until his death at the age of nearly eighty-eight. I went on exploring every field and footpath in the parish, yet repeating the same favourite walks time after time and feeling, like Richard Jefferies, that 'I do not want change: I want the same old and loved things, the same wild flowers, the same trees . . . and I want them in the same place.' I read all I could find about the history of South Mimms. I compiled album after album of newscuttings relating to the contemporary life of the parish and indexed them carefully. I spent many hours in the cold vestry poring with numbed fingers over the parish registers, which open in 1558, and studying their sad record of poverty, of visitations by plague, smallpox, and cholera, of occasional burials of highwaymen shot at Mimms Wash, of the burial in 1665 of over a hundred nameless fugitives from the Great Plague of London, and of the long and pathetic procession of children who died (as most people died in past centuries) in infancy.

Early in the nineteen-twenties I invented the title of 'Patriarch' for Allen Hay. It had no reference to age, but was in part a jocular conferment of high ecclesiastical rank, above an archbishop, and partly a serious recognition of the autocratic patriarchal rule which he exercised over us. He drove us hard at times and made us do things which clerics with far larger churches and congregations either never attempted or abandoned as impossible. Was there, for instance, another parish church in the land where the choir was expected to render a full choral service at ten o'clock every Bank Holiday in the year, including even Boxing Day? Yet we came, and I have seen nearly twenty men and boys in the chancel on such occasions. We were ordinary lay people, not particularly pious, and as fond as anyone of the secular festivities of Bank Holidays; but he had made his church and its services so beautiful, and had so magnetic a personality, that we could not stay away.

Life with Allen Hay never lacked colour, certainly, but occasionally it was less colourful than outsiders imagined. There was, for instance, a baseless but firmly held belief in the neighbourhood — it has been held in other places about other clerics — that he rode a donkey round his church on Palm Sunday every year. One Saturday in the spring some years ago, when I was getting my hair cut at Barnet by a man who did not know me, he remarked that the next day was Palm Sunday and that the Vicar of South Mimms would therefore be riding round his church on a donkey. When I asked him his authority for this statement he replied that it was common knowledge and had long been so. I answered, with some vehemence, that I had taken part in the Palm Sunday procession at South Mimms for many years, and had even marshalled it, but there never had been a donkey and never would be one. I thought that would convince him, but events showed that I was mistaken. By coincidence, I had my hair cut on the day before Palm Sunday in the following year by the same barber. He did not remember me, and told me exactly the same story. He probably still tells it and still believes it.

Until 1925 South Mimms church was lighted entirely by paraffin, except that there were, of course, candles on the altars and that the choir stalls had candles as well as paraffin lamps. The brass lamps, hanging from the roof by three-branched chains, certainly harmonized well with the ancient building, yet it was not everybody who liked them.

The choirboys naturally liked them, because there was always a chance that one of the lamps would be turned up too high and belch black smoke over the head of some unsuspecting worshipper. Sometimes if the preacher was a visitor, he might be flattered by the apparently close attention that the boys were paying to his discourse, when all the time they were watching a flaring lamp just over his head and hoping that the glass would split with a loud crack before he could finish his sermon. The boys liked the lamps most of all at *Tenebrae*, because then one or two of them might be deputed to go round the church and put them out during the singing of the Benedictus; and if they were skilful they would turn them down to a point where they were not quite extinguished but would make gurgling groaning noises during the rest of the service.

The women of the congregation, on the other hand, disliked the lamps intensely. They asserted that the oil had a nasty smell, that Frederick Roland White (our sacrist, verger and parish clerk) overfilled them, and that the overflow dripped on to their hats and coats during the service and on to the pews at all times. It might have been expected that Frederick Roland would dislike the lamps, too, and would favour replacing them by electricity, seeing that the replacement would save him a good deal of work and obviate numerous unwelcome complaints from irritated members of the congregation. He had been heard to say, too, that in his opinion electric lamps would look just as well as paraffin lamps. Yet everybody knew that he was opposed to a change, although he did not explicitly say so.

The reason for his conservatism was that he was very susceptible to cold and that paraffin lamps raised the temperature of our chilly medieval church a little, whereas electric lamps would not do so.

Accordingly, when he heard that the patron of the living was going to present electric-lighting apparatus to the church, he was not enthusiastic. He was no more so when the installation was complete and the Vicar announced that the electric light was going to be switched on for the first time at Evensong on Christmas Eve, after suitable dedicatory prayers.

A pleasant ceremony has been attached to Evensong on Christmas Eve in our parish church ever since 1698, when a Mimmsian, one John Bradshaw, died, bequeathing a sum of money to pay for a sermon to be preached at that service every year and for a loaf of bread to be given to everyone present. Allen Hay nearly always chose the same text for the Bradshaw sermon — 'Let us now go even unto Bethlehem'. He chose it because, as he explained to us at the beginning of the sermon, the word 'Bethlehem' means 'House of Bread'. After the sermon he blessed the loaves and distributed them from the chancel step to members of the choir and congregation.

We looked forward to Christmas Eve in the year 1925 with more than the usual interest, because of the impending inauguration of the electric light. There were two sets of switches — one close to the main door of the nave, the other in the chancel. When the belfry clock struck the hour we emerged from the vestry in procession and groped our way through the dark nave, for there was no light except from the altar candles and the two others that accompanied the processional cross. When we reached the nave door the donor and his wife joined us, the Vicar opening his *Priest's Prayer Book* and, after searching for some time, read such prayers suitable to the occasion as he could find in it. At the end of the prayers he made a sign and the donor switched on the new nave lights. The procession then turned round and began to make its way slowly up the nave to the chancel, where, after further prayers, the donor's wife was to switch on the remaining lights.

Unfortunately, the Vicar (as so often happened) had forgotten to say anything about his intentions to the verger; so he, full of zeal and anxious only to do the right thing, rushed ahead to the chancel, switched on all the lights, folded his arms, and stood waiting for the procession to arrive, conscious of having done his duty in excellent time. He therefore felt decidedly hurt when the silent, slow-moving procession reached the chancel and the Vicar, in a cold stage-whisper that could be heard all over the church, said, for no apparent reason, 'Now switch them all off again.' The bewildered and humiliated Frederick Roland did as he was told; the ceremony already enacted at the nave door was repeated, the chancel lights were officially switched on, and we all went to our stalls and sang Evensong.

A hymn followed, and then came the Bradshaw Sermon. Instead of the customary 'Let us now go even unto Bethlehem' the Vicar gave out a text from St Matthew iv, 16: 'The people which sat in darkness saw great light'. To prepare the ground thoroughly for the spiritual lesson he was going to draw, he began by sketching the long history of the lighting of our church, from the primitive rushlight to the paraffin lamp. Paraffin, he emphasized, was considered wonderful in its time but was now antiquated. It was evil-smelling, messy, ruinous to hats and clothes, and liable to fail at any time, but science had come to the rescue. One could never tell, he said, when a paraffin lamp would go out; but, with this wonderful electric light. . . . He waved his hand grandly towards the wonderful electric light and at that very moment it fused, plunging the church at once into a darkness broken only by the light of the altar candles.

The astonished Vicar stared into the blackness of the nave, in which he could distinguish the ghost-like faces of his flock. For a tense moment or two no one stirred, and he felt he must be dreaming. Then one of the congregation coughed and he realized that he was awake. Turning towards the chancel he said, in a feeble voice, 'Bring me a candle'; and Frederick Roland, with what seemed like slow delibera-tion, struck a match, lit a candle in one of the little square wooden candlesticks which we had thought would never be used again, walked slowly with it to the pulpit and handed it up to the Vicar.

As he did so, some of us noticed that, although the verger was in no way to blame for the failure of the light, his wax-like and normally placid and saintly face wore a faint but unmistakable smile.

On one of the few occasions when Allen Hay did not himself preach the Christmas Eve sermon the preacher was the Reverend William Clarke, for many years Vicar of the adjacent parish of Ridge. He opened his sermon with an account of the orgies that had accompanied those pagan forerunners of the Christian festival of Christmas known as the bacchanalia and saturnalia. He then proceeded to exhort his congregation, composed mainly of children and working-class women.

'Good people,' he pleaded, 'you will not convert your Christmas into bacchanali*ah* and saturnali*ah*, will you? The bacchanali*ah* and saturnali*ah* were a disgrace even to pagan Rome. Do not let it be said that the people of this parish are celebrating bacchanali*ah* or saturnali*ah*. Let us all remember that bacchanali*ah* and saturnali*ah* are abominable substitutes for the Christian festival. There has been for years a deplorable tendency in this country to convert Christmas into bacchanali*ah* and saturnali*ah*. We must strike a blow for their dethronement.'

The Vicar of Ridge was noted for his caustic wit and for being a man of few words. When I was standing at the churchyard gate with Allen Hay one summer evening William Clarke came driving up the village street in his pony and trap on his way home. He pulled up just opposite us, and the following dialogue took place:

'Good evening, Hay.'

'Good evening, Clarke.'

'I've just seen one of your parishioners along the road – a Mrs Mitchell.'

'Yes?'

'She said to me, "I'd like to see you in that ditch, and that old devil, the Vicar of South Mimms, along with you".'

'Oh, yes.'

'Good night, Hay.'

'Good night, Clarke.'

Mrs Mitchell, however, who left the village a year or two later, bore no animosity against anyone. Some years after her departure, when Allen Hay was in London for the day and was walking along Oxford Street, he heard a loud scream of 'Well, I never! If it ain't the old Vicar!' and the buxom Mrs Mitchell rushed forward, threw her arms round his neck and kissed him.

Both Allen Hay and William Clarke were members for some years of the Barnet Board of Guardians, whose area included South Mimms, Ridge, and other villages. Their duties involved the supervision of the Barnet Union workhouse and its infirmary. During the nineteen-twenties a Government scheme came into operation for improving the administration of the Poor Law and removing the social stigma attaching to admission to infirmaries. One result of this was that the Barnet infirmary was renamed the Wellhouse Hospital, which rapidly became celebrated for the skill of its medical staff and the high standard of its nursing.

William Clarke strongly disapproved of the change of name and status, which he thought likely to make the working classes get above themselves. He therefore lost no opportunity of belittling the Wellhouse Hospital, which he continued always to call 'the workhouse infirmary'. One day, at a meeting of the Guardians, he went so far as to assert that he would rather die in a ditch, with a tarpaulin over him and his old dog beside him, than enter the Wellhouse Hospital.

Some time afterwards a man was found ill in a ditch at Ridge, and he was taken to the Wellhouse Hospital, where his name was found to be William Clarke. This led to an interesting discussion at the next meeting of the Guardians, before the Vicar of Ridge arrived.

According to the local newspaper, one of the Guardians asked, 'Were the dog and tarpaulin there?'

Allen Hay said, 'I have not seen our respected colleague for some time, and it would be a remarkable coincidence if two William Clarkes were found in a ditch in a sparsely populated parish. I mention this because the man concerned was conveyed to the Wellhouse Hospital, and I am sure we should all protest against such an enormity to one of our colleagues.'

To this the Relieving Officer replied, 'I assure the Vicar of South Mimms that the man found in a ditch was not his brother Vicar from Ridge. He was a labourer who had been sleeping rough.'

Another Guardian therefore suggested that the local paper should be asked to make it clear that the Vicar of Ridge was still in good health.

When the Vicar of Ridge arrived in the board room he was greeted with cheers. Legend says that he asked the meaning of 'this unseemly merriment'.

In 1926 Allen Hay persuaded me to apply to the bishop for a lay reader's licence. The application was granted and the licence authorized me, *inter alia*, to give addresses in the parish church. Allen Hay, who underrated his own ability as a preacher, was not slow to take advantage of my new status, but it was rare for him to give me as much as a week's notice if he wanted me to speak. Usually, he told me only the day before, or even on the day itself. Sometimes he would even send a message to me across the chancel during Evensong, asking if I would give an address at that very service. I declined. Nevertheless, as he passed by me on his way to the pulpit a few minutes later during the singing of the hymn before the sermon, he would sometimes even then pause, turn a sorrowful face to me and say, 'Are you quite sure you won't say just a few words?' Once, about a year after I received my licence, I was assisting him at the wedding of a friend of mine. When the time came for the address ordered by the Prayer Book, he made the congregation sit down and told them that I was going to address them. He then sat down firmly in his stall. For a few seconds I tried to sit him out; but, knowing what a determined man he was, and not wishing to cause a scene at a wedding, I capitulated. On my way to the pulpit I wondered whatever I could say. A verse of the psalm which we had just recited came into my mind, 'We wish you good luck in the name of the Lord', and I managed to embroider on that text for a few minutes.

He was equally casual with the clergy. Sometimes, about the middle of Lent, he would exhort his flock to get ready for Holy Week and Easter. 'Be sure to come to the Three Hours' Service on Good Friday', he would say, 'I am asking Father Mayhew to conduct it. He has a long way to come, and I want him to have a good congregation.' When Palm Sunday morning arrived he remembered that he had forgotten to invite the prospective preacher for the following Friday; and so, when giving out the notices in church, he would say, 'Don't fail to come to the Three Hours' Service on Friday, dear people. Father Mayhew will conduct it, I hope.' The story can best be ended by quoting from a letter which I received from the Rev. A. F. Mayhew after Allen Hay died. 'More than once', he wrote, 'I had a frantic wire from him on a Maundy Thursday, "Can you take the Three Hours' for us to-morrow?" Of course I could not, at that eleventh hour.'

During the annual church meeting at Easter 1928 Allen Hay remarked that there had not been a wedding in the parish for over twelve months. The local weekly newspaper reported him as saying, 'It is not that the young women of South Mimms are not comely: I am sure young men would find excellent wives here. Possibly the men are shy, but I would remind the young ladies that it is Leap Year.'

The popular dailies, with characteristic exaggeration, came out with such headlines as 'Village where nobody weds' and photographs of 'The Matchless Maidens of Mimms'. Some of the papers, whether intentionally or by accident, stretched the Vicar's 'twelve months' to 'twelve years'. He was soon bombarded with letters — some serious, others facetious — from unmarried men all over England and abroad, asking to be put in touch with the matchless maidens. There were so many applicants that he had to announce that there were not nearly enough unmarried women to go round. Upon that, unmarried women from all over the world wrote asking to be put in touch with the unmarried men and he received over a thousand letters in all.

When the first marriage for eighteen months took place at South Mimms that autumn, the church was packed to the doors. Scores of people had to stand, and there was another crowd outside who were unable to get in. I was in the chancel, helping the Vicar. He had declined to take any of the usual fees for performing the ceremony, but towards the end of the service he announced that there would be a collection for the restoration of the church. He then turned to me and told me to take it. As collections were unknown at weddings, and as most of the congregation were merely inquisitive gapers who would probably resent being asked to give, I did not like the prospect. I therefore tried to escape by saying that the collecting plates were in the vestry and I could not get to them beeause of the crush.

'Then take one of those', he said sternly, pointing to the three big brass dishes, about eighteen inches in diameter and over three centuries old, which stood in their usual place on the Nameless Tomb in the sanctuary. I took one, and forced my way round the packed church while a hymn was being sung. Some of the congregation were, as I expected, indignant, and said, 'We've never heard of a collection at a wedding before', to which I could only reply, 'Well, you've heard of one now'; but most of the congregation subscribed very willingly. Next day a newspaper carried the headline, 'Hay makes hay at wedding.' So far as I know, this was the first collection at any wedding, but I believe there have been wedding collections at other churches since, and indeed there is no reason why there should not be.

24

The 'Matchless Maidens of Mimms' caught the public fancy partly because the saga of the Archdeacon's Horse had made the name of the parish well known a couple of years earlier.

To understand the full significance of the saga, it is important to remember that the parish of South Mimms, although its boundary is only about four miles from the city of St Albans, and although it is surrounded on the north, the west, and even on the south by parishes in the diocese of St Albans, is nevertheless in the diocese of London and the archdeaconry of Hampstead. To make things more complicated, the Archdeacon at the time did not live in his archdeaconry, but south of it, at St James's Rectory, Piccadilly, in the heart of London and about fifteen miles from South Mimms.

The whole saga grew out of one small incident at the Easter Vestry and annual meeting of the Parochial Church Council at South Mimms in 1926. The meeting was characterized by the gravity that normally reigns on such occasions until copies of the church accounts for the previous year were circulated and the Vicar asked for comments on them. I asked for an explanation of the item 'Visitation Fee, 18s.' which appeared in the expenditure column. The Vicar replied that it was an annual fee paid to the Archdeacon and that it was a very ancient one, paid by every parish in the country. He believed that it originated in the distant past, to compensate the Archdeacon for feeding and putting up his horse when visiting the parishes in his jurisdiction. Upon my asking when the Archdeacon last visited South Mimms on a horse, I was told that that had not happened within living memory. The church-wardens, in fact, added that nowadays they had to go up to the Archdeacon in London, and pay their own fares into the bargain, although the affair was still called a Visitation.

In view of these facts, I proposed a resolution that, as long as the fee was levied and paid, the Archdeacon should be requested to visit the parish at least once a year on horseback. Archdeacons, I pointed out, with their gaiters, breeches, and short cassocks ('aprons') still wore riding dress. They should live up to their gaiters and cease to be walking sartorial falsehoods.

My proposal having been seconded, Allen Hay put it to the meeting at once and it was carried unanimously. A reporter of the local paper, who was present at the meeting, brought the resolution to the notice of his chief. The latter, thinking that it might interest the British public – and his thought proved to be correct – communicated it to the Press Association, and they to the newspapers of the British Isles.

The first intimation that the Archdeacon had of the new duties expected of him arrived on the following day, when he was kept busy at the telephone answering journalistic enquiries about when he was going to visit South Mimms on a horse. Puzzled by all this, he left the house to avoid further enquiries, only to fall into a bevy of Press photographers and interviewers waiting outside.

Next day, all the papers in London and most of those in the provinces came out with a report on the situation, under such headlines as 'Strange Request to Archdeacon' and 'Archdeacon Requested to be Equestrian'. South Mimms became the centre of interest in the country, particularly when a few days later *The Times* published a delightful fourth leader on the subject. It was an excellent piece of humorous writing and was afterwards reprinted in anthologies of English prose. I was much flattered when people accused me of writing it. I wish I had done so.

For some time afterwards the correspondence columns of *The Times* were occupied with letters from rural deans and country parsons who, taking the matter very seriously, congratulated the South Mimms Parochial Church Council on what they called its fine stand against archdiaconal exactions. The celebrated ecclesiastical lawyer Lord Phillimore, however, took a different view, solemnly explaining that we had no reason to be dissatisfied, seeing that we enjoyed the services of an Archdeacon for a mere eighteen shillings a year. His letter nevertheless revealed the interesting fact that the unfortunate Archdeacon received only two of the eighteen shillings, the rest going to legal officials. What Lord Phillimore did not realize was that we were not interested in the fee: what we wanted was the horse.

The Archdeacon meanwhile merely remarked that he fully appreciated the humour of the situation. When asked what he would do if we refused to pay the fee next time it was due if he had not meanwhile visited us on a horse he said that time would tell. The newspaper discussion lapsed after a run of about a month, and we thought that was the end of the whole matter.

In September of the same year, however, the newspapers contained an announcement that the Archdeacon had become engaged to be married. The Vicar decided to hold a meeting of the Church Council on the following Sunday evening after church to consider the situation. Unfortunately, before Sunday came he had to leave for Switzerland, to visit a sick relative, but he gave me instructions to hold the meeting in his absence.

When we met at the Vicarage on the Sunday evening I read out the notice of the Archdeacon's engagement and reminded the meeting that he had not carried out our request to visit the parish on a horse. Probably he could not afford one, I said. If so, still less would he be able to afford one when he was married. I therefore proposed that we should give the Archdeacon a wedding present and that it should take the form of a horse.

This resolution was carried unanimously and a Horse Committee was elected forthwith, with the Vicar as president, the curate (the Rev. Benjamin Fenwick) as vice-president, and myself as secretary and treasurer. I collected a token subscription of sixpence from everyone present, issued receipts, and the meeting adjourned.

Most of us, I think, contemplated nothing larger than a model silver horse as a wedding present for the Archdeacon, but the newspapers chose to think otherwise, and some of them took the matter very seriously. A number of them published illustrated interviews with the Archdeacon, some of the details being obviously journalistic fakes, though others were as clearly due to the Archdeacon's sense of humour. Where, he reasonably asked, was he to keep a horse in Piccadilly? How was he to make his way on a horse through the ceaseless motor traffic of Central London? Besides, it was so long since he had ridden a horse that he trembled at the prospect. As one journalist put it, the prospective horse was to him nothing but a nightmare with which he was loath to be saddled at a time when he was just going into double harness.

The Vicar, who was following the newspaper correspondence from abroad, apparently decided that things were getting embarrassing for the Archdeacon. Early in October *The Times* published a letter from him, stating that, since the Archdeacon had shied at the horse, and since the horse would undoubtedly shy at the motor traffic in Central London, the Horse Committee had decided to give him a car instead, and subscriptions could be sent to me as treasurer.

The Horse Committee, however, had not been consulted about the proposed change and were reluctant to adopt it, though they already foresaw the probability of having to do so later. We were also being besieged daily by Press reporters and photographers, clamouring to be

Plate VII

NFORMAL PORTRAIT OF F. B.
by Narraway, 1966

F. B. in female costume, 1955

F. B. wearing Doctor of Letters gown and bonnet

The Fellows' Garden in winter

Plate VIII

present when the horse was presented to the Archdeacon. One enter-prising insurance agent even wrote to me asking if he could have the privilege of negotiating an insurance policy on the life of the horse, to be handed over to the Archdeacon with the animal.

Knowing that we should have to capitulate before long, but deter-mining first to be even with some of the very serious-minded journalists who were clamouring for news and regarding us as unsophisticated simpletons, we announced on October 10th that we were going to Dyrham Park Farm the following afternoon at two o'clock to select a horse for the Archdeacon.

We went, and found a bevy of reporters and photographers waiting for us. The farmer, William Fraser, who was in collusion with us, pro-duced one or two cart-horses, quite unsuitable steeds, for us to consider. We examined them with deliberation and the reporters solemnly wrote down that we found them 'unsuitable for the purpose in view.'

We then went back to the farmyard, where we saw a horse looking out of his stable door, the top flap of which was open. His name, Tony, was chalked on the lower flap, and by a stroke of luck a piece of chalk was lying on the ground in front of it. 'This is obviously the horse we want', I said. 'Let us change his name to Gaiters.' The committee approved the change, and I rubbed out the old name and chalked the new one on the door. Gaiters was brought out of his stable and was trotted up and down the farmyard. One of the reporters asked his age. M. H. Benbow, who was a farm bailiff and a member of the Horse Committee (our Equine Adviser), looked at Gaiters' teeth and pro-nounced him to be 'a bay gelding, rising five years'. This the reporters solemnly wrote down, though for all most of the company knew Gaiters might have been sinking sixty-five. After he had been photo-graphed in various attitudes the committee adjourned.

The next morning's papers were full of portraits of Gaiters. One of them inevitably showed our Equine Adviser 'looking the gift horse in the mouth'. In another, the curate was shown giving him a feed from a sieve, the legend being 'Filling Archdeacon's Gaiters'. However, when a representative of *The Barnet Press, Finchley and Hendon News, South-gate and Edgware Chronicle,* and *General Advertiser for North Middlesex and South Herts* asked the Archdeacon whether he would accept the horse if offered, his answer was, as they say in Parliament, in the negative, and his refusal was broadcast in the B.B.C. news bulletin that evening.

L

Apparently the Vicar, who had by this time migrated from Switzerland to Jersey, heard the broadcast, or read about the Archdeacon's refusal in the next day's paper. At any rate, he sent me a cable stamped with a laconic brevity. It ran:

DROP GAITERS CONCENTRATE ON CAR ARCH EVIDENTLY PERTURBED.

We thereupon surrendered, as indeed we had already decided to do, in order to avoid any further annoyance to the Archdeacon. The subscriptions already received, and others which came in later, were given to the Archdeacon to help towards the cost of a car which, he said, would carry a metal horse as its emblem.

The news of the change from a horse to a car naturally took a little time to penetrate into some quarters. Some weeks later, for instance, when I was at Cambridge, I received a letter from Benbow saying that several horse-dealers had called on him. They stated that they had been to Dyrham Park Farm and examined Gaiters but did not consider him good enough for an archdeacon. In short, they wanted to sell him another. 'I told them', said Benbow in his letter, 'that Gaiters was good enough for an archbishop and that in any case they must apply to the treasurer. So I've sent about half-a-dozen of them on to you.' I was relieved when I read his postscript, which ran: 'Don't worry about those horse-dealers. I told them you were at Oxford.'

I met the Archdeacon for the first time some years later, when he came to preach at South Mimms. He was a most urbane man, and we all enjoyed his visit. In after years, when I had become churchwarden of the parish, I had to attend his Visitation, which was held in a London church, and he made me tell the story of the horse to the officials who were with him. I cut it as short as I could, as there was a long string of churchwardens behind me, waiting their turn to pay their eighteen shillings.

25

One Sunday morning those of us who were in the choir-stalls in South
Mimms church noticed a stranger in the congregation. He was an elderly
man with a flowing white beard and he followed the sermon and every
detail of the service with the closest attention.

As we left the church after the service the Vicar was standing by the
door. He shook hands with the stranger, who returned his greeting by
saying, 'I like your church very much. I'm coming again next Sunday.'

'Good', said the Vicar. 'Come into the choir, will you?'

The stranger, not knowing our Vicar's impulsive ways, was obviously
somewhat startled at this unexpected invitation; but after a slight
hesitation he answered: 'Thank you very much. I shall be glad to come.'

'Splendid', said the Vicar. 'Now come into the Vicarage and meet my
wife: she's our organist.'

When they got into the drawing-room the Vicar introduced the
stranger by saying, 'This gentleman is coming into the choir next
Sunday'; whereupon the organist, who was severely practical, turned to
the stranger and asked, 'Can you sing?'

He was silent for a while. His beard moved up and down while he
swallowed twice, and then he said, 'Well, I think I can, but my wife and
daughter say I can't.'

'I see,' said the organist. 'Then it's not much use your coming into
the choir, is it?'

The Vicar coughed and said firmly, 'I have already arranged for him
to come into the choir next Sunday', and the organist said no more.

From that time onwards the newcomer sat in the choir-stalls twice
every Sunday. He lived miles away — we never remembered where —
and in spite of his age always came and went by cycle. When the
morning service was over he used to go into the vicarage for a little chat
and then cycled to a roadside café near Hatfield, where he took lunch
and tea. Having finished his tea he used to cycle back to Mimms again
and sit on the churchyard fence, sometimes for an hour or more, until
it was time for Evensong. His cycle stood by him; and from its handle-
bars, suspended by a loop, hung a flat tin tied very elaborately with a
long piece of string. Every now and then he would laboriously untie the
string, open the tin, and take out an acid drop or some similar sweet,

which he sucked cautiously, as if he was afraid that it might be poisoned. The tin was then carefully tied up again and hung on the handle-bars; but it was always untied, and the contents proffered, whenever anyone stopped to speak to him. This addiction to sweet-eating led to his being generally known in the village as 'Old Sweetie'; and the Vicar, who never could remember his real name, used to address him formally — and with obvious approval — as 'Mr Sweetie'.

Mr Sweetie's favourite topic of conversation was the excellence of the food provided (particularly at tea-time) at the little café which he frequented. 'I had ten slices of bread-and-butter today,' he used to say, 'with plenty of jam, three pieces of cake and four cups of tea — big cups, too — all for one-and-three. Dirt cheap, I call it.' He was much less communicative about himself; but it became known in time that he had been an inmate of a mental asylum, that in consequence many of his former friends and acquaintances now shunned him, and that he, being a sensitive man, felt this very keenly.

It was no wonder, then, if, receiving such a welcome as he did in our village, he felt that he had stepped into Paradise, Singing, moreover, was one of his chief joys, and he was delighted beyond words when he was so unexpectedly made a member of the choir.

It must nevertheless be confessed that everyone was not equally delighted. The organist, for instance, stamped her foot one Sunday after church and exclaimed:

'I will *not* have that old Sweetie in the choir any longer.'

The Vicar merely took a pinch of snuff and said, 'You will.'

'But he makes such a dreadful noise,' she continued.

'The Almighty likes it,' he answered.

'He may do, but nobody else does,' the organist asserted.

One must admit that Mr Sweetie's voice, though of fairly good tone, was abnormally strong and was used without restraint. It would be less true to say that he sang than to say that he roared and bellowed, nor could he be induced to practise moderation. His methods, too, were most unconventional. He preferred, for instance, to do the greater part of his singing with his eyes shut, repeating whatever his neighbours had sung one beat before. If he sang from a book he was generally careful to sing the same hymn as the rest of the choir, but as often as not sang a different verse. In processions, too, his common practice of walking with his eyes shut often produced disturbing results. Sometimes he would leave a gap of five or six yards between himself and the man in front. At other times he walked too quickly, cannoned into the man in front of him, and dropped his book with a crash. Such practices as these naturally endeared him greatly to the choirboys, even though they displeased the organist and some of the congregation.

He was missing one Sunday. When he reappeared a week later he explained that he had been to church at Stoke Poges for a change.

'And do you know', he said, 'before the service had gone on long one of the churchwardens came and asked me to stop singing. He said I was upsetting the congregation.'

'What did you do?' the Vicar asked.

'What did I do?' said Mr Sweetie. 'Why, I said to the churchwarden, "What does it say in the hymn?" and he said to me, "What hymn?" so I said to him, "Why, the hymn that says 'Louder still and louder praise the precious blood' ".'

It was a long time after that before Mr Sweetie stayed away from us again, and then it was an accident that kept him away. He went cycling one day and was free-wheeling down a hill with his eyes shut when he crashed into a wall. He was picked up unconscious and was taken to the local hospital. Some days later a police message reached the Vicar, who went to see him at once.

'I'm very glad you've come, Vicar,' said Mr Sweetie. 'I wouldn't have liked anything to happen to me until I'd made sure that you knew how to find that café where I have tea on Sundays. The last time I was there I had nine slices of bread-and-butter, any amount of jam, three pieces of cake, and four or five cups of tea — big cups, too — all for one-and-three. Dirt cheap, I call it. You'd better take the address down.' And the Vicar wrote it down.

A few weeks later Mr Sweetie was back in his old place in the choir, and for a good many Sundays he roared as loudly as ever. Then, one week-day, news came that he had been found dead at the bottom of a hill, with a battered cycle beside him.

He was buried in our churchyard. The whole choir attended the funeral service — men as well as boys. Before we left the graveside the Vicar made us sing Hymn 99:

> Lift ye then your voices,
>   Swell the mighty flood:
> Louder still and louder
>   Praise the precious blood.

One or two persons lacking in imagination gnashed their teeth when they heard what we had sung, and called it blasphemy for us to have sung it; but others nearly wept.

When the Vicar heard of these criticisms he said nothing; but a year later, when the anniversary of Mr Sweetie's death came round, he made us all go out into the churchyard after Sunday morning service, stand round the grave, and sing again Hymn 99:

Louder still and louder
Praise the precious blood.

In the late nineteen-twenties I began to write a history of South Mimms, paying special attention to such subjects as local government, the village school, health, and housing, which are commonly ignored in local histories. Heffers of Cambridge agreed to publish the book when it was ready. When dealing with education, I found the parish school-master's log-books, dating from 1870, most useful and interesting. No other source could have provided such valuable material for a detailed study of the struggle for elementary education in an English village – a struggle waged and won by a few resolute people against the combined prejudices of parents and employers.

In 1929 I made the welcome discovery of a pile of old minute-books of the parish vestry meetings, dating back to 1727. They were at the bottom of our big medieval church chest, which had not been opened for years, under layers of discarded hymn-books, worn-out hassocks, moth-eaten curtains, and other rubbish, and were mildewed and malodorous. I found the study of these month-by-month records of the life of the parish in past ages utterly absorbing, particularly during the Napoleonic period. They helped me to understand for the first time what the French Revolutionary wars had meant to the ordinary stay-at-home Englishman. I took the books to the vicarage and worked at them there for about fourteen hours a day for a week or more, only stopping to go reluctantly to bed or when Allen Hay dragged me away for a church service or a meal. When I had finished studying and copying from them a friend told me that I looked pale and ought to go away for a change of air. I answered that if I had not had a change of air I had had what was more unusual and perhaps even more beneficial – a change of time; for I felt that I had been living in the past.

My researches into the history of the parish inevitably took me to Knightsland, a late medieval or early sixteenth-century farmhouse standing in a hollow in the fields, a mile from where we lived, and visible from my bedroom window. Next to the house, and perhaps as old as it, stood a great barn with a framework of huge oaken timbers. It was so large and lofty that a loaded waggon of hay standing inside it looked quite small. The house, although it was in a bad state of repair, was a charming one, with a big stone-floored kitchen and a dining-room that was lined from floor to ceiling with linen-fold panelling of the early sixteenth century. A spiral staircase led to the bedrooms, which had great wide floor-boards of oak and were fitted with panelled powder-closets. In one of these bedrooms a series of sixteenth-century mural paintings, depicting the parable of the Prodigal Son, was discovered behind the panelling in 1933 — too late, unfortunately, for mention in my history of the parish. Above the bedrooms were big attics, with the same great oaken floor-boards and Tudor arched doorways. If ghosts exist anywhere, Knightsland must surely be haunted. I accordingly made it the setting for a ghost story which I wrote about the ill-fated admiral, John Byng, who bought the house about 1750 and is said to have lived in it while Wrotham was being built for him on higher ground half a mile away.

I very frequently walked down to Knightsland across the fields from home, to take tea or spend the evening with the bachelor farmer Walter Mossman, who gave me the freedom of his house and farm. He was one of the most gentle, humane, and open-minded men I have ever known. His gentleness and humanity were obvious from his speech and from his behaviour to both human beings and animals. One day, for instance, he noticed a sick hedgehog near his house. Most farmers would have ignored it. Some, I fear, would have kicked it out of the way. Walter Mossman took a saucerful of milk to it twice a day until it was well and went its own way. I have known few men so remarkably free from prejudices, whether political or social, as Walter Mossman, and he had no superstitions. He was unusually well-informed on current affairs, having read *The Times* daily for years; but he had practically no time to spare for any other reading, owing to the very long hours he worked, on seven full days a week. There was little fear of not finding him on his farm, at whatever time or on whatever day one called, because he rarely left it. I never remember his sleeping a night away from home. He did, however, once take a day off to pay me a visit at Cambridge — a great compliment to me, as I never knew him to go so far from home on any other occasion. At one time he used to attend the Wednesday cattle-market at Barnet fairly frequently and sometimes stayed to lunch or tea with farming friends at the *Salisbury Arms*; but later he abandoned even that brief outing. Yet, although he became more and more of a stay-at-home, he lost none of his breadth of mind or charm of manner, nor did he give a less warm welcome to anyone who called on him at Knightsland.

His sister, Kate Mossman, who was also unmarried, kept house for him and was a most hospitable person, delighting in company. She was a warm-hearted, simple soul and, unlike her brother, full of superstitions, believing firmly that the sun puts fires out, that the weather changes with the moon, and that various crops must be sown at certain phases of the moon.

One day when I called at the farm during a long spell of wet weather she said, 'Never mind. The weather will be fine after next Tuesday.'

'What makes you think that?' I asked.

'I don't think it. I know it,' she replied, 'because there's a new moon on Tuesday.'

'The Astronomer Royal has told me that a new moon doesn't make any difference at all to the weather,' I said.

'Then he must be a most unobservant man,' she asserted.

Her brother laughed. 'Don't be a fool, Kate,' he said. 'The Astronomer Royal has all his life been trained to observe and he is paid large sums for doing so.'

'Then,' she said, turning to me, 'you must have misunderstood what he said.'

I assured her that I had not done so, and added that when he next came up for a feast — he was an Honorary Fellow of the College — I would ask him to give it to me in writing. He did so, on official paper headed 'From the Astronomer Royal, The Royal Observatory, Greenwich.' When I told him I would let him know what Kate Mossman said, he answered, 'You needn't bother. This note won't make the slightest difference.'

I posted his letter to her, and when I called at Knightsland during my next vacation she said to me, 'Thank you for that letter. I shall keep it. It's nice to have a letter from the Astronomer Royal in the house.'

'But what have you to say about what he says in the letter?' I asked.

'Well,' she answered, 'I know he's a very clever man; but, you know, the weather *does* change when there's a new moon.'

Walter and Kate Mossman were alone on the farm at night, except that Arthur Gaylor and Tom McElroy occupied two disused pigsties in the farmyard. Tom had come from Ireland years before to work at Knightsland during the hay-making season and had stayed there for good, although he now worked elsewhere. Irish though he was, he was a very quiet and unsociable man, except when he was in drink. Throughout the winter he sat in the kitchen every evening, studying *The Times* from end to end, including the Court Circular, on the contents of which he could have passed an examination.

Arthur Gaylor came up from Bedfordshire every summer for the hay-making season or rather longer, and then returned to his home at Clophill. Unlike Tom, he was a most sociable man and did not seem to read anything. He looked the simple countryman of pastoral poetry, but inwardly was full of guile. This quality was particularly evident on Saturday nights, when he called at the tap-room of a Barnet public-house a little before closing time with a sack of vegetables. He got good prices for them, on the ground that they were 'fresh-cut in Bedfordshire to-day'; but he had in fact just bought them privately from a green-grocer, who was glad to sell them to him very cheaply at that late hour.

Arthur Gaylor used to show great tact and histrionic ability in getting rid of undesirable trespassers who came to roll and picnic in the meadows at Knightsland just before hay-harvest. His usual method of dealing with them was to ask them politely whether they knew that they were occupying the bull's favourite exercise-ground, and to warn them that he might arrive at any moment. The intruders generally decamped without waiting to thank him, but on at least one occasion he was given half-a-crown in gratitude for the information.

During the course of my researches into South Mimms history I encountered, in various documents and at various times, over twenty ways of spelling the name of the parish. I had to decide which of these to use in the title of my book and its pages when not quoting from sources. The decision was not easy, because four different spellings were still in common use. As the Rural District Council, the Post Office, the Ordnance Survey, the local newspaper and a large number (if not a majority) of the inhabitants all used the spelling 'Mimms,' I adopted it for my book. Allen Hay, however, was a fanatical supporter of the spelling 'Mymms', and when I incautiously showed him a proof of the first few pages which had arrived from the publisher his indignation knew no bounds. He gave me no peace until I telegraphed to Heffers, 'Spell Mymms with "y" throughout except when quoting from documents.' To this day, I sometimes find that I have not the courage to spell it any other way, even though Allen Hay is now dead.

A book of that kind could only be published by subscription, and Allen Hay was indefatigable in obtaining subscribers. Without his help — for instance, in urging his Sunday congregation week after week not to forget to order a copy — it probably would not have been published at all. Q wrote an introduction to it, making a most conscientious tour of the parish with me before doing so. A pupil of mine drew a map of the parish to make end-papers for the book. By an interesting coincidence, one of the few private houses that he marked and named on the map became my home years later when I married.

When *South Mymms, the Story of a Parish*, appeared in 1931, one observant reviewer remarked that it closed with an interesting list of subscribers. He was right, and yet he was less than right because it was much more than interesting. It must have been an almost unbelievable list to anyone who did not know Allen Hay, containing as it did the names (selected here in alphabetical order from about 300) of Count Ascoli d'Ascoli, Mrs Bramwell Booth, Cardinal Bourne, the Archbishop of Canterbury, the Bishops of Durham, Exeter, and London, Signor Enrico Maccario, the Marchesa Menabrea di Val Dora, Monsignor G. Roverio, the Bishops of St Albans and Salisbury, Sir Hugh Walpole, and the Bishop of Willesden.

Few of these subscribers knew either South Mimms or the author of the book and some of them had never heard of either until Allen Hay told them. The presence of their names in the list of subscribers is a record of his heterogeneous friendships and acquaintances in England, of chance meetings in trains, of a holiday (evidently a busy one) that he spent on the Italian Riviera that year and, above all, of the ease with which he could induce anybody to subscribe to anything. To get subscriptions for such a work even from a number of Anglican archbishops and bishops whom he had seldom or never met required initiative; to induce a cardinal and the widow of a Salvation Army general to subscribe required something more than initiative; but to sell copies of an unpublished history of an obscure English parish to a number of Italian priests and noblemen must be an achievement unique in the annals of salesmanship. He could have sold ice to Eskimos, even in the depths of the Arctic winter.

26

The year 1930 marks a turning-point in my life for more than one reason, but chiefly because it was then that I was appointed to a lectureship at Jesus and granted something which I desired more than anything else on earth — rooms in college. A new block of nearly fifty sets of rooms, designed by Morley Horder, had been completed at Jesus that summer, and I was the first to move into it. My rooms were on the top floor of Staircase 8, with a pair of angels, carved in stone by Eric Gill, just below my windows; so that, as Q put it, I was 'a little higher than the angels'.

On one side I looked into Chapel Court, with the east end of the chapel facing me. On the other side I looked on to Butt Green (soon afterwards incorporated in our Close) and Midsummer Common; but it would have mattered little to me where my rooms were situated so long as they were in the college. Bliss was it in that place to be alive, and it has been so ever since.

I had for some time — I cannot now remember how long — held the rank of Director of Studies in Modern and Medieval Languages at Jesus. My promotion to a College Lectureship made no difference to the work which I was already doing, but it had the great advantage of giving me some financial stability, as it brought me a minimum annual stipend. The change did not interfere with my teaching at Pembroke College, which went on as before until H. G. Comber died in 1935.

I became Librarian of the College at the same time and held the office for fifteen years. It was a very pleasant office. It gave me the oversight of what was then a small library for undergraduates and also of the larger Old Library, which is one of the glories of the College, housed as it is in a charming late-medieval building with an open-timbered roof. Each of its windows contains two cockerels facing one another, with scrolls coming out of their beaks in typical medieval style. Each scroll carries a quotation from the Latin Bible, indicating the subject of the books that were originally placed on the shelves below. The contents of the Library included a human skeleton which appears to have been at the College ever since the seventeenth century, a fine box of mathematical instruments which belonged to Roger North, who entered the College in 1667, a number of incunabula, and about eighty medieval manuscripts, among them an illuminated Bible of the thirteenth century.

One of the pictures in this Bible is described by Montague James in his catalogue as 'a devil'. I am confident, however, that it is no devil, but King Nebuchadnezzar after he had become like a beast of the field, because it faces the Book of Daniel, has a sub-human pig-like face and animal's claws, and yet is wearing a crown.

Comparatively few books in the Old Library are of later date than the eighteenth century. One of the more modern ones is a first edition of Coleridge's *Kubla Khan*, at the end of which poem there is a criticism of it written in pencil in a contemporary hand: 'The writer of the above had much better have kept his sleeping thoughts to himself, for they are, if possible, worse than his waking ones.' Among the older books is a copy of the Nuremberg Chronicle, printed in 1497. This outline of the world's history is lavishly illustrated with woodcuts, including views of important cities. One woodcut is used seven times. It begins as Troy, becomes in turn Pisa, Verona, Ravenna, Tivoli, and Toulouse, and makes its last appearance as London.

My move into college rooms was simultaneous with a new development, not only of my work for the College, but also of my University work. Medieval Latin Literature had recently been added to the syllabus of the Modern and Medieval Languages Tripos, and also of the English Tripos, as one of the several alternatives open to candidates for Part II. There appeared, however, to be no one available to lecture on the subject other than G. G. Coulton, who was already fully occupied. I was invited to fill the gap. The invitation came from Coulton on behalf of the Faculties concerned, and I naturally accepted it with alacrity.

I lectured twice a week. One of my difficulties was to know what pronunciation of Latin to use. I had been taught both the 'old' pronunciation and the reformed classical pronunciation at school, but neither of them was suitable for Medieval Latin, with its rhyming verse, which sometimes ceases to rhyme if either the 'old' or the classical pronunciation is used. This dilemma led me to carry out some research into the history of Latin pronunciation during post-classical times, both in England and elsewhere. I found the subject fascinating, and was glad to discover that the compromise pronunciation which I had begun to use for my lectures was, so far as one could tell, identical with the pronunciation used in medieval England. The results of my research were published in 1934 by the Cambridge University Press as a small book entitled *Latin in Church*. Later research confirmed the conclusions which I then drew, so that when an enlarged edition of the book appeared more than twenty years later I had nothing to retract.

As I have said, G. G. Coulton was instrumental in my being appointed to lecture on Medieval Latin. I well remember my first meeting with him. It was at St John's College, in his rooms on the top floor of what is still called New Court, though it is not the newest court now, nor was it even then. I remember the beautiful views of the Backs from his window, and the walls lined with books and rows of large cubical biscuit-tins. Each tin was suitably labelled, and into it, from time to time, he dropped slips of paper containing material for forthcoming historical works or controversial pamphlets on such subjects as 'Romanism and Truth.' Even the chairs were loaded with books and papers, and he had to clear one of them before I could sit down.

I met Coulton many times after that – as a co-examiner for the Tripos, at college feasts, at his house, and elsewhere. Always, like Braunholtz, he was a mirror of gentleness and courtesy. Once, when an enclosed Roman Catholic nun, who was a friendly correspondent of mine for years, put some hagiographical question to me which I was unable to answer, I advised her to write to Coulton. She replied that she could not think of approaching so dreadful a person, such an appalling enemy of the faith, and so on. I answered that she was quite mistaken about him and once more advised her to write to him. I added that if she wished she could tell him what she thought of him as plainly as she had told me, and that he would nevertheless send her a courteous and full answer to her question, even if it entailed a couple of visits to the British Museum to get the necessary facts. He would undoubtedly have done so, but she never wrote to him.

My routine when I moved into College was much the same from day to day. Morning chapel (which I did not attend every day) was followed by breakfast in my rooms, or in Hall with the rowing men if they were in training. In those days breakfast was not provided in Hall for anybody else, at any time of the year. The morning was filled with lectures and individual tuition, followed by lunch at high table, in my rooms, or at the Footlights, who in those days rented a club-room and stage in Corn Exchange Street. Lunch in Hall generally resulted in an adjournment to Q's rooms for a glass of port. After that, Bernard Manning and I frequently spent an hour together, studying and translating some of that vast repository of medieval lore and Biblical exegesis, the *Glossa Ordinaria*, long ascribed to Walafrid Strabo. I then went to the boathouse or the towpath for an hour, had a few undergraduates to tea, and did some more teaching. Evening chapel (if I attended it) was followed by dinner in Hall. Then came coffee and conversation in the Combination Room, or more entertaining in my rooms, or a meeting of some University or College society, at Jesus or elsewhere.

Sometimes, at these after-dinner meetings, I would take my turn by reading a paper on some medieval subject, such as the Troubadours, which I illustrated by singing some of their songs in Old Provençal to the original melodies. My favourite items were Bernart de Ventadorn's plaintive love-song *Can vei la lauzeta*; Peire Vidal's lively *Pos tornatz sui en Proensa*; Guiraut de Bornelh's lovely dawn-song, *Reis glorios*; Marcabrun's recruiting song for a crusade against the Spanish Moors, in which he points out the advantage of not having to cross the sea in order to fight the infidel; Gaucelm Faidit's lament on Richard of England, which moves one still, after the lapse of seven-and-a-half centuries; and Jaufre Rudel's song about his distant love, the theme of so many commentaries, poems, and plays, from the twelfth century to the twentieth. To these in later years I often added Arnaut Daniel's clever but somewhat absurd sestina, *Lo ferm voler*, and the Monk of Montaudon's *Enueg*, which is a simple but entertaining list of his dislikes.

At less serious gatherings I would read a paper on another of my favourite subjects — the English Music-hall Song, illustrating it by selections from comic songs or sentimental ballads (sometimes burlesqued) of late Victorian or Edwardian times. Meetings of this latter kind soon became known in the College as the Real Folklore Society, and I sang in appropriate costume, male or female, with Bernard Manning as compère and Alan Pars as my accompanist. Songs like *The Diver* and *Pansy Faces* cried aloud for burlesque; but I preferred to sing *Thora* (based on a sentimental novel by Hall Caine) and *If those lips could only speak* quite seriously, as also *The man who broke the Bank at Monte Carlo*. I believe this to be essentially a pathetic song, and I think I succeeded in getting my audience to accept it as such. My favourite comic items included Fred Earle's *Seaweed,* Billy Williams's *Save a little one for me*, Frank Coyne's *You've got a long way to go*, George Bastow's *Captain Ginger*, and Marie Lloyd's tribute to the marriage of Alphonso XIII of Spain in 1906 — *Tiddley-om-pom*, with its tripping tune and rollicking double rhymes:

Oh! the folks they do go on so
In the land of King Alphonso.

Another society which I founded about this time was called the
Jesus Melodramatic Union. Its title explains its object. It did not last
long, but it gave two or three performances of Henry Arthur Jones's
celebrated late Victorian melodrama, *The Silver King*, which, as George
Sampson says, 'raised melodrama almost to the level of art'. I played
the title role and so had the pleasure of declaiming the magnificently
hyperbolic line, 'O God, put back thy universe, and give me yesterday!'
The part of the Silver King's little daughter, Cissie, was played by an
undergraduate, J. N. Duckworth.* He was as plump and rosy-cheeked
as a Della Robbia cherub but had to say, 'I'm starving, Jakes. I've had
nothing to eat for three days' – an assertion which brought down the
house. Vyvyan Cox, afterwards a well-known producer of broadcast
plays, acted the part of the Silver King's wife, Nellie; and the part of
my faithful henchman, Jakes, was played by my pupil, D. C. C. Trench,
afterwards Sir David Trench, Governor of Hong Kong.

Noel Duckworth spent much of his time in my rooms. He was very
popular in the College, in which he was commonly called – I should say
miscalled – 'the Bastard.'

One morning when he called on me my old friend Vincent
Robinson, who had retired from his grocery business at Barnet at an
early age and settled at Cambridge, happened to be paying me one of
his frequent visits. Admirable man though he was, he was most conventional and possessed little sense of humour, as this visit showed.

When Duckworth had gone, Vincent Robinson said to me, 'What a
pleasant young man!'

'Yes', I said. 'He has a very unusual nickname, too', I added,
thinking that he would be amused to hear it.

'Has he?' asked Robinson, 'What is it?'

'Oh, he's always called the Bastard', I answered.

On hearing this, the sober Vincent Robinson almost fell out of his
chair.

'What?' he gasped. 'Dis-s-s-GUSTing! Dis-s-s-GUSTing! I'm very sorry
for him, very sorry for him indeed, having to go through life with that
dis-GUSTing nickname; and you tell me he's going to be a clergyman,
too. Dis-GUSTing!'

I assured him that Duckworth, far from disliking his nickname, was
rather pleased with it; but nothing would convince him that this could
be so, and he went away with a sorrowful face, loudly protesting his
shocked disapproval.

* Afterwards Canon J. N. Duckworth, Chaplain of Churchill College.

Noel Duckworth was a distinguished Rooster, and I was intending to present him at the end of that term with a jocular coat of arms, emblazoned with references to his undergraduate activities, such as was my custom to present to the Presidents and others who had deserved well of the Roost. As I cannot paint, I used to make a pencil sketch and hand it to Vincent Robinson for reproduction in correct heraldic colours. He took great interest in the work, and he knew his heraldry so well that I could foresee a difficulty about Duckworth's Rooster arms. I knew that Robinson would resolutely refuse to include in the design any of the usual signs of illegitimacy, such as a bordure compony or wavy, or a baston sinister. At the same time I realized equally well that, if there were no marks of bastardy in the arms, both the recipient and the Roosters as a whole would be very disappointed.

I decided to solve the problem by using a significant motto. Being aware that Robinson knew very little Latin, I chose the motto *Galli nothi optimi sunt*. Having made my sketch, I showed it to the artist who, as usual, asked the meaning of the various charges. Coming at last to the motto, he said, 'My Latin is a bit rusty. What exactly does this mean?'

'Oh,' I said, 'it means "Cocks of mixed breed are best." You see, his father and mother came from different counties.'

'Most appropriate,' he said, 'most appropriate.'

I was afraid that when he got home he would consult a Latin dictionary and find that the usual translation of the motto was 'Bastard cocks are best.' Fortunately, he did not, and so the Robinson honour was satisfied, and Duckworth and the Roost were able to rejoice in his (purely heraldic) illegitimacy.

Another of Vincent Robinson's outstanding characteristics was his pessimism. If anyone asked him whether he did not agree that something or other was beautiful, he would generally qualify his assent with some such phrase as 'in its way' or 'while it lasts,' or 'It's a pity it's so small.' One day in May when he came to see me the sun was shining brilliantly, the grass in the college courts was a vivid green, the flowers in the borders were in full bloom, and the birds in the flowering chestnuts on the Close and in the Fellows' Garden were singing in loud chorus.

'What a perfect day!' I said.

'Yes-s-s-s,' he answered, 'in its way, while it lasts. It's a pity all this blossom lasts only about a fortnight. It's soon gone. In a few weeks we shall have the longest day here. Then the nights will soon start drawing in. Before we can look round we shall have those long, dark, damp winter evenings here again. They're beastly, and I HATE 'em,' he snapped – in the third week of May.

Once, when I was seriously ill, he opened the conversation by saying, 'My goodness! You *do* look ill. I've never seen you look like this before.' He capped this by saying, just before he went, 'I *do* hope you'll recover. It will be a very sad day for me if you don't.' I realized that this was a great compliment but I thought he might have kept it until later.

Owing to lack of means in my undergraduate days, and to timidity afterwards, it was not until 1932 that I joined that well-known society whose full title is 'The Cambridge University Footlights Dramatic Club'. The club had been founded in 1883 for the production of light original plays and has numbered among its members Jack and Claude Hulbert, Richard Murdoch, Harold Warrender, Julian Slade, Jimmy Edwards, Jonathan Miller and Tim Brooke-Taylor. Its chief function when I joined was, as it has been ever since, to produce a May Week revue. I joined the club through the instrumentality – I needed little persuasion – of one of my Pembroke pupils, John Coates, who was President in 1932-33 and had seen me performing in a Rooster revue. The Footlights played in the (Victorian) New Theatre in those days: the Arts Theatre did not open until 1936. In collaboration with John Chaplin and Michael Killanin (both of Magdalene) I helped to write the script of the 1933 Revue and played several parts in it, including one as a policewoman. The revue was called *No More Women*, because in the previous year women had been included in the cast for the first time; but as the play was not a success, the club had reverted to an all-male cast in 1933. Women were not re-introduced for another twenty years or so.

When *No More Women* was in rehearsal I generally lunched at the club's premises in Corn Exchange Street, where in those days we had our own little theatre and stage. After lunch and a rehearsal I often cycled with the Jesus boats to Baitsbite and back. One afternoon we ran into a heavy shower and I arrived back in Cambridge in a ragged greasy raincoat and an ancient battered hat, with my shoes and trousers coated with mud.

I had for some time been badly in need of a haircut and the first night of *No More Women* was close at hand. I accordingly made my way to the nearest barber's shop, pushed open one of the swing doors and went in.

I realized at once that I had gone to the wrong shop. The walls were decorated with posters advertising race-meetings and hunt balls. They

M

were hung with antlers, foxes' masks, riding whips, and binoculars. The shop was clearly the daily resort of the nobility and gentry of the hunting, shooting, and fishing fraternity.

There were no customers when I entered, but there were four assistants on view. One was sitting down, reading a newspaper. Another was sharpening a razor. The third and fourth were looking out of a window and carrying on a conversation.

None of them took any notice of me when I went in, which was not surprising, considering my tramp-like appearance. I took off my battered hat and muddy raincoat, hung them up, and sat in one of the vacant chairs. After a minute or so, one of the conversing pair turned to me and, raising his eyebrows, said, 'Haircut?'

'Yes, please', I said.

He got slowly to work with an air of 'It irks me, but I suppose I must do it.'

A minute or two later there was a commotion in the shop. The two men who were sitting down sprang up, rushed to the swing doors, pulled them open, bowed as a customer walked in, said 'Good afternoon, my lord' and remained respectfully standing while he took a chair.

I recognized him at once. He was Michael Killanin, a youthful peer of the realm, who obviously came to this shop every day for a shave. For some time he could not see who I was, though I could tell that he was trying to do so. At length, when one of the assistants changed his position, he recognized me and said, 'Well, I'm dashed! It's *you*, Freddy, is it?'

I was conscious immediately of a more delicate touch on my hair than before as my hairdresser got on with his work. Killanin and I chatted until his shave was finished, when he said 'See you at lunch at the club tomorrow' and went out.

Even when he had gone no one ventured to sit down. When my haircut was finished one of them fetched my filthy raincoat and helped me on with it, another respectfully presented my battered hat. Then, as a climax, when I felt in my numerous pockets for some money, I found I hadn't a farthing with me.

'I'm very sorry,' I stammered. 'I've come out without any money. I'll bring it along later.'

'That's all right, sir,' said one of them. 'There's no hurry. Any friend of his lordship —.'

I felt he was almost inclined to add 'need never bother to pay', but he didn't finish his sentence. I walked grandly out, with a bowing assistant holding a swing door on each side of me.

I told Michael Killanin about my adventure at lunch next day. We agreed that it would make an admirable sketch for a May Week revue, without any touching up, adding only a song with the refrain 'The British nation dearly loves a lord.'

On Sunday evenings I continued to attend chapel at the Oratory House, where I was cantor until the place changed hands in 1939. I generally stayed to dinner, returning to College soon afterwards for a meeting of the Roosters. As in past years, the Roost continued to demand urgent reforms, such as the abolition of the law of gravity, and to debate such important motions as 'We are the lost ten tribes'. The club also developed in new directions. Once a year we held a Bizarre Bazaar and Sale of Work, which was generally opened by Q with a witty speech, and had various side-shows. At one of these, T. L. T. Lewis (afterwards well known as a surgeon) performed the feat of drinking a pint of beer while standing on his head. Once a year also we staged a Rooster Revue, in the form of a burlesque on the history of the College, with plenty of topical references and songs. A large part of the population of the College, both senior and junior, attended the performances. One of my songs, which I sang disguised as 'Sister Betsy Co-ed', an alleged nun of St Radegund's Priory, was to the tune of the Victorian music-hall song, *The Man on the Flying Trapeze*:

> We nuns at Saint Radegund's, down Jesus Lane,
> Are ruled by a prioress, and find it a strain.
> If we ask for an exeat, she says in a pet,
> 'It's not been invented yet'.
> She seldom will give us an absit
> And never a late leave at all;
> So, if we come in after midnight,
> We have to climb over the wall.
> We climb up the wall with the greatest of ease,
> We get over the spikes and we drop from the trees.
> Last night, when she caught me, she hissed in my ears,
> 'You're gated for fifty years' . . .
>
> No Jesus man yet has been thrust into jail,
> And no Jesus tutor's been called on for bail.
> No Jesus man yet in the stocks has been set,
> For Jesus is not founded yet.
> John Alcock, the bishop, dislikes us:
> We're full of misgivings and fears;
> For, if he turns us out, there's no Girton

To go to, for four hundred years.
   If he turns us out of here, where shall we go?
There's no Girton College, or Newnham, you know,
   He's quite the most horrible bishop we've met:
He'll found Jesus College, you bet.

On both Sundays and week days, if I was free, I paid visits to Q and Bernard Manning shortly before they went to bed, because they both liked company while they were undressing. I went to Manning's rooms first, because he, being a semi-invalid, was usually the first to retire. When I had seen him to bed I went to the other end of the College, to Q's rooms. The ceremony there was much more elaborate and took about three-quarters of an hour. It was much like a one-man play. As his bedroom opened straight out of his keeping-room he would alternately disappear into the wings and reappear framed in the doorway, holding a pair of socks or trousers or a shirt in his hand while he delivered an epigram or a brief homily. He would then disappear again, and the sound of a muttered 'Damn!' from behind the scenes would indicate that he had stubbed his big toe against a chair-leg or some other obstacle. As he undressed from below upwards he looked a comic figure when he stood in the doorway in his shirt-tails, with bare feet and bare legs, and yet (if it was a feast night) in full evening dress down to the waist. When the play was ended he would get into bed and dismiss his audience.

One day at the end of term I chanced to call on Q just as he was about to leave for home, so I walked with him to the gate and saw him into his car. There I handed to him the spare bowler-hat with which, for some unknown reason, he generally travelled. (He possessed black, grey and brown bowlers for particular occasions.) He was obviously pleased with this send-off. I therefore made a point of calling on him the following term at the time when I knew he was going down. On this occasion I went with him all the way to the station, where I saw him into his train. Within a year or two this had developed into a grand ceremony, in which the chief officers of the Roost all took part and sometimes a car-load went to the station with him. The going-down ceremony was repeated every year until Q died, and the officers of the Roost came to regard attendance at it as part of their duties.

When we arrived at the station Q was in no hurry. A porter piled his luggage on to a trolley and we patrolled the platform, with the stationmaster in attendance, looking for a suitable compartment. Once, when the porter had transferred the luggage to what he thought was a suitable compartment, he had to take it out again when Q came up. We then patrolled the platform until a compartment of which Q approved was found. Meanwhile passengers were putting their heads out of windows all along the train, wondering what was causing the delay.

I have been told that the same ceremony took place at Par, the main-line junction for Fowey, when Q left there for Cambridge at the beginning of each term.

27

In the summer of 1932 my parents moved their home for the last time
– from the working-class Puller Road to The Avenue, which was entirely middle-class. The two elderly spinsters who lived next door
showed their intense abhorrence of their new neighbours. They were
very devout women, devoting their spare time to raising money for
missions to the Jews and getting other people to make shirts for Zulus;
but they could not bear to have for neighbours anyone who belonged
to the same social class as Christ, as my father so obviously did.

It had done me good to live in a small working-class house during
vacations to the age of thirty-eight, but there were disadvantages. For
instance, I had to share a bedroom with my brother. I also shared with
him the small shed which he and a carpenter friend had built in the
garden, so that he might have somewhere to conduct wireless experi-
ments, and I to write, as there was no room indoors. For some time I
did most of my writing in the shed, but it was very cold in winter, very
hot in summer, and had no space for books. I had to keep some of
these in our joint bedroom, the remainder in the tiny overcrowded
family sitting-room. The frequent journeys backwards and forwards to
fetch books or papers did not make literary composition easy.

The new house in The Avenue was much more commodious than the
old. Both my parents were pleased to possess a larger garden than
before, though it was still a small one. My father was delighted to have
a cellar in which to store his home-made wine and vegetables and an
attic in which to keep the varied lumber which he loved to accumulate.
My brother and I now had a room each, and the house satisfied two
conditions which to me were indispensable: it was within the ancient
boundaries of the parish of South Mimms and it commanded the ever-
entrancing view across the parish to the top of Ridge Hill which I had
always loved.

During that same summer I moved out of the 1930 building in
Chapel Court at Jesus to the 1640 range in First Court, where I had a
set of rooms on the top floor of C Staircase. When Claude Elliott heard
of the impending move he said to me, 'The old buildings have glamour,
I know, but the new building has hot and cold laid on; and hot and cold
laid on are worth a lot of glamour.' As I relished the thought of living in

the older part of the College, and also of being on the same staircase as Q, I chose the glamour. With the aid of a gas-ring (later, of an electric kettle) I soon got used to the absence of hot and cold laid on. It was true that I now had to walk across two open courts to get a bath, and that my new bedroom was so narrow that it would take only the smallest of chairs at my bedside, but I never regretted the change.

Mrs Mitchley, our bedmaker, had worked on C Staircase for many years. She was admirable in every way and Q called her 'The Best Bedmaker in Cambridge'. I abbreviated this to 'The B.B.C.' One evening a year or two later, when term was well under way, someone in the Combination Room asked me whether I had heard when Q was likely to come up. I answered 'The B.B.C. says he is coming tomorrow.' — 'What!' my colleague said, 'Do they broadcast it now?'

I had a finer outlook on C Staircase than I had had in Chapel Court. My front windows looked across the flower-edged lawn of First Court to the Fellows' Garden and the nunnery buildings, with the battlemented chapel-tower and the tall graceful spire of All Saints' Church rising in the background, one on each side of the great gate of the College. My back window looked down on to the formal flower-beds and clipped hedges of Pump Court and gave me a glimpse into the Close and across it to Jesus Green, where I could see the almond-trees blossoming every spring. My bedroom, being at the end of the range, commanded a view of a part of the Close where the grass was allowed to grow high every year and was then converted into hay. There I picked handfuls of golden buttercups for my rooms in May, big ox-eye daisies in June, and masses of ragwort in July, successfully passing these off on uninitiated enquiriers as rare Hungarian flowers grown under glass. Beyond the Close lay the hockey field, and in the background rose the big tower of St John's College Chapel. From its roof, if the wind was in the right quarter, I could hear the choir singing carols at noon on Ascension Day.

As on most staircases in the College, there were six sets of rooms on C Staircase, two on each floor. On the ground floor there were an undergraduate set and the undergraduates' Common Room. The middle floor was occupied by Q's rooms and a guest room. My neighbour on the top floor was Nairne, who had now resigned from the Regius Professorship of Divinity but still lived in college during term, and during vacations in the cloisters at Windsor Castle. On my first evening in my new rooms Nairne and I came out of our doors simultaneously to go to Hall. When we were part of the way down the stairs he said, 'Oh, dear! I've forgotten about my teeth,' and went back to his rooms. I naturally imagined that he meant he had forgotten to put his false teeth in and had gone back to fetch them; but I found by observation in the course of a few days that he meant the opposite. He had gone back to leave his teeth behind, because it was his rule to take them out before meals. As he ate very little, it did not make much difference whether he wore them or not, except to his appearance.

My rooms were immediately over Q's, and Nairne's were over the Fellows' Guest Room. This room had been furnished to suit Q's taste and had a carpet and wallpaper of a curious shade of red. He used the room so much that some wag nicknamed it 'the Q-bicle'. He always referred to it as 'my dining-room', and kept many of his books there, and his clothes in the wardrobe of the guest's bedroom. If any Fellow housed a guest in it (as he was entitled to do), and if the guest stayed more than two or three days, Q would say with indignation, 'That devil —— has had a man in my dining-room for the last fortnight.' It was in 'the Q-bicle' that the Red Herrings generally met once or twice a term for dessert and wine. Q greatly enjoyed these functions. They acquired even greater zest for him, as for the other members, when Sir Herbert Richmond, who had been appointed Professor of Naval History in the University and elected a Fellow of the College, became a member of the Red Herrings. As we sometimes called Q 'the Red Knight' (from his title in the Cornish Gorsedd, his hair having been red before it went grey), and as Richmond had been an admiral, I nicknamed him 'the Blue Knight'.

One frequent occupier of the Guest Room was another knight – at least, he became one a few years later. This was Sir William Nicholson, the distinguished artist, who had some years previously painted portraits of Arthur Gray and Tommy Watt for the College. He had now been commissioned to paint Q's portrait for the Roosters and stayed in College during his visits to Cambridge for the purpose. Eighteen months elapsed between the first sitting and the last, partly because Nicholson and Q possessed artistic temperaments which clashed at times. Most of the sittings were held in the Guest Room – hence· the curious red background to the portrait – but some of the later ones were in London. On one occasion for which a sitting had been arranged Q waited in his rooms all day for 'that devil Nicholson', who was meanwhile waiting for Q in his studio at Chelsea.

Another frequent occupier of 'the Q-bicle' – too frequent for Q's liking – was F. J. Foakes Jackson, who had been a Professor in the

United States since 1916 but was a life Fellow of the College and frequently returned to it during his summer vacations. It was he who persuaded the College to celebrate the centenary of S. T. Coleridge's death a year in advance because he was going to be in England that summer. He also persuaded the College to give a dinner as part of the celebration. The guests included many prominent literary men, and also David, the Cambridge bookseller, who immediately after dinner fell asleep at table with a cigar in his mouth. He slept all through the speeches and through the reading of a sonnet which one of the guests, Gilbert Coleridge, had written in honour of his ancestor.

Foakes Jackson was in some ways the eccentric and absent-minded don of popular legend. Even Nairne, who had been one of his pupils back in the eighteen-eighties, found him trying at times. One morning, when Foakes Jackson discovered that he and Nairne had both been invited to a feast at the same college, he called on him and asked him whether he was going to accept the invitation. Nairne replied that he had not yet decided and Foakes went away. An hour or two later he came back and repeated his question. Nairne replied that he still had not decided and asked Foakes to go away, as he was busy. To his surprise, Foakes came back a third time before lunch and asked the same question. Nairne, becoming suspicious, asked him why he was so anxious to know, and Foakes answered, 'Well, you see, I thought that if you weren't going you would lend me your scarlet gown.' 'I didn't want to go to the feast at all,' said Nairne, when telling the story afterwards, 'but I decided at once that I must go, because if I hadn't gone I should have had to lend him my beautiful scarlet gown, and I knew that he would clean his false teeth on it before he left the table.'

Nairne would occasionally talk about his undergraduate days at the College. He weighed so little, he said, that his services as a coxswain were in great demand until an unfortunate occasion when his boat was rounding Grassy Corner when rowing a course. He steered so badly, he said, that he did not merely hit the bank but ran his boat right on to the land and it was smashed to pieces.

'And, do you know,' he said, 'those rowing men were *so* cross with me.'

Those who are familiar with the ways of rowing men can easily picture the scene. A member of the crew evidently went up to Nairne after the accident and said, 'I hope you don't mind my mentioning it, cox, but I really am rather annoyed at what has just happened.'

Upon this, another member of the crew no doubt added, 'At the risk of repeating what has just been said, I feel bound to say that your coxing this afternoon was rather unsatisfactory.'

Nairne's seemingly artless ways were sometimes most effective. Once, at an evening gathering at which he was present, someone told a rather 'blue' after-dinner story. Two other stories of the same kind followed, each of them being longer than the one before it. When the laughter had died away after the third story, Nairne took a pinch of snuff and said, 'I heard *such* a good story the other day. Oh! it *was* a good story.'

Here everyone grew rather alarmed, wondering whether the saintly Nairne whom all revered was possibly going to kick over the traces and add to the blueness, and hoping that he was not.

'Yes, it *was* a good story,' he continued. 'It was quite short, and there was nothing about sex in it, and nothing about the lavatory. It was the sort of story that makes you realize what a beautiful world we live in; and the worst of it is ——' (here he looked despairingly round) 'I can't remember it. I can't even remember what it was about. Can any of *you* tell me?'

Complete and painful silence reigned. Nairne took out his watch, looked at it, and said, 'Dear me! It's nine o'clock. I must be going', and went.

Nairne often entertained the Combination Room with his experiences as a parish priest. One of his stories showed that, although he had been born and bred in Hertfordshire, there was a homely phrase in use in the county which he had never heard until he became Rector of Tewin.

One of his women parishioners, he told us, called on him one day to ask his advice about her next-door neighbour, whom she found very trying.

'The other day, Rector,' she said, 'she called me all the B's.'

Nairne, thinking that he had not heard her correctly, said, 'Called you *what*?'

The woman repeated, with a shocked expression on her face, 'She called me all the B's.'

Nairne was nonplussed and asked her what she meant. She explained that her neighbour had used foul language to her; whereupon he advised her, if anything of the sort looked like happening again, to go indoors and take no notice.

'When the woman had gone,' Nairne said to us when telling the story afterwards, 'I sat and thought about that curious expression, "She

called me all the B's." I began to consider its etymology, and I came to
the conclusion that it originally meant calling someone by offensive
epithets all beginning with the letter B. I thought about it for a long
time; but, do you know, I could only think of three.'

Both Nairne and Q were very fond of Okey, of whom I saw a good
deal about this time. Like Nairne, he had resigned voluntarily from his
Professorship, but still spent a considerable part of each term in his
rooms at Caius College, where I visited him frequently. He kept his
eightieth birthday in 1932. Unlike Nairne, he was sad, nervous, and
sometimes depressed in his later years. I found that he was cheered if I
induced him to talk about his early life and his experiences as a basket-
maker, and I persuaded him to take up basket-making again as a hobby.
When he had turned eighty-two he made a waste-paper basket and gave
it to me, together with a smaller older basket. He had made this in 1910
to illustrate the article on basket-making which he contributed to the
eleventh edition of the *Encyclopaedia Britannica*, where a drawing of it
is reproduced.

I took care to let Nairne and Q see the basket that Okey had made
for me and, as I expected, they were envious. I let Okey know this and
(again, as I expected) he made a basket for each of them, to their
pleasure and his own. In his letters to me about the baskets, the crafts-
man and the man of letters were blended in one. 'Please make all
allowances for my bad handwriting in willow as in literary scripture', he
wrote. 'This badly written work,' he called one of the baskets, 'work
which in my younger days would have brought the yard-stick across my
back.'

What might be called Okey's last public appearance was probably at
a tea-party in my rooms in the early spring of 1935. I had gathered a
number of his admirers together – Q, Nairne, Herbert Richmond,
Conrad Skinner, Robert Gittings (at the time a Research Fellow of the
College), and Michael Killanin, who was then an undergraduate at
Magdalene and more than sixty years younger than Okey. Okey
recovered his old spirits as soon as he entered the room and saw the
company eager to greet him, and he was the life and soul of the party.

Towards the end of that term I walked almost daily with him along
the Backs at Trinity, up and down among the flowering crocuses wide
open in the brilliant March sun, while he talked about his early life.
That was the last I saw of him. He was taken ill during the Easter
vacation and died at his Kentish home in May, *integer vitae scelerisque
purus*, true to his own nature from the beginning of his life to the end.

Nairne survived Okey by less than a year. He died at Windsor during the spring vacation of 1936 and was buried in the village churchyard at Tewin. J. M. Edmonds, who was a great admirer of Nairne, sketched some of the many facets of his character in *Chanticlere*:

> Elf, angel, artist, theologian, Latinist, in his own dear childish way a *poseur*, shrewdly wrong-headed, optimistically pessimist, idealist and yet somehow practical, a man of petty enthusiasms, expunger of commas, user of hand-made notepaper, praiser of manner rather than matter, disconcerting admirer of the bizarre, yet passionately convinced of the worth of learning and the goodness of beauty, finder of excuses for every man but one, wry smiler at himself, a kind of spiritual *bon viveur*, a mystic who walked with men, a pagan who communed with God.

28

I had for some time felt that, if I outlived Nairne, I should like to move across the landing into his rooms, which Foakes Jackson had occupied before him; and as soon as they had been redecorated after his death I did so.

My bedroom now looked into Pump Court; but I still had a good, if indirect, view of the wild part of the Close, with the hockey-ground and St John's Chapel beyond it. Otherwise the outlook from my rooms was much the same as before. I had gained a room by the move, having now a small dining-room between my even smaller bedroom (about eight feet square) and my keeping-room. Considering the amount of entertaining that I did, it must have been an advantage to Q (though he had always been most uncomplaining) to have me no longer immediately over his head. It was certainly an advantage to me to be over the Guest Room, because it was unoccupied as often as not. It was also an advantage to possess an even larger keeping-room than before, because my entertaining seemed to increase every term. So did my collection of ornamental cockerels of every size, design, material and colour. Old Jesus men sent them to me from all over the world, until I had about 600 of them and new shelves had to be fitted to accommodate them. In course of time they included such out-of-the-way items as an earthenware cockerel about 2,500 years old from Cyprus, a brass cockerel some 500 years old from Ceylon, a witch-doctor's stick from East Africa, a wooden cockerel from Pitcairn Island, and a large cockerel carved from a block of anthracite by a South Wales mining-mechanic and presented to me by the National Coal Board.

In May 1937 I was elected a Fellow of the College. There was the usual brief ceremony in Chapel a day or two later, at which I read a Latin declaration of obedience to the statutes and ordinances of the College and was then admitted to my Fellowship by the Master. When he proposed my health in the Combination Room that evening with one of his usual felicitous speeches, a merciful tradition precluded me from replying.

As mine was what is called in the Statutes an Official Fellowship, it carried with it a stipend, together with a seat on the College Council. I of course possessed also the right, common to Fellows of all classes, to a free dinner in Hall every day, but had to pay for drinks and all other meals. It was my duty, so long as I remained the Junior Fellow, to pour out the wine in the Combination Room and to fix the College seal to leases, agreements, presentation to benefices, and similar legal documents on behalf of 'the Master or Keeper and Fellows and Scholars of the College of the Blessed Virgin Mary, Saint John the Evangelist, and the Glorious Virgin Saint Radegund, commonly called Jesus College, in the University of Cambridge.'

In the same year as my election to a Fellowship the Cambridge University Press published my book *The Medieval Latin and Romance Lyric to A.D. 1300*, in which I tried to trace the evolution of lyrical poetry in Latin and the various Romance languages during the Middle Ages. This was followed two or three years later by *A Short History of Jesus College*, based on the talks which I gave while conducting undergraduates or outside visitors round the College. In the spring of 1939 I paid two visits to London, in order to give a couple of broadcast talks on Medieval Latin Hymns and Sequences. Apart from that, I seldom went to town except for the annual dinner of the Jesus College Society, which in those days was held just after Henley Regatta and was attended by old Jesus men of many generations. I rarely stayed a night away from Cambridge during term, but I stole away for half a day in mid-May occasionally, so as to be in Mimms Wood when the bluebells were in their prime. I went back to Cambridge from such visits feeling that I had seen a vision, even a miracle; and that, like other men who have seen miracles, I could not explain it to anyone else.

I was doing a good deal of acting and singing at this time, sometimes outside the College — at Footlights smoking concerts, for instance, or as the Drunken Porter in a performance of *Macbeth* at the A.D.C. Theatre — but more often inside the College walls, at performances of the Real Folklore Society or in Rooster revues. In these I occasionally played a serious part, such as Archbishop Cranmer in a verse monologue written by Robert Gittings; but naturally there was little room for serious items in an undergraduate revue. One day, Arthur Gray, who was afflicted with deafness in his old age and in any event had little ear for music, asserted that he had heard me singing a Latin hymn in a part of the College adjacent to the Master's Lodge. What he heard was in fact Marie Lloyd's song *A little of what you fancy does you good*.

My singing during vacations at this time consisted almost entirely of church music, of which I always had a full quota during the Easter vacation. Wherever else I might be at other seasons, Allen Hay expected me to be at South Mimms throughout Holy Week and Easter every year, so as to act as master of ceremonies during the elaborate services at the parish church, to be cantor at *Tenebrae*, and to sing the glorious *Exultet* for him on Easter Eve, which I did for the last twenty years of his life. I have continued singing it every Easter Eve until now.

I have never yet been able to decide which I enjoy singing most — medieval church music, troubadour music, or music-hall songs of the Victorian-Edwardian Golden Age.

When Steve Fairbairn died in 1938 Arthur Gray was over eighty-five but had not had a day's illness in his life and was full of vigour. Having been elected under statutes which laid down no retiring age for the head of the College, he could hold office as long as he lived, and he had no intention of resigning. Once, when he had a suspicion that the Fellows wished him to resign, he made a speech at a bump supper — he was always admirable on such occasions — which had a deeper meaning than the assembled undergraduates realized.

'I am *Master* of this College, gentlemen,' he said. (Applause.) 'I am con*tin*uing as Master of this College.' (Loud applause.) 'I in*tend* to be *Master* of this *College* as long as there is *breath* in my *body*.' (Tremendous applause.)

Arthur Gray was very tough and rarely wore an overcoat out-of-doors, even on the coldest days of the piercing Cambridge winters, when the hardiest undergraduates were muffled against the frost. Very abstemious in both eating and drinking, he was an almost incessant smoker. When I spent a week with him at a hotel at King's Lynn in the spring of 1938 my chief duty (though I was never told so) was to see that his lips were never without a cigarette.

Despite his age, his voice was clear and loud, as was shown to my embarrassment one day while we were staying at Lynn. We had gone to tea at another hotel, in order to have a change and (the Master said) to see the garden there. When we had returned from the garden and had reached the foot of the main staircase of the hotel where the manager, the head waiter, the receptionist and other officials were standing together, respectfully studying the Master's venerable figure, I said to him, 'Here's the tea-room, Master.'

He glared round him and said, in the loudest tones and with that strong emphasis on every third or fourth syllable which was habitual with him, '*I* don't *like* the *look* of this *place*.' (I tried to look as if I could not hear him.) 'Let us go somewhere *else* to tea.' (I tried vainly to look as if I had never seen him before.) '*Sure*ly you can find a *tea*-shop.

Any tea-shop would be *better* than *this*.' I almost ran to the front door, while he plodded firmly behind me with his stick, delivering his final charge as he went: 'Be*sides*, we've *seen* their *gar*den, which is what we *came* to see.'

Despite his age and his strong antiquarian interests, Arthur Gray was a restless reformer to the end, the most revolutionary member of the society of dons over whom he presided. Like Okey, he did not believe in the myth of 'the good old days'. 'They were *not* good old days,' he used to say, 'they were *bad* old days.' He had certainly known the College in its bad days when he was a young don. At that time the College (including the Master, so it was said) was dominated by the overpowering personality of Red Morgan, the Dean-cum-Senior-Tutor, who allowed the undergraduates to do very much what they liked. The result was that the College fell into disrepute; and Arthur Gray, who as Junior Tutor tried to administer an antidote to Red Morganism, became very unpopular with the undergraduates. He did not mind unpopularity. As Nairne used to say, no one could have endured hardship more gallantly, but he resented the harm done to the reputation of the College. 'Red *Mor*gan did more *harm* to the College than anyone else *ever* did', he used to say. To the end of his life, he could always be roused to wrath by any mention of the repugnant name. Anyone who did not know might have thought that Red Morgan's enormities had been perpetrated a few weeks previously, whereas he had been dead for well over forty years.

One story that is told about Red Morgan must have been unknown to Arthur Gray, or he would surely have repeated it many times. It alleges that when Red Morgan was a schoolmaster during the interval between his graduation and his return to the College as a Fellow, one of his colleagues died, leaving a widow totally unprovided for. Red Morgan thereupon stepped gallantly forward, started a subscription list on the lady's behalf and did not relax until he had collected a considerable sum. He then married the widow.

At the last graduation lunch that Arthur Gray attended he described himself as 'a great traditionalist and a great radical'. There was much truth in his self-description, but he was an iconoclast rather than a radical. His iconoclasm had perhaps begun when he decided that he had to smash the idol of Red Morganism, and had then become inveterate in him. It was strongly evident even where one would never expect to find it. His *Earliest Statutes of Jesus College*, for instance, published in 1935, seemed to have been produced with the intention of throwing doubts on John Alcock's right to be honoured as the founder of Jesus College and to suggest that it had been founded by someone else, whose name had never previously been mentioned in connection with the founding of the College, even by Arthur Gray himself in his published history. His animus against Alcock at this time was so strong that one would not have been surprised, on returning to Cambridge after a vacation, to find that he had surreptitiously removed the statue of the bishop from its niche over the great gate.

In his later years he dined less frequently in Hall than formerly, and even when he came he seemed to eat practically nothing. Often, however, he joined us in the Combination Room after dining (or perhaps not dining) at the Lodge. On these occasions his conversation was as lively as ever and his reminiscences of Cambridge eccentrics as entertaining as they had always been.

Q, on the other hand, dined in Hall every evening, unless he was dining out of College or entertaining guests in 'the Q-bicle'. He was the slowest eater I have ever known, and when he was dining in Hall the meal always took at least ten minutes longer than when he was not. Even when dinner appeared to have ended, he would often sit for some minutes 'fiddling with his wretched wine', as Nairne used to say when he was itching to get away to a meeting of the Clouds.

One of my pleasantest vacations was spent at Q's beloved Fowey in the summer of 1938, when he was Mayor. The Dutch novelist Maarten Maartens had described him many years before as 'King of Fowey in a quiet way', and during the year of his mayoralty he appeared to deserve the title more than ever. It was a delight to accompany him on his daily walk through the main street of his miniature kingdom, with his subjects greeting him all the way, to sit with him in the barber's shop while he was being shaved with a grave air and at the same time with a twinkle in his eye, to listen to him discussing business with officials of the tiny borough at the Town Hall, to watch him choosing regatta prizes at the Yacht Club, and above all to see his affectionate yet always reverential attitude to his wife.

Q never resided at Cambridge during the Long Vacation. Nothing could ever tear him away from Fowey then. It is nevertheless a very pleasant time to be at Cambridge, and a don has more leisure then than during an ordinary term. In August 1939, Bernard Manning and I took advantage of this leisure to carry out a plan on which we had been meditating for some time. We visited every parish church and college chapel in Cambridge and wrote a report on them, calling ourselves the

N

William Dowsing Society, after the Puritan iconoclast who had visited the churches of Cambridgeshire and Suffolk in 1643 under the orders of the Long Parliament, to deface or remove objects of reputed superstition. Dowsing had kept a journal of his tour, with such entries as this:

> At Little Mary's we brake down LX. superstitious Pictures, some Popes & Crucyfixes, & God the Father sitting in a chayer & holdinge a Glasse in his hand.
> At Peterhouse we pulled down ii mighty great Angells with wings, and divers other Angells, & the IV Evangelists & Peter with his Keies over the Chappell Dore, & about a hundred Chirubims and Angells.

The William Dowsing Society in its report employed similar language and spelling like this:

> *Saint John's College* hathe a most decente & statelie Chapel, though divers in their folly mislike it. Yet it seemede bare in ye middes, by reason y^t they cherisshe here a beggarlie superstition concernynge Vistas & hadde hid awaye ye brave & comelie Lecterne. We did sette it back in his proper place.

> *Holie Trinitie Chirche* . . . . . We espied nigh on .ccc. copies of a Booke of rhymes & ditties entituled *Songes of Prayse*. When we hadde made a fyre in Markett Street, we caste thereon ye saide bookes & made a myghtie greate blaze of ye same.

> At *Saint John's Churche* in ye Hills Road we digged up all ye tiles before ye Altar & did out divers foolishe Banners. Item, we brake downe & utterlie destroied .i. superstition called a Children's Corner.

> In ye chapel at *Ridley Hall* we turned ye lecterne straight. We tooke· awaye therefrom .i. superstitiouse booke called ye Revised Version & did put ye Bible in place thereof.

> From ye Chapell of *Westcott House* we took out ye Revised Version & destroied .xLvj. tip-up Seates. Item, at ye gate of ye House we utterlie destroied & abolishede .i. foolish Coney & .i. superstitiouse Pigge.

In short, we expressed our dislike of various ecclesiastical usages which were popular at the time; and, although one of the two members of the Society described himself as 'a believer in east worshippe and dropping worship' and the other as 'a painfull and fanatical upholder of Master Calvin', only one very brief passage had to be omitted from the report through any disagreement between us. Our 'Narracioun' was published by instalments in the *Cambridge Review* and soon afterwards reprinted as a pamphlet, with the title *Babylon Bruis'd & Mount Moriah Mended.* To our surprise, a number of reprints were called for during the next twelve months and it is now in its eighth impression.

One unexpected and very pleasing result of the publication of *Babylon Bruis'd* was that the authorities of Westcott House, far from resenting our remarks about their iron boot-scrapers (one in the form of a rabbit, the other of a pig) forthwith elected me a member of their council. During my period of office I visited the House and its chapel very frequently and had the privilege of becoming friendly with two celebrated men – Charles Raven, the Chairman of the Council, and B. K. Cunningham, the Principal.

29

Just before the outbreak of war in the autumn of 1939 the number of men in residence at Jesus College, excluding dons, was little less than 300. By the end of the war it had fallen to a bare hundred.

Most of the war-time undergraduates were cadets, sent to Cambridge for a six-months' university course as part of their training before being commissioned. The remainder — the only ones in residence for any length of time — were mostly men taking degrees in medicine, natural sciences, or mechanical sciences before being drafted into national service. It was they, in conjunction with such dons as continued in residence, who were responsible for keeping the College traditions going and for helping the short-course men to get as much as they could out of their brief stay in the University. Most of the academical societies, social clubs and games clubs were in fact kept going throughout the war, and *Chanticlere* was published every term without a break — perhaps the only College magazine at Cambridge of which that could be said. Roosting was so popular with the short-course men that we had to hold two or three Roosts a week to satisfy them.

Although the number of undergraduates, after about the first twelve months of the war, was small, the College was nevertheless always full, as half or more of our buildings were occupied by a detachment of the Royal Air Force. The advance guard arrived within three days of the outbreak of war. Next day about 250 others joined them — officers and other ranks. There was a moving scene in the College Hall that evening, when our guests lined the walls and our venerable Master welcomed them with a charming speech, just as he had welcomed the men billeted in College in 1914.

At first the officers, being few in number, dined with the Fellows at high table. They soon became too numerous for that and migrated to another part of the College to dine. The other ranks had their meals in Hall throughout the war, at a different time from the members of the College. Owing to difficulties about the service of meals in the middle of the day, the College lunch for two years or more was served in the premises of the Pitt Club, of which we obtained a lease when the Club closed down at the beginning of the war. Later, we were ejected from the Pitt, which the Government converted into a British Restaurant, where a tenpenny lunch was served daily. Q commemorated this transformation in four lines of light verse:

Though our Club has had notice to quit,
Yet as Britons we still claim admittance;
So our last one-and-eightpence we'll split
And we'll feast at the Pitt for a pittance.

A rearrangement of Air Force meal-times enabled us to return to Hall for our lunch.

We made many friends among our guests. They played numerous games on the Close, against the College and against other opponents. They attended College concerts and services in our blacked-out Chapel and some of them were elected to College clubs. One of our guests, D. M. Balme, who was serving in the ranks at the time, was not strictly speaking a guest at all, being already a member of the College and indeed a Fellow of it. Once, in the darkest days of the black-out, he was put on guard with a fixed bayonet outside the Porter's Lodge, where his own colleagues, not even knowing that he was in Cambridge, passed him without recognizing him. I do not remember seeing him there — perhaps because my distinguished colleague, Professor C. H. Dodd, and I, regarding it as an indignity to have to produce passes to enter our own College, normally came in through the Fellows' Garden with our private keys.

About half-way through the war our guests were reinforced by a detachment of the Women's Auxiliary Air Force, who likewise were billeted in College. The R.A.F. had, from the first, publicly advertised their presence to potential bombers by erecting a flag-pole on the Close and flying their pennant from it, but we were not allowed to mention their presence in print, or even the presence of the W.A.A.F. I managed, however, to hint at the latter in one of the annual reports of the Jesus College Society, copies of which were sent to all the members, in England or abroad. I remarked in it that 'in one respect, part of the College has reverted to conditions which prevailed before 1496', which was the year that the nuns left. I was surprised to find how many old Jesus men failed to understand the allusion.

Early in the war the medieval glass in our Old Library and the Burne-Jones windows in the Chapel were sent away into the country, and the majority of the College portraits and medieval manuscripts were dispersed, so that they might not all be lost if things came to the worst. There were 424 air-raid alerts at Cambridge during the war, during which the enemy dropped 118 high-explosive bombs and about a thousand incendiaries, and twenty-nine persons were killed. The Round Church, the Union Society and houses in Jesus Lane were hit, but the College buildings came through the war unscathed.

Arthur Gray, who celebrated his eighty-seventh birthday a few weeks after the arrival of the Air Force, did not live much longer but was active to the very end. He continued to preside over the meetings of the College Council and to act as though it were legally a despotism instead of a democracy. He seemed impervious to the climate, and continued to walk slowly through the College courts and the town streets without an overcoat in what was one of the bitterest winters ever known. In February he sauntered through the courts during a heavy snowstorm with his jacket and even his waistcoat unbuttoned. He continued to smoke cigarettes all day long and to delight the Combination Room with his admirable stories of Cambridge characters of the past seventy years and with his denunciations of Red Morgan. In March 1940 he made one of the best bump-supper speeches he ever made, weaving into it the pathetic story of the aged Barzillai the Gileadite and holding his undergraduate audience to the end with his oratory, his humour, and his obvious devotion to the College. He died in his sleep on April 12th, having worked even on the day of his death. At his funeral, the coffin was wheeled through each of the College courts in turn, with the Fellows walking behind. This practice at the burial of Masters of Jesus was carried out at Dr Corrie's funeral in 1885 'according to custom', but no one knows when the custom originated. Now that there is a retiring age for Masters the custom has been extended to the funeral of former Masters, to prevent it from dying out.

A few weeks later we met in Chapel at noon to elect a new Master. As the Senior Fellow, Foakes Jackson, was in America, Abbott, the next senior, who had lived in retirement at Barnet ever since 1932, came up to preside over the election. When we had in turn read a declaration, as required by the statutes, that we would 'disregard all personal considerations whatsoever and have regard only to the welfare of the College', we recorded our votes on paper and they were counted by Abbott and the Junior Fellow, D. M. Balme. Abbott then declared Dr W. L. H. Duckworth elected, and he forthwith made the lengthy declaration in Latin required by the statutes and was admitted to office as thirty-third Master or Keeper of Jesus College.

The new Master was already seventy years of age and could not have been elected but for wartime statutes. He had been born on St Boniface's Day 1870 and was therefore christened Wynfrid — the saint's original name — though his family always called him by his second name, Laurence. Everybody liked him. Tall, spare, and very abstemious, he was a mirror of old-fashioned courtesy, with a gentle humour of an unusual kind. He had been admitted to the College in 1889, had been a Fellow ever since 1893, and had a great knowledge of the College and its traditions. Unlike all his predecessors in the Mastership, he was a Doctor of Medicine and also a Doctor of Science, and a good deal of the precise language which he used in his scientific lectures had become absorbed into his ordinary speech and writing. This mode of expression, which perhaps began as a jest, had long since become second nature. However it began, the result was that he never seemed to say anything in one word if he could say it in six, or to use a short word if a long one would do.

At meetings of the College Council, for instance, he would never say 'You will remember,' but 'It will be within the recollection of the Council, will it not?' Q used to wink hard at me across the table, and make it difficult for me to keep a straight face, when the Master referred to 'water for purposes of drinking', or described a boys' camp as 'a camp for juvenile individuals', or translated a tenant-farmer's application for a new cowshed into 'a request for an additional shelter for the accommodation of his herd'. One of his best efforts in circumlocution was printed in *Chanticlere* in 1937, before he became Master, in the form of an article on repairs to the Chapel. He wrote:

> There is no respite in respect of minor operations. Occasionally the need for perfecting or renewing the defences on a relatively large scale becomes irresistible. The year 1815 illustrated the point, by activity manifested in the employment of an Italian firm to cover with Roman cement the whole of the southern aspect of the building. . . . There are circumstances in which not even Roman cement can resist decay indefinitely, and in the present instance the passage of time witnessed the development of a certain incompatibility between the Italian cuticle and the native British substratum. Decay and disintegration are natural enough, yet [probably] Nature was not without the aid of human agents in effecting the final unauthorized detachment of the cement. The trouble started at the gargoyles, whence streams of rain-water were projected with such great force and momentum as to explain amply a mode of incidence of the damage which had seemed rather capricious.

One evening in the Combination Room he told us how, some years before, a don had taken his son to the barber for a haircut.

'The artist,' Duckworth said, 'was much too dilatory for the impatient parent. Having endured the agony for some minutes, he sprang from his seat. "Give me those scissors," he shouted. He snatched the shears from the hand of the astonished artist and completed the operation himself.'

'Were you there?' I asked.

'Indeed I was,' said Duckworth. 'I myself had gone there for purposes of tonsure.'

Under Duckworth, as under Gray, the social life of the College managed to struggle on, despite such obstacles as rationing, scarcity, fire-watching, and air-raids. We still held our two chief feasts, the Rustat and the Audit, even though the fare became more and more attenuated as the war went on. They provided useful opportunities for getting to know the Air Force officers, for entertaining American officers stationed in England, and for keeping in touch with our Honorary Fellows, such as W. R. Inge, 'the Gloomy Dean', who continued to attend feasts until he was about ninety, walking the mile-and-a-half from the railway station and carrying his suitcase. He said little, being afflicted with acute deafness in his old age; but he would stand by the Combination Room fire after dinner, blinking like a great cat and uttering occasional witticisms.

Two other Honorary Fellows who continued to visit the College during the war were among the most eminent lawyers of their time. One of these was Lord Thankerton, who had been bottom of the list in the Law Tripos in 1894 but had nevertheless risen to be a Lord of Appeal in Ordinary. His hobbies included knitting, at which he was an expert, though I do not know whether he practised the art while sitting on the bench. The other was Lord Justice Luxmoore, who frequently stayed in the Guest Room on my staircase and whom I came to know well. During his undergraduate years in the eighteen-nineties he had been less distinguished for work than for Rugby football and his practical jokes, one of which became famous. He and a friend had climbed to the College roof one quiet Sunday afternoon to pour a bucket of water down another man's chimney, but poured it down Luxmoore's own chimney by mistake. Not surprisingly, he went down with only a pass degree, but he made good by his native ability and hard work. He was one of the most enlightened, kind, and unassuming men I have ever known, and one of the most lovable, and I shall always hold his memory in great affection.

Many former members of the College who had taken their degrees before the war and had gone to the ends of the earth were now back in England on war service and few days went by without a visit from at least one of them. Two or three of them might appear together at a meeting of the Roosters. Another, who had perhaps come almost direct from a bombing raid, might appear unexpectedly at a 'shoal' of Red Herrings, where the pre-war port and punch had perforce been replaced by a small ration of cider, and the sweepstake which had formerly been won by guessing the number of leaves on a pineapple was now decided by guessing the number of pages in one of Q's books.

Among the serious societies which continued to meet regularly was the Jesuits (the Jesus College Historical Society). After Bernard Manning's death it met in my rooms. I have a very clear recollection of a meeting of the society at which Edward Welbourne, Fellow (afterwards Master) of Emmanuel, read a paper — or, rather, gave a most entertaining talk. He spoke very rapidly for an hour and forty minutes, without using a note or pausing for breath. I should add that when he had finished the audience stayed till midnight to take part in the discussion aroused by his talk.

Another society which met three or four times a year in my rooms, and indeed was founded there in 1942, was the John Mason Neale Society. Its objects were to perpetuate Neale's memory and to study his life, works, and chief interests. That is to say our scope included anything ecclesiastical. We excluded only the formal study of theology, since it was already catered for by a large number of societies at Cambridge and elsewhere. Our first speaker from outside Cambridge was, appropriately enough, Clement Webb, the philosopher, who was a godson of Neale and consequently was now nearer eighty than seventy years of age.

When the society grew in numbers we had to move to a bigger room; but at the time of writing we still meet in Jesus College — in the Prioress's Room. Our present President is Dr Geoffrey Bushnell, Curator of the Museum of Archaeology and Ethnology*. Our first was my friend P. G. Ward, Rector of Harston. He was succeeded after some years by Bruce Dickins, Professor of Anglo-Saxon and a Fellow of Corpus. After him came C. P. Hankey, Dean of Ely, tall, charming, and very dignified, but without any starch. He used to say that, knowing my predilections, he never dared come inside the walls of Jesus College unless he was wearing his decanal gaiters.

My links with Ely Cathedral, which I had known ever since 1914 and

* Reader in New World Archaeology and a Fellow of Corpus.

visited many times since, were greatly strengthened in 1941, when
Edward Wynn became Bishop of Ely. I attended his consecration by
Archbishop Lang in Westminster Abbey on July 25th and his enthronement at Ely on August 7th, the festival of the Name of Jesus. The day
had been specially chosen by him for the ceremony because of his triple
connection with Jesus College, as sometime Scholar, as Chaplain
(ordained priest in the College Chapel itself), and now as Visitor.

The vast cathedral was packed from end to end. The service opened
quietly with the choir singing the psalms 'O how amiable are thy
dwellings' and 'I was glad when they said unto me' far down at the west
end of the cathedral, the voices getting gradually louder as the procession made its way slowly up the grand Norman nave. It closed with
the triumphant strains of Stanford's 1898 *Te Deum*, accompanied by
organ, orchestra, and trumpets ringing from the triforium, while the
newly enthroned bishop stood in his cope and mitre before the high
altar with his canons round him. The beautiful and dignified service was
characteristic of the Anglican rite at its best, being fundamentally
medieval yet true to the spirit of the early church and also of the
post-Reformation church down to the twentieth century.

One striking feature of the enthronement ceremony passed un-
noticed by the Press. The new Bishop of Ely had attended the same
school and was a Fellow of the same college as his illustrious seven-
teenth-century predecessor, Matthew Wren, who had been imprisoned
for sixteen years by the Puritans and had returned to his diocese in
triumph at the Restoration. Bishop Wren's crozier, which had been
preserved for three centuries at Pembroke College, was lent to the new
Bishop for the occasion and was carried by him throughout the ceremonies, but no journalist was sufficiently wide awake to discover and
publish so interesting a fact.

Edward Wynn was the first Bishop of Ely who did not live in the
unwieldy medieval Palace, which had become a home for crippled
children soon after the war began. When the war ended he continued to
live in the smaller medieval house which he had occupied from the first,
the former Deanery. He extended to me the great privilege of staying
with him whenever I wished, and I revelled in the numerous opportunities which this gave me of attending services in the cathedral and of
absorbing some of the spirit of Ely, a place 'concerned less with time
than with eternity.' For a Jesus man, it was a particular pleasure to
attend early service in John Alcock's tiny chantry, where the founder
of the College lies buried under a tomb carved with cocks' heads.

I soon came to know the head verger, Mr Whetstone, who was devoted to the cathedral and was a mine of information about its traditions. He generally (if not always) wore a black suit with a stiff tight-fitting single collar and very broad black tie. Anyone who did not look very closely would imagine that he was wearing a clerical collar and stock and treat him accordingly. Once, in fact, when I was travelling back from Oxford by train in the black-out and Mr Whetstone got in at a wayside station, the American airmen who were occupying all the other seats in the compartment were so impressed by his manner and his conversation that they assumed him to be the Bishop of Ely, and I basked in reflected glory.

The first time I stayed at Bishop's House we had just finished tea when Mr Whetstone arrived to conduct the Bishop to the cathedral for Evensong. He looked very impressive in his cassock, gown, and top hat, as he walked solemnly ahead of the Bishop, carrying his silver wand with great dignity. While we were going down the steps at the front of the house and through the garden I walked beside the Bishop, because he was talking to me; but as soon as we reached the street I naturally fell a step behind. The Bishop, noticing this, turned half round towards me and said, 'You can walk beside me till we get to the cathedral.' Then (apparently noticing some slight movement of his escort's head) he added quickly, 'That's all right, Whetstone, isn't it?' The Head Verger, still plodding gravely on, turned his head very slightly to one side and then to the other. I could not see his eyebrows, but I could almost feel them rising as he answered respectfully, but slowly and in a hollow tone, 'As —— your —— lordship —— wishes.' There was no mistaking his meaning. The Bishop did not utter another word all the way to the cathedral, and I stayed where I was. When we got back to the house after the service I said to the Bishop, 'You will never again dare to invite a layman to walk beside you on your way to the cathedral, will you?' – 'No,' he answered fervently, 'never.'

The diocese of Ely contains no town of any size except Cambridge, but it has several small ancient boroughs which are understandably proud of their history and status. Among these are Huntingdon and Godmanchester (or Gumster, as it was and is sometimes still called), which are separated from each other only by the River Ouse but until very recently were two different boroughs. Huntingdon, with only a few thousand inhabitants at the last census, must be one of the smallest county towns in England but is obviously a town. Godmanchester, on the other hand, which is even smaller, has no street of shops and does not look like a town. Yet, as a borough, it was senior to Huntingdon. It must therefore have been galling to the Godmancunians (or Gumcestrians) when their Arcadian borough was mistaken, as sometimes happened, for a mere suburb of Huntingdon, or was otherwise slighted.

It was consequently with feelings of apprehension that when Edward Ely, not long after his enthronement, was instituting my friend Ralph Gardner as Vicar of Godmanchester in the presence of a congregation which filled the church, I heard him in his sermon refer to the ancient borough of Godmanchester as 'this lovely village.' He paused at the end of that sentence, and one could have heard a pin drop. I wondered whether the veins of the mayor, aldermen and councillors assembled in the front pews would burst with indignation or whether the Bishop would be stoned as he left the church. Fortunately nothing untoward happened. I told the Bishop afterwards of my fears; and I noticed that when next he preached at Godmanchester he referred to it twice as 'this ancient and beautiful borough.'

Bernard Manning, who had long been my closest friend, had been absent from the enthronement ceremony at Ely — not because he was too staunch a Nonconformist to attend but because he was at his home in Westmorland at the time and unwell.

He had been spiritually a stalwart but physically a weakling all his life. During 1941 his health deteriorated rapidly and we were unable to carry out a suggestion put to us that the William Dowsing Society should visit Oxford and produce a sequence to *Babylon Bruis'd*. He returned to Cambridge for the Michaelmas Term, carried on with his tutorial work, and was able to attend the meetings of the Jesuits, the Roosters, and a small society which we had formed to study and translate the works of St Augustine. During the second week of November, however, he was taken ill again, and in the third week was removed to a nursing home, where he died peacefully on December 8th.

Uncompromising Congregationalist though he was, requiems were said for him in High Anglican and Roman Catholic churches. They were a tribute to the life he had led and to his unfailing championship of the Christian religion, regardless of sects or factions. His death was a great blow to the College and to me personally, but I was merely one of many who had leaned heavily on this physical weakling when in need of support. I wrote a biography of him which was published during the year after his death.

30

In the autumn of 1942 I became Editor of the *Cambridge Review*, founded in 1879 and reputed to be the oldest University weekly in existence anywhere. It had had a distinguished history and has always exerted a much greater influence than its circulation figures might lead one to expect. The list of its past editors included men with such varied after-careers as Walter Raleigh, the literary critic and Professor of English Literature at Oxford; Erskine Childers, the Irish Republican who was shot by order of a Free State court-martial in 1922; John Ellis McTaggart, the philosopher, some of whose lectures I had attended (but not understood) in my undergraduate days; Neville Figgis, the Mirfield Father and historian; Stephen Gaselee, the kindly gourmet, Medieval Latin anthologist, and Keeper of the Papers at the Foreign Office; and Michael Redgrave, the actor.

The *Review* has always been an unofficial publication, owned by a self-perpetuating committee of dons, who appoint the editor and leave him a free hand. The normal period of office is a year. I held office for six years. There was no money in it, as the saying goes: I was paid £30 a year for the first two years and £40 a year for the remaining four.

The paper was printed and published by the well-known firm of William Heffer and Sons, of which Ernest Heffer was at the time managing director. I had known him for years already, but as Editor of the *Cambridge Review* I inevitably came into closer contact with him than ever. He was a big, breezy man, with his own special type of humour, which often took the form of pretending to be a bully. It was sheer pretence, for he was a most kind-hearted, generous man and nothing delighted him more (as I found from experience) than if someone saw through his pretence quickly and paid him back in his own coin. He was a model employer, and I am confident that every one of the firm's large battalion of employees lamented his death soon after the war. He could, however, be very obstinate, particularly if I asked him to approve of some *Review* expenditure which he considered unnecessary. On receiving a refusal I used to raise my voice in protest and thump the table between us. His reply to that, on one occasion, was to ring the bell for his private secretary. When she appeared, he said with solemn voice, 'Miss Southwick, send out at once for a soap-box.' —

'A soap-box, Mr Heffer?' — 'Yes, a soap-box. The Editor of the *Review* wants to address a public meeting.' To this the embarrassed Miss Southwick replied, 'Oh, Mr Heffer!' and retired to her own office.

Most of my editing was done from my rooms at Jesus College, but on Thursday afternoons I used to go to Heffers' printing-works to make up the week's issue for publication on Saturday. The printing was in the hands of E. J. A. Fabb, who now held an appointment with Heffers but had formerly been in business as a printer on his own account, in succession to his father. He and his father between them printed every issue of the *Review* from its foundation until the son's retirement from active work in 1946 — a total of 1,650 numbers.

It was impossible for me to get secretarial help of any kind during the war years, except for the voluntary help of my old friend, Vincent Robinson. Like myself, he could not use a typewriter but (fortunately for me and for the *Review*) he had taught himself shorthand in boyhood and could still write it rapidly. He used to write out my letters in a copper-plate hand from his shorthand notes and bring them to me next day for signature. Without his help, I do not see how the *Review* could have continued.

On looking through the *Review* files of my time I am gratified to see what a galaxy of talent I had in my contributors: G. M. Trevelyan, Sir Herbert Richmond, David Knowles, Charles Smyth, Zachary Brooke, Harold Darke, Sir Arthur Eddington, Charles Raven, Muriel Bradbrook, Basil Willey, A. H. Ramsey, Edward Welbourne, Frank Kendon, Q, Herbert Butterfield, S. C. Roberts, G. G. Coulton, Edmund Blunden, Mary Ellen Chase, Sir Albert Richardson, C. H. Dodd, Frederic Raby, Sir Ernest Barker, D. A. Winstanley, Sir Harold Spencer-Jones, John Burnaby, and many others. G. R. Owst would walk more than a mile in the middle of the night in order to return a proof in time. P. F. Radcliffe was my never-failing music critic, Denys Wilkinson and Claude Havard my indefatigable sports editors. Elizabeth Sewell, just starting to write, contributed entertaining light verse. Walter Roberts wrote admirable narrative verse on English rural life, reminiscent of Crabbe.

I nevertheless found difficulty at times in getting enough material for publication. One great stand-by was the University Sermon preached at Great St Mary's every Sunday and traditionally reported in the *Review*, in whole or in part, according to its length. 'A new University Preacher', Mr Fabb used to say, 'will preach five or six columns, a canon or dean four, a bishop not more than three, an archbishop only

two-and-a-half or even two', though Archbishop Fisher's celebrated
appeal to the Free Churches to 'take episcopacy into their systems' ran
to four columns. On the other hand, a Select Preacher would sometimes
let me down by delivering less than the Fabbian quota, and I would
have to labour far into the night to make good the deficiency from my
own pen. On one of these occasions – it was at a time when nothing
seemed to happen except in this or that 'sector', and when Lord
Woolton was Minister for Food – I made up for the brevity of the
University sermon by bringing Henry Cary's *Sally in our Alley* up to
date and adding to it a few lines of a revised version of Gus Elen's song,
If it wasn't for the 'ouses in between, like this:

SARAH IN OUR SECTOR

Of all the girls whose speech was plain,
    There wasn't one like Sally:
She wasn't uppish, or too vain
    To live down in our alley.
But since the war reports she's read,
    Our Sarah is correcter:
She hasn't moved her board or bed,
    But she dwells in our sector.

Until she read communiqués
    My pretty little Sally
Lived in the East End all her days:
    She hung out in our alley.
But Sarah now such words derides;
    She'll bluster and she'll hector
Till I agree that she resides
    In London's Eastern Sector.

When pretty Sal I used to chase,
    Her speech, though plain, was pleasing.
She'd sometimes say: "I'll smack your face
    If you don't stop your teasing."
But Sarah now without a doubt
    Speaks English that's selecter.
She says: "I'll fetch you such a clout
    Right in your facial sector."

If Sal at supper used to take
    Too much, when she had eaten
She'd say: "I've such a belly-ache:
    Lord Woolton's got me beaten."
Now Sarah often ends a feast
    By saying, sweet as nectar:
"Oh! what a pain in the middle east
    Of my abdominal sector!"

Oh! we hope we'll soon be married by the rector:
 In our sector there's a house on which we're keen.
  With a tele-lens projector
  You could see the Western Sector,
 If it wasn't for the sectors in between.

I had scarcely taken up office as Editor of the *Review* when I began a campaign against the so-called University of Sulgrave, which had just come into existence. It had borrowed its name from Sulgrave Manor, the Northamptonshire home of the Washington family, and its declared intention was to confer 'degrees' (for what they were worth) on American soldiers, who were stationed in England at the time in large numbers. Its organizers, however, were Englishmen of no academical standing whatever, and it was discountenanced by real universities, both of the United States and elsewhere. The names of its organizers were already familiar to me: they had been among the leading lights of a thing called the Intercollegiate University — its very title was Gilbertian — the head of which for many years was a bogus archbishop.

The leaders of this new contingent from the academical underworld were in some ways simple-minded. When I first attacked them, for instance, they threw out dark hints that if I was not careful I would get — it was intended to be a terrible threat — a letter from their solicitors. They did not know that I was being advised daily by no less a legal authority than Lord Justice Luxmoore, who was staying in College at the time. I soon received the support also of Wilson Harris, Editor of *The Spectator*, and of that stalwart champion of so many good causes, Sir Ernest Barker, a close and lasting friendship with whom was one of the most pleasing outcomes of my editing the *Review*. Sometimes I supplied *The Spectator* with material for anti-Sulgrave articles, sometimes I wrote them myself. It was amusing to get private letters from readers of the *Cambridge Review* asking me whether I had noticed that *The Spectator* was running a campaign similar to my own. Before long, questions were asked in Parliament about Sulgrave, and it voted itself out of existence.

During my first year as Editor of the *Cambridge Review* I was still smoking fifty or more cigarettes every day, as I had done for years without intermission. I became ashamed of being a slave to tobacco and in the summer of 1943 decided that something must be done about it. After several ineffectual attempts to cut my smoking down I decided that I must abandon it altogether. Several times I decided that I would stop smoking 'next week' and even 'tomorrow'. At last I decided to

Plate IX

INGHAM LODGE

VICTORIAN EVENING GROUP, 1965

Plate X

THE ROOMS AT 13 CHAPEL COURT

Left: View from the window

Below: Muriel and F. B. in the Keel
Room, 1967

stop without waiting for tomorrow and did so. It was such an important event for me that I remember the date and even the exact time. It
was on Thursday, June 17th, 1943, at eight o'clock in the evening. I
have never smoked since.

I succeeded in breaking so strong a habit only because I remembered
Dryden's line, 'Men are but children of a larger growth', and applied it
to myself. I accordingly made no resolution to give up smoking for
good, but merely to try to go without it for a day. During that day
(which was difficult enough) I was 'kidding' myself — I think that
colloquialism is permissible and even indispensable here — that I would
be able to smoke all day next day. Having got through the first day
without smoking I decided to make it two days, then three, then a
week, a fortnight, a month, three months, six months, and finally a
year; and all the time I was telling myself that I would be able to smoke
as usual next week, next month, and so on. Within six months I was
cured. I would not take up smoking again now on any account. Life is
much simpler without it.

During the first six months, however, my output of work was
halved. Smoking does not, as is often asserted, help anyone to work;
but I had associated smoking so closely with my work — which, after
all, consists mostly of talking, reading, and writing, all of which can be
combined with smoking — that when I stopped smoking my work
wanted to stop too. Wilson Harris had commissioned me in June to
write an article for *The Spectator* in commemoration of Q's eightieth
birthday, which was to fall on the following November 21st. I intended
to write it in July, to get it out of the way, but could not write a word.
The same thing happened in August and September. I knew that if I
smoked ideas would come, but I did not want to give in. October came,
and the Michaelmas Term with it, but I still could not write a word, and
often sat with a blank sheet of paper in front of me, and a pencil in my
hand, for three hours at a stretch. November came, and when the last
possible day for sending in the article had almost arrived I got des-
perate. I consulted my friend and colleague Eustace Tillyard, and told
him that I would take whatever advice he gave me. I felt, I said, that I
must either start smoking again or write to Wilson Harris to say that I
could not write the article after all. He advised me to do the latter and
added that in the circumstances it would not be discreditable for me to
do so. That broke the spell. I went back to my rooms to write a letter
to Wilson Harris, but wrote the article instead, straight off, without
difficulty. After that, I had no more trouble.

By this time, the fourth year of the war, petrol was so severely rationed that, except during air-raids, the English countryside was enjoying a peace such as it had not known for years. When I went home, I found the roads and lanes, though so near London, delightfully free from traffic. It was possible to walk in safety and comfort even along the main road linking Barnet and South Mimms with St Albans. One could hear the song of birds in places where it had been drowned beneath the roar of traffic for years. Where all odours had long been obliterated by the foul smell of petrol fumes, now

> Only the scent of woodbine and hay new mown
> Travelled the road.

Allen Hay, who was now nearer eighty than seventy, was as irrepressible as ever. I shall never forget one Sunday evening when I was at home. We were in church and had come to the end of the First Lesson when the air-raid warning sounded. He announced 'We will sit quietly until the all-clear goes.' We did so, and listened to the firing of guns and the dropping of bombs. Then there came a lull. We could hear an aeroplane zooming faintly overhead and wondered somewhat anxiously what might happen next. Then we heard something that broke the silence and relieved the tension: it was the sound of the Vicar taking snuff – first one nostril, then the other. Everyone smiled and felt at ease at once, and no one was surprised that the all-clear was sounded almost immediately.

In the autumn of 1943 I was elected Pro-Proctor of the University and, in accordance with the normal practice, became Proctor a year later. Both officers are nominated by the colleges in turn and then (as a formality) elected by the Senate of the University. The Pro-Proctor is a mere upstart, dating only from the year 1818, but the office of Proctor is one of the most ancient in the University, dating back to the thirteenth century. The names of many Proctors are known from the year 1314, and the lists are complete from 1441 onwards. John Fisher, the victim of Henry VIII, was Proctor in 1494, and Nicholas Ridley, the victim of Mary Tudor, in 1533. Members of my own college who had held the office included the Puritan John Dod, who preached a celebrated Sermon on Malt to some ill-mannered undergraduates; John Duport, one of the translators of the Authorized Version of the Bible; and, in the early nineteenth century, Thomas Castley (called Ghastly, because he looked it), Thomas Dickes, who suggested that the chapel tower at Jesus should be pulled down because (he alleged) it made his chimney smoke, and Thomas Gaskin, a shoemaker's boy who 'spent all his spare time in working sums with an awl on leather', was sent to Cambridge by a private patron, and became distinguished both as a mathematician and as a classical scholar.

The Proctors are the representatives (*procuratores*) of the Masters of Arts of the whole University and originally had charge of the finances. They were no doubt elected to keep an eye on the Chancellor and other more or less permanent officers who might be tempted to misappropriate the common funds or override the rights of the Masters.

All that most people know about a Proctor today is that he patrols the streets of Cambridge after dark, wearing gown, square cap, and bands, accompanied by two university constables (paid employees, nicknamed 'bulldogs'), and that he can fine, gate, or rusticate undergraduates and Bachelors for breaches of university discipline. His duties, however, are far wider than that. He keeps an eye on the relaxations of undergraduates, who may not hold a dance, a dinner, or a party outside college walls, or keep or drive a car, without his permit, and he keeps in touch with the city police. He attends all Congregations of the Senate and the Regent House, wearing gown, square cap, bands, hood, and ruff. His book of obsolete statutes is carried through the streets behind him by one of the bulldogs, who on such occasions wear long blue cloaks — so long that the skirt has to be held over the arm to prevent it from trailing on the ground.

The Proctor attends the University Sermon at Great St Mary's on two Sunday afternoons during term, wearing gown and bands, and with his hood 'squared', which converts it into a shoulder-cape. On Ash Wednesday he reads the first part of the Litany in the same church, wearing ruff instead of hood. He also attends the Assize Sermons (three a year), calling first, with the Vice-Chancellor and heads of colleges, at Trinity College Lodge, where the representatives of the University are presented to the Judge of Assize. The Mayor and Corporation have meanwhile assembled at the entrance to the College, waiting their turn to be presented. The retiring University procession meets the advancing City procession about the middle of Great Court, where there is much hat-raising, bowing, and smiling, plus a certain amount of winking between friends.

At these Assize processions and on other special occasions — when the Chancellor is present, for instance — the Proctorial constables carry ceremonial weapons. These are a linstock, a partizan (short pike), a halberd, and a metal tube about a yard long, called 'the butter-measure'. This is supposed to have been used by the Proctors, as supervisors of the sale of food in the local shops and markets, in the days when butter was sold at Cambridge by length, cut from long rolls, instead of by weight. Readers of Q's parody of Wordsworth will remember the lines:

> For I loved Cambridge, where they deal —
> How strange! — in butter by the yard.

Butter was sold by length at the College Buttery until just before my undergraduate days. It is difficult, however, to see how this particular instrument could have been used for measuring butter, and there are those who assert that it was used for quite a different purpose — to measure the depth of liquids in casks. The linstock, before it became a purely ceremonial instrument, was used to hold lighted tow for the firing of cannon.

There are always two Proctors at a time. Whichever of the two became a member of the Senate first is the Senior Proctor, but he is merely the first of two equals. Both Proctors, or their approved deputies, must be present at every Congregation of the Senate before any University legislation can be passed or any degree conferred. The Senior Proctor reads out the proposals, which are called Graces. If there is no opposition the Junior Proctor calls out 'placet', and the Grace has become an Ordinance. The Proctors preside over the formal election of a Vice-Chancellor in June and install him on the first weekday of October, first jointly occupying the throne during the brief interregnum after the previous Vice-Chancellor has vacated office.

The election of the Vice-Chancellor is a farce. The Council of the Senate is required by statute to nominate two heads of colleges as candidates for the office. One of these two is to be elected by members of the Regent House, voting by secret ballot. By law, either of the two could be successful; but it is always understood that the first on the list is to be elected, and that the second of the two will become Vice-Chancellor after him. There would be pandemonium if the second on the list were chosen.

Notice of the date of election is given, and the notice states that the poll will be open in the Senate House from 1 p.m. to 3 p.m., but that the poll may be closed at any time if no one has come to vote during the previous ten minutes.

The Registrary, the Proctors and the Esquires Bedell assemble in the Senate House for the election. No one else comes. When the clock of Great St Mary's strikes one, these five officials record their votes and drop their papers into the ballot box. They then stand, watch in hand, until ten minutes past one, when the poll is declared closed, the secret ballot-box is opened, the ballot-papers are taken out, the votes are counted, and the first man on the list is declared elected. The same procedure is followed annually in accordance with statute, although everyone knows that when a Vice-Chancellor is elected he is always re-elected for a second year of office.

Once when I was Proctor a man wearing an M.A. gown walked into the Senate House about nine minutes past one on election day. There was panic for a while, lest our lunch should be delayed by an extra ten minutes. Conversation between the caller and an Esquire Bedell revealed, however, that he thought that members of the Regent House were expected to come and vote. When the facts were explained to him, although he was assured that he had a right to vote, he apologized and went away. We then closed the poll and went to lunch.

All Proctors and Pro-Proctors have the legal right to enter any theatre, cinema, dance-hall, or other place of entertainment at Cambridge at any time, with their constables.

There are a number of firmly held and oft-repeated but baseless legends about Proctors. One asserts that an undergraduate wearing a specified dress can, under the terms of an ancient statute of the University, require a Proctor to clear Petty Cury for archery practice for him. This is patently absurd, seeing that Cambridge, like other towns, had its archery butts in a retired spot, for the very reason that archery practice in or even near a densely populated street like Petty Cury would have been highly dangerous. One would also like to see an undergraduate 'requiring' a Proctor to do anything. The area reserved for archery practice at Cambridge is still called Butt Green and is now part of Midsummer Common.

Another legend asserts that any undergraduate can (again, under the terms of an old statute) stop the Proctor on his way to Great St Mary's on Sundays and require him to read the Collect for the day from the big Prayer Book which one of the constables is alleged to be carrying behind him on a chain. A variant of the legend asserts that the book is a Bible, and that it is consequently one of the Lessons for the day, not the Collect, that the undergraduate can require the Proctor to read to him. Both versions are again obviously absurd, seeing that the book is neither Prayer Book nor Bible, but a collection of obsolete statutes of the University from its foundation to the year 1784. When I was Proctor I repeatedly offered fifty pounds to anyone who could find in this very book any authority for these alleged undergraduate privileges. No such authority is to be found there, or in any later statutes, but people will go on believing these silly superstitions, because they like to believe them.

Another oft-quoted fable asserts that an ancient statute of the University requires every bedmaker to be old and ugly. The alleged words of the statute — *senex et horrida* — are even quoted as 'evidence', but the fifty pounds which I have several times offered to anyone who can produce the statute has never yet been claimed. The legend is obviously baseless, seeing that bedmakers are not appointed by the University at all, but by the colleges. The University is not concerned with them in any way. No university, moreover, is likely ever to have passed such ridiculous and insulting legislation; and bedmakers are in any event indistinguishable from the rest of the women of Cambridge (whether of the University or the Town) by either age or beauty. Yet this absurd story will continue to be told, and printed in books and articles about Cambridge, some of them written even by senior members of the University. Dons can sometimes be as credulous as barbers' assistants with their stories about Palm Sunday donkeys.

My colleague in the Pro-Proctorship and Proctorship was E. E. Raven (affectionately called 'Dave'), who was Dean of St John's and a brother of Charles Raven, Master of Christ's. He was a charming man. I should have enjoyed being Proctor in any event, but with him as my senior colleague the experience was doubly enjoyable.

Both of us found the office entertaining at times, as well as enjoyable. A particularly amusing incident occurred one evening when I was not on Proctorial duty but was presiding over the Roosters in my rooms at Jesus. I was conducting Rooster examinations and wearing the Presidential gown sprinkled with red cocks' heads and the ludicrous cap shaped like a cock's comb. An undergraduate whose face was vaguely familiar came in late. Thinking that he was a Freshman and a candidate for emperchment, I told the officers to find him a perch and hand him a copy of the *Codex Gallorum*; but all my questions to him drew a blank. After further discussion at cross purposes, I found that he was an Emmanuel man whom I had caught without a gown in the streets some evenings before. He had called in response to a Proctorial summons and either he or I had made a mistake about the time. Until he discovered what was going on, he must have thought a Proctorial court a very strange affair. I did not fine him.

The numerous American soldiers stationed in or near Cambridge during the war were often interested observers of University customs and some of them acquired considerable knowledge of them. One evening, when I was writing down the name and college of a gownless undergraduate on King's Parade, an American soldier stepped forward from the interested group of spectators and quite politely asked if he might say something. He wished to inform me, he said, in defence of the undergraduate, that he had seen him wearing a gown only a few minutes before and that it had been stripped from him just round the corner by some Americans who wanted it as a souvenir. He felt bound to tell me this, he added, because the undergraduate had obviously said nothing about it, for fear of getting the Americans into trouble.

'I am afraid,' I answered, 'that you have come too late. If you had been here only a minute earlier, you would have heard the under-graduate admit that he left his gown in his rooms before he came out this evening; but I am sure that he, like me, greatly appreciates your kind attempt at international co-operation.'

Q did not survive his eightieth birthday by many months. He returned to Cambridge from Fowey in January 1944 for the Lent Term, wearing (as usual) a suit of brighter colours than most men dared to wear, carrying in his hand the spare bowler hat, and accompanied by a large quantity of luggage.

For some weeks he carried on much as usual. He attended meetings of the College Council, winking at me when the Master referred to 'timber in the form of trees', and to the misuse of 'conveniences in the form of gas rings' by some members of the Women's Auxiliary Air Force quartered in College. He entertained a good deal, and in conversation continued to ride some of his favourite hobby-horses, such as the excessive number of lectures attended by undergraduates. Two lectures a week, he said to me one day, were enough for any man. In international affairs, he regarded the Jameson Raid as the turning point from the peaceful world of his earlier life to the warring world of his later years, and he expressed his detestation of Cecil Rhodes. 'To think', he said, 'that there is a statue of him outside Oriel, facing the statue of the Virgin Mary!'

Towards the end of February he was obviously unwell. He went down for the last time on March 1st and died at Fowey on May 12th. I wrote a biography of him which was published in 1947 and compiled a Q anthology which appeared a year later; and I had the privilege of speaking when memorials to him were unveiled in Truro Cathedral in 1945 and at Fowey in 1948. I stayed with the Bishop (J. W. Hunkin) at Lis Escop during that and subsequent visits to Truro. He differed greatly in his ways and outlook from his predecessor, Bishop Frere, with whom I had formerly stayed at Lis Escop, but there are few men to whom I have taken such an immediate liking as I did to Bishop Hunkin when I first met him, shortly after Q's death.

When Q died the country round Fowey and elsewhere along the south coast was packed with troops, and the harbours with ships, for the invasion of France, which began on June 6th, 1944.

In the following March the Air Force and its auxiliaries evacuated Jesus College. Despite the oft-repeated stories of vandalism that were told about troops billeted in beautiful old buildings, there was not a scratch on the panelling or the venerable oak tables of our Hall when our lodgers moved out of college that spring, although they had used the Hall every day for five-and-a-half years.

When the war ended (except with Japan) on May 8th, 1945, Cambridge played its full part in celebrating the arrival of the day which had so often seemed as if it never would come. My memory of the day is a welter of many sights and sounds. I remember the music of the bells of Great St Mary's in full peal during the morning after long silence; peripatetic music provided by the Home Guard, the Cadet Corps, and a band of girl pipers; wedding music during the afternoon in Magdalene Chapel, to which I had gone for a friend's marriage; the summoning of the Proctors to the Guildhall at four o'clock to appear on the balcony with the Vice-Chancellor and the Lord Lieutenant while the Mayor addressed the vast crowd which had gathered on Market Hill – a close-packed crowd which filled every corner of the market-place and overflowed into the adjacent streets and on to the roofs, a crowd brilliantly variegated with women's summer dresses of every conceivable colour.

After the Mayor's proclamation we made the Guildhall our Proctorial headquarters for the rest of the day. I remember some scores of service men and civilians who danced for the whole of the hottest hour of a hot afternoon, hand in hand in rings round a burly smiling negro, his hat decorated with coloured paper streamers and his hand beating time with a miniature Union Jack; the Master proposing a toast in Hall that evening; Market Hill packed again to its utmost capacity to hear a broadcast of the King's Speech; the torch-light procession which drew most of the crowd away afterwards to a huge bonfire on Midsummer Common; the delight and the cheers of those who stayed behind and watched a dozen airmen, commando men, and American soldiers climb up the front of the Guildhall to the balcony with the greatest ease and disappear into the building, from which they made their exit by the stairs; the undergraduate who climbed up after them; the bow which he made to the applauding crowd when he reached the balcony; the astonishment on his face a few moments later when he found that he had walked into the very room where the two Proctors and the Chief Constable were in consultation; and the walk back to Jesus College in the small hours through streets where lights were still shining from many uncurtained windows and through college courts where friendly searchlights were playing on flowering chestnuts and laburnums.

The crowd on Market Hill that day was intensely interesting to watch at all times, but never so much as when it stood still and some ten thousand faces were upturned to the Guildhall balcony to listen to the Mayor's proclamation or the broadcast of the King's speech. To have been on the balcony then is to have had an unforgettable experience. One was face to face with a representative section of the common people of England, whose easy-going ways Hitler had despised, whose courage Mussolini had derided, whose determination was unknown even to themselves, and whose courage and determination had beaten Hitler and Mussolini to the dust. One remembered what the common people of England had suffered, and one remembered those men, of both town and gown, who had loved Cambridge and its beautiful ways, who had so often crossed Market Hill on their way to shops and offices, to lectures, to Hall, to Chapel, or to the river, and who would never come back from the war to cross it again. *Quorum animis propitietur Deus.*

Of the 124 Jesus men who are known to have died in the war there was none for whom I had a greater affection than I had for Peter Thorne, William Wallace Anderson, or Lambert Charles Shepherd.

Peter Thorne, the youngest of the three, did not come up from High Wycombe Grammar School until 1940. He read for the English Tripos and had rooms on my staircase, immediately under Q. He was a versatile man: he rowed in the College first boat, was a wing forward in our first Rugby side, sang in the Chapel choir, edited *Chanticlere* and was a leading Rooster. In the summer of 1943 he went into the Air Force and soon afterwards was sent to Canada to be trained. He wrote to me from Canada, enclosing an article for the *Cambridge Review*, and saying how much he had enjoyed life at Cambridge. 'Rowing, Reading, and Roosting – all at Jesus. What more could a man want?' he wrote. When he arrived back in England he was commissioned and took part in operations against Germany. Early in 1945 he was killed in action, leaving a widow and an infant daughter. Tall, fair, of fine presence and of magnificent physique, he was outstanding intellectually also. A born leader and teacher, and mature beyond his years, if he had lived he must have risen to eminence, whatever career he followed.

> Jeune, brave, riant, libre, et sans flétrissures,
> Je vais m'asseoir parmi les dieux, dans le soleil.

Wally Anderson, an Australian, came up from Parramatta in 1933. He was a man of most genial and sunny temperament and made an unusually large number of friends – not merely among the Roosters (of which club he was President) and in the Boat Club, but in the College as a whole. After taking his degree he went back to Australia and worked

in his father's firm at Sydney until the outbreak of war, when he joined
the Royal Australian Air Force. In the winter of 1940-41 he arrived in
England as a pilot officer, and on two occasions when on leave revisited
the College. One of his visits happened to coincide with a bump supper.
Although war-time bump suppers were inevitably celebrated with
considerable restrictions and severely attenuated fare, his pleasure at
being present was delightful to see; but, alas! he was killed that summer
in a bombing raid on Germany. He had left a letter to be delivered to
his family if he did not return. His father afterwards sent me a copy of
it. It was a beautiful letter, one of the most moving documents that I
have ever read, and I wept as I read it.

Lambert Shepherd, called 'Bush' by all Jesus men who knew him,
was a man of outstanding ability and marked personality. He came up
from Shrewsbury School in 1929 as a Scholar and resided four years,
reading Classics and English. Tall and lean, with eyes which went
'googoo' (as his friends termed it) when he was in his cups, he rowed in
the first May boat, and in the crew which won the Ladies' Plate at
Henley, and was President of the Roosters. His home was in Ireland
and, although he always stoutly denied having any Irish blood, he had
acquired the casualness that is supposed to be an Irish characteristic.
His luggage, for instance, seemed to have a knack of arriving at college a
fortnight or more after term began. His friends alleged that, until the
luggage arrived, he wore the same suit and the same underclothing every
day; and that when it did arrive he did not unpack it for another
fortnight but kept it under his bed, opening one suitcase or another to
take out a handkerchief, a shirt, or whatever else he wanted, as required.

He showed his casualness also in his treatment of books, which he
hardly ever returned to the College Library until they were long over-
due and he had incurred heavy fines. One day he asked me what was
done with the fines. I answered that we used them to buy new books
for the Library, and that his fines were a considerable asset to it.

'If that's so,' he said, 'I think you might put a label inside the books
which you buy with my money, to say that they were presented by me.
I've noticed labels of that sort in other books.'

'I'm sorry, Bush,' I said, 'but there are too many for that. We should
have to employ an extra library assistant.'

After he went down he became a journalist — first at Belfast, next at
Manchester, and finally in London, from which he often revisited the
College. On one occasion he brought with him a friend who had never

been to Cambridge before and who was greatly looking forward to seeing the wonderland of Jesus College which Bush had so often described to him. He had even been promised – he could hardly believe it – a night in that Elysium. Unfortunately, Bush left his application for rooms in College so late that there was none for either of them and they found themselves disconsolately leaving College at midnight with their luggage. Bush was sure that his old landlady, Mrs Hopkins, would put them up in her house in Jesus Lane, but when she was roused from her sleep she said that that was impossible, as her house was already full to overflowing. Further inquiries at house after house along Jesus Lane brought further refusals, the tone of which became sharper and sharper as the night wore on. The night watchman at the Lion Hotel was decidedly acid in his refusal, somewhere about 2 a.m. Finally, Bush took his guest and luggage to Midsummer Common, where they spent the night on the cement floor of a public convenience. I have forgotten the date when this happened, but could rediscover it without difficulty, because it was within a week or two of the time when S. C. Roberts published his book called (even more appropriately than its author could have realized) *Introduction to Cambridge.*

During the evacuation of the hard-pressed British forces from Dunkirk in 1940 Bush, who was at the time a civilian, accomplished a remarkable feat: he twice rowed a small boat all alone across the English Channel from Dover, bringing several British soldiers back with him each time. He joined the Navy soon afterwards and in 1941 was killed in action in H.M.S. *Hood.*

I often think of him, perhaps most of all when we meet in our candle-lit chapel at College for the annual Commemoration of Benefactors. After the reading of a Lesson from the Book of Ecclesiasticus and the singing of the anthem, *The souls of the righteous*, the Dean reads out a long roll of benefactors to the College. It begins with Malcolm IV, King of Scotland and Earl of Huntingdon, who endowed the Priory of St Radegund during the reign of King Stephen, and goes on by way of John Alcock, Bishop of Ely, who refounded the Priory as a College; Thomas Thirlby, Richard Sterne, Tobias Rustat, and many others, who added to its endowments; William Boldero, sometime Master, who enriched the College Library; until at last it reaches 'Lambert Charles Shepherd, sometime Scholar here, who bequeathed all his English books to the College Library'; and so it comes about that many books in the library are inscribed with Bush's name as donor after all.

32

After the War of 1939-45, as after the Napoleonic Wars and the War of 1914-18, the resident membership of the University grew considerably. The increase was greatest during the first few years, owing to the presence of a large number of men whose academic careers had been interrupted or delayed by war service. It would have been difficult in any event to find accommodation for all the undergraduates at Cambridge, particularly as many of them were now married men with children. What made the situation even more difficult was that many Civil Servants, evacuees, refugees, and others who had found temporary homes in the town during the war did not leave it until some years after it ended. The result was that some undergraduates had to keep 'residence', not merely outside the precincts of the University (which extended to a distance of three miles from Great St Mary's Church), but even outside the boundaries of Cambridgeshire — in Huntingdonshire, Suffolk, Essex and Hertfordshire. A few married men had to live in caravans and even in houseboats on the Cam.

It was noticeable how well these undergraduates, of very different ages, social backgrounds, and experiences, settled down together. Men who had held commissions for several years and fought on more than one front, objectors to military service, men who had begun residence before the war, married men with families, boys straight from school, men from the big public schools and from unknown municipal secondary schools, rich men and poor men — all these lived together in amity. Before the war, when undergraduates were much more homogeneous in age and social background, the life of the University had unfortunately been disfigured at times by outbreaks of intolerant hooliganism. This had shown itself particularly in the organized smashing of political meetings, no matter how moderate, of which the hooligans disapproved. The smashers were always public-school men, though it is right to add that they formed only a minority of their class and that certain enlightened public schools were always conspicuous by their absence from the barbarian ranks.

The post-war generation of undergraduates from the public schools were undoubtedly much more tolerant than the pre-war generation. One of the few instances to the contrary that I can remember at my own college occurred in 1945, when an old Jesus man, Leslie Symonds, who had just been elected Socialist Member of Parliament for Cambridge, was hissed by some of the undergraduates when he appeared at high table as my guest. His memory may have gone back then to an incident in his undergraduate days about 1930, when his oak (the outer door of his rooms) was screwed up in the hope (ungratified, as it proved) of preventing him from speaking at a Labour Party meeting that day. An admirable example of the normal post-war spirit was provided by two Jesus men, one of whom was the chief organizer of the Conservative undergraduates in the University, the other of the Socialists. They became close friends and, at their own request, shared a set of rooms in College, on the ground floor of my staircase. I never discovered which was the Conservative end and which the Socialist end of their joint settee or whether, to save time and money, they sent out rival political leaflets in the same envelope.

Even when the men of the big post-war 'bulge' had gone down, the University continued to be considerably larger than it had ever been before the war. This was mainly because of the great increase in the amount of financial help given by national and local government bodies to the cause of higher education. State Scholarships had been given before the war, but there were far more of them now; and if a College Entrance Scholarship was inadequate for maintenance the State was prepared to make good the deficiency. Among those undergraduates who were not up to Scholarship level the scales were still tipped against the poor man, but the composition of the University nevertheless became much more democratic than it had ever been. Boys from the working class were now able to enter it in considerable numbers for the first time. The competition for places became in consequence very keen, and the former stream of wealthy or middle-class men who had entered the University with no intention of working for anything more than a pass degree was now suppressed in favour of men reading for honours, regardless of social class.

A further increase in the size of the University came about (though it brought no more people to Cambridge) when the two women's colleges, Girton and Newnham, were incorporated in it after a separate existence of over three-quarters of a century. Their members had received titular degrees ever since 1921, and since 1926 they had been eligible for membership of Faculties and Faculty Boards and for all teaching offices in the University. Yet, even if they were Professors, they were still non-members of the University, without a vote in its

internal affairs. The inconvenience and injustice of this absurd situation
had made a change inevitable, and in 1947 proposals to incorporate the
two colleges in the University were brought forward.

I was present at the meeting fixed for discussion of this proposal in
the Regent House. When the Vice-Chancellor called for comments there
was a long silence. It was broken at last by a friend of mine, who
opposed incorporation on the ingenious plea that it would be unfair to
the women, as they would have to work much harder than before,
though he did not make it clear how this would come about. He had
not intended, he said, to speak 'so early' in the debate. When he sat
down again he must have felt himself a kind of *Athanasius contra
mundum*, because no one else uttered a syllable and the meeting ended.
Those who had attended it in the hope of entertainment were disappointed. At a subsequent Congregation a Grace for the incorporation
of the women's colleges in the University was carried without
opposition.

This almost complete lack of opposition to the change did not
surprise me at all. I had signed the petition which had first caused the
question of incorporation to be brought forward, but as Editor of the
Cambridge Review I naturally invited correspondence from both sides. I
did not get even one letter in reply. Only when the Grace had been
carried did I get some doggerel verses from a country parson. In them
he expressed his pained regret at the defeat of the anti-feminine cause
which, he said, had been upheld by 'the blood and tears of sixty years'.
I was tempted to publish the verses, mercifully suppressing the author's
name. If I had done so, I would have added a comment that no one but
the writer of the verses had heard of any blood being shed on either
side during the long history of the struggle for incorporation, and that
if any tears had been shed they would have come with more justice
from the supporters of the women's cause than from its opponents; but
I resisted the temptation.

When women took part in a University procession for the first time I
was on duty as a Steward of the Senate House. Part of my duty was to
see that academical dress was worn properly — for instance, that only
those who were officiating in any way should keep their heads covered.
I noticed that a Professor from one of the women's colleges did not
take off her square cap as she came in with the procession. She was an
Oxonian by origin and was no doubt unconsciously following the
custom of her old university, where women wear unstiffened square
caps and keep them on during ceremonies. I asked her to remove her

cap and she did so, with some embarrassment. My action received the approval of the authorities (of both sexes) and it became a rule for square caps and doctors' bonnets to be worn or removed without regard to the sex of the wearer. This seems to me more reasonable than the Oxford custom. It avoids confusion and sex discrimination. It helps to maintain an ancient University custom, and it has the practical advantage of making it easy for everyone in the Senate House to see who is officiating on any occasion. One can tell at a glance, for instance, who is presenting for degrees, since all Praelectors are wearing caps, regardless of sex.

The great increase in the amount of State help given to the University after the war led to the establishment of new chairs and lectureships in subjects which had previously been starved, and I was one of the beneficiaries. The number of undergraduates reading Medieval Latin for the Modern and Medieval Languages Tripos and the English Tripos had grown so much by this time that an official University Lectureship in the subject was created in 1946 in my favour, with a full stipend. Although its establishment had taken a long time — I had been lecturing in the subject for sixteen years — Cambridge has the credit of having been the first university in any country of the British Commonwealth to found an official Lectureship in Medieval Latin. Medieval Latin studies at Cambridge were immeasurably strengthened in 1948 when Dr F. J. E. Raby, who had an international reputation as a Medieval Latinist, left the Civil Service and came into residence as a Fellow of Jesus, of which he had been an Honorary Fellow for some years.

Frederic Raby had taken his first degree from Trinity College in 1910. He then left Cambridge for the Civil Service and toiled for thirty-seven years in the Ministry of Public Buildings and Works, conscientiously and efficiently; but he was before all else a scholar and a medievalist. While he was still in the Civil Service he produced his *Christian Latin Poetry in the Middle Ages* and its companion *Secular Latin Poetry in the Middle Ages* in two volumes. These works, totalling about 1,300 quarto pages, opened a completely new world of Medieval Latin literature to English readers and put him in the forefront of the world's medievalists.

After knowing him for some years through his writings I met him in the flesh through the medium of Edward Wynn, who was Raby's contemporary at Cambridge and, though they were at different colleges, had attended the same lectures. Before the end of our first meeting I realized what an asset he would be to Cambridge, which he ought never to have been allowed to leave, and how he would love to return to the academical life. I therefore determined to get him elected to an Honorary Fellowship at Jesus as soon as possible and later, as soon as he could leave the Civil Service, to an ordinary Fellowship. I told B. L. Manning of my ambition. He strongly approved and aided and abetted me. As I have already recorded, we were successful.

Raby was a great asset to the College, with the life of which he identified himself completely. He delighted in the teaching of medieval history, and his pupils repaid him with devotion and affection. On the other hand, he could never be induced to give a lecture. I once persuaded him to read a paper to the Jesuits; but, even when facing that small band of undergraduates, he was so overcome with nervousness that I was never so callous as to ask him to read another paper, and it is most improbable that he ever read one anywhere else, though he must have been frequently invited and even pressed to do so.

To my great pleasure, he kept on the same staircase and landing as myself, in the rooms which I had occupied until Nairne died. This was a great boon to me, as he was one of the most widely-read men to be met anywhere. He was a mine of information, not merely on medieval Latin literature and every kind of ecclesiastical subject, but also on the classics, on Dante, on English and French literature, on philosophy, art, and architecture. We were constantly in and out of each other's rooms, and he lunched with me practically every day of term until he died.

Raby played cricket, took little interest in rowing, and disliked acting and singing. His only sartorial peculiarity was that he wore brocade waistcoats. He wrote (almost illegibly) always with his left hand, and took snuff, though only once a day, in the Combination Room after dinner.

I differed from him on all those points, but we had many other interests in common. He was, for instance, a keen Anglican, and a member of the Friends of Little Gidding and the John Mason Neale Society. We were on the committee of the Alcuin Club together and were both vice-presidents of the Hymn Society. I cannot imagine why I never (so far as I can remember) canvassed him to join the Cambridge Heraldic Society, which I feel sure he would have enjoyed. I never posted a book-review, an article, or a letter to a paper without first showing it to him for his opinion, and he was so humble that he returned the compliment.

Raby was fond of society and never missed dining in Hall without good reason. When he became one of the senior Fellows he was in his

P

element if it fell to him to preside over high table. He was particularly fond of quoting from St Augustine, Dante, George Herbert, and Dr Johnson. Among modern authors he quoted freely from Max Beerbohm and P. G. Wodehouse, and from the quaint sayings of his lifelong Quaker friend and disciple, Harold Rossiter-Smith, whose devotion to him was an inspiration to the friends of both of them. He had a wonderful way with children, whom he treated as his equals and contemporaries. An abiding memory of him will be of small children calling at the house of this scholar of international repute when he was in his late seventies and asking, 'Please can Dr Raby come out to play with us?'

33

I continued to give my University lectures within the walls of my own College after 1946, as I had always done, but I migrated from an ordinary lecture-room to a room in the Cloisters, called the Prioress's Room. This delightful room, with its open-timbered roof, old-fashioned fireplace, and portraits of College worthies hanging from the walls, provided a much more appropriate setting for lectures on medieval literature than a bare room in a centrally heated block of University lecture-rooms would have done. My audience appreciated the padded seats, the carpet, and the coal fire, and the University was relieved of the burden of fitting me into one of its overworked lecture-rooms. It even paid a fee to the College for allowing one of its rooms to be used for a University purpose. I find that a mention of this last point helps visitors to grasp the relationship between the University and the colleges, which the uninitiated otherwise often imagine to be merely departments of the University, instead of the self-governing corporations, *imperia in imperio*, that they are.

On October 1st, 1945, 'Dave' Raven and I performed our last official act as Proctors by installing the Master of Clare (Sir Henry Thirkill) as Vice-Chancellor with the ancient ceremonial, in succession to Dr Hele, Master of Emmanuel. We then vacated office, but I was immediately sworn in again as Pro-Proctor, because Sidney Sussex College, whose turn it was, had done me the honour of nominating me as their representative. My colleague this time was James Stevenson of St John's, afterwards a Fellow of Downing, with whom my relations were most happy. As I had taken my Master of Arts degree before him, when we became Proctors a year later I was the Senior and he the Junior. I was delighted to be in office again.

My second tenure of office as Pro-Proctor and Proctor proved as enjoyable as my first. There were fewer complications now that the big contingents of American airmen had left Cambridgeshire, but there was still plenty to do. As always, the Proctors worked in complete harmony with the local police. The Chief Constable, B. N. Bebbington, happened to be not only a member of the University but also a Jesus man and a Rooster to boot, so that he and I had many interests in common. When patrolling the streets of the town on winter nights, I often called at his house in Park Street for a brief respite. There we had more than one profitable discussion about the state of crime in Cambridge over a cup of coffee, or laid plans for circumventing the hotheads, of both town and gown, who could always be relied on to cause trouble, and make fools of themselves, on such occasions as the Fifth of November.

The serious side of the Proctorial office was sometimes irksome, but unpleasant incidents were far outnumbered by pleasant ones. Our relations with the undergraduates were very cordial. We often looked in at their dances, to chat with the organizers and wish them well, though occasionally the appearance of the Proctor with his constables caused alarm at first among the uninitiated and also perhaps among those who had guilty consciences. Sometimes during these visits I took off my gown and bands and danced for a few minutes. On one such occasion I committed the *faux pas* of handing my partner back, not to her partner for the evening, but to the rival whom he had supplanted.

One day the Vice-Chancellor handed me the typescript of the Footlights' proposed May Week revue and asked me to censor it for him.

'With pleasure,' I said, 'but I feel I ought to mention that I am a member of the Footlights.'

'I know that,' he said. 'That's why I've asked you to censor it.'

I took the script away and locked it in a drawer in my rooms. As I was very busy at the time I forgot the censoring until one day the secretary of the Footlights called on me.

'The Vice-Chancellor is keeping the revue a long time,' he said. 'Do you think you can do anything to speed it up?'

'I feel sure I can,' I answered. As soon as he had gone, I took out the script, read it through, blue-pencilled some parts of it and returned it to the Vice-Chancellor, who sent it back to the club.

A few days later the Secretary called on me again. 'The Vice--Chancellor has sent the revue back,' he said, 'but he's blue-pencilled quite a bit of it.'

'Well,' I said, 'everybody knows him to be a reasonable man; and in any case you'll either have to revise those parts or cut them out altogether.'

A revised text was submitted and the script went on its journeys again — without delay this time. A few further excisions were made and the rest of the text was approved.

One amusing event which occurred during my second proctorship was the playing of an absurd game called 'Foot-the-ball'. It had been invented by some genius at Caius. There were three balls, three goals, and three teams playing against each other simultaneously on a single pitch on Parker's Piece. The novelty of the game, coupled perhaps with an announcement that the three balls would be kicked off by the Mayor, the Senior Proctor, and the Chief Constable, attracted a large crowd of spectators. When I was asked to take part in the kick-off I readily agreed, particularly as I was told that the Mayor and the Chief Constable would be doing the same. When I arrived at the ground the Chief Constable came up to me and said, 'I knew it would be quite in order for me to take part in this, because the organizers told me that you and the Mayor were doing so.' I came away from the match with the Mayor, who remarked thoughtfully, 'I wondered at first whether to take part in the kick-off or not, but I agreed to do so when they told me that the Chief Constable and you were going to be in it.'

Proctorial duty was least agreeable during the early months of 1947, when the English winter was the most severe within living memory. For practically the whole of the Lent Term we did not see a blade of grass in the college courts at Jesus, or on the Close, owing to repeated snow-falls and frosts. The thaw which set in towards the end of term was accompanied by very heavy and continuous rain. As a result, Cam-bridgeshire suffered severely from floods — in the Fens, disastrously so. Queens' and other colleges along the Backs were invaded by the floods and parts of them could be reached only by boats, but at Jesus we were more fortunate. The Cam, it is true, expanded into a lake, covering Jesus Green and Midsummer Common and stretching right up to the College boundary; but, owing to the foresight of the founders of the Priory of St Radegund in building on slightly higher ground, the College itself escaped flooding.

One day in February that year, when we had had ice and snow for weeks, I was miserably patrolling the streets of Cambridge with my two 'bulldogs,' Reg. Johnson (the senior of the University force) and Donald Tarrant. I remarked that I had had more than enough of that bitter weather.

'That's all right, sir,' said Johnson, 'we shall have good weather after Tuesday.'

'What makes you think that?' I asked.

'Because there's a new moon on Tuesday,' he said, 'and when the moon changes the weather always changes.'

I assured him, as I had assured Kate Mossman at Knightsland some years before, on the authority of the Astronomer Royal, that a change of moon did not make the slightest difference to the weather, but he was obviously unconvinced.

'You'll see what happens when the new moon comes in,' he said confidently. 'We shall get good weather then.'

The new moon, however, came in with a blizzard. When snow had fallen almost continuously for nearly twenty-four hours I rang up St Catharine's College, where Johnson worked in the day-time, and asked for him. The porter on duty soon brought him to the telephone. He was rather anxious, wondering whether there was an undergraduate riot or something of the sort requiring our immediate attention.

'What's the matter, sir?' he asked eagerly.

'Nothing,' I answered, 'nothing. I only wanted to point out to you how much the weather has improved since the moon changed.'

He laughed. 'You've got me there,' he said.

Snow fell every day for about a week after that, and every evening I rang him up to point out the improvement in the weather. I expect that the good Reg. Johnson (one of the best constables the University can ever have had) soon forgot the snowfall and remained unshaken in his belief.

James Stevenson and I vacated office as Proctors in October 1947, after installing Dr Charles Raven, Master of Christ's, as Vice-Chancellor. We continued, however, as Additional Pro-Proctors for another year, in accordance with custom.

I was therefore still in office when I took the degree of Doctor of Letters in February 1948. This was naturally a great event for me, giving me as much pleasure as my election to a Fellowship had done. As on the two occasions when I had been installed as Proctor, I gave a party at Jesus on returning from the Senate House and had the pleasure of entertaining a large number of friends who had been present at the ceremony.

In the following April women became members of the University. The Mistress of Girton had already consulted me about details of academical dress for women, but gowns were not made compulsory for them until October, when I had gone out of office. I therefore never had the privilege of 'progging' any of my numerous Girton or Newnham friends for being without a gown or indeed (I regret to say) for any other reason.

During that same Easter term I was, strictly speaking, guilty of a breach of University discipline myself. The ordinances require doctors to wear their scarlet gowns and velvet bonnets with gold cord and tassel whenever they appear in public on a Scarlet Day. There are always several Scarlet Days during the Easter Term and on one of them I was on pro-proctorial duty. Yet it seemed wrong to wear a scarlet gown — particularly a Litt.D. scarlet, which is perhaps the most vivid of all gowns, being scarlet all over — to patrol the streets that evening, when I might have had to enter a public-house to deal with an undergraduate. I therefore wore my black gown, but on a strict interpretation of the ordinances I should have reported myself to the Vice-Chancellor for doing so.

Except for an infrequent appearance on such occasions as the Fifth of November, I performed no proctorial duties after October that year. I would most gladly have taken office for a third time a few years later, when my college wished to nominate me again, but my medical adviser peremptorily forbade me to do so.

34

All Masters of Jesus College, up to and including Arthur Gray, were appointed under statutes which allowed them to stay in office for life, but the reformed statutes of 1926 introduced a retiring age for all future Masters. Dr Duckworth consequently vacated office in 1945, became a Fellow again, and lived in College until he died in 1956.

For the second time in five years, therefore, we met in chapel at noon one day to elect a Master. Abbott again presided over the election, but this time the junior Fellow who helped him to count the votes was A. W. Lawrence, Professor of Classical Archaeology, who a few years later followed D. M. Balme to the new University of the Gold Coast. We elected Eustace Tillyard, who had entered the College in 1908 and had been Senior Tutor throughout the greater part of the war. A Doctor of Letters and a specialist on Shakespeare and Milton, he enjoyed an international reputation for scholarship. Like Arthur Gray, he was a Liberal in politics, whereas Duckworth had been a strong Tory.

As a result of the general reshuffle of offices which accompanied the end of the war and the change in the Mastership, I became Steward of the College.

The duties of a Steward (or Domestic Bursar, as he is called at some colleges) vary in details from college to college. At Jesus they are very wide, including as they do the security of the college, the supervision of the kitchen, buttery, wine cellars, Combination Room and other common rooms, the planning of feasts (including the seating), the maintenance of the courts and gardens, the housing and feeding of vacation conferences, and the engagement, payment and promotion of the numerous employees. The Steward, in short, represents the College as tenant. The Bursar represents it as landlord and is responsible for the maintenance of the buildings, just as he is for the external property of the College.

The Steward, being responsible for the catering (albeit through the medium of a Manciple or of a Catering Manager) has the most thankless of all College offices; for even dons are known to grumble about the food, and there are undergraduates at every one of the twenty colleges in the University who are firmly convinced that the food provided at their own college is the worst in Cambridge.

One of the pleasantest features of my nine years' tenure of the Stewardship was that it brought me into close contact with the employees of the College. In August every year I invited them all to come to tea with me in Hall, to bring a guest each — wife, husband, or anyone they wished — and to enjoy the freedom of the Fellows' Garden and other parts of the College for a few hours. It was delightful to see how greatly they valued the opportunity of showing the College to their relations and friends. Many of them had spent the whole or the greater part of their working lives within its walls and were as devoted to it as any don or undergraduate could be. Few of them were well paid, and those who were employed in the kitchen or buttery had to work a long split day, with six full working days a week, Sunday often being one of the six.

The years immediately after the war were very crowded ones for me. I was simultaneously Proctor and University Lecturer, Steward, Keeper of the Records, and Director of Language Studies at Jesus, and Editor of the *Cambridge Review*. When I came in from proctorial duty about midnight I had to correct proofs for the compositor to collect on his way to Heffer's printing works in the morning, or write letters, so that I rarely went to bed before two o'clock. Even when I resigned the editorship of the *Review* and vacated the proctorship in 1948 there did not seem to be any more leisure. This was because, like other dons, I also held a number of unpaid offices, each of which was small in itself, but in the aggregate they consumed a great deal of time.

I was, for instance, Treasurer of the Jesus College Amalgamated Clubs — an office which required almost daily attention, and which I held for twenty-five years and thoroughly enjoyed. It led to my appearance in court in 1955 as defendant in an action brought by a Cambridge townsman. He claimed that his motor-launch, moored to the river-bank at Grassy Corner, had been damaged by a Jesus boat when the latter had been bumped in the May Races three years earlier.

The plaintiff could not sue the University of Cambridge, as it could not be held legally responsible for damage caused by any of its members during athletic contests. For the same reason, the Master and Fellows of Jesus College could not be sued. The University Boat Club could not be sued either, as it did not exist legally, neither did the Jesus College Boat Club, since no one could define which of the undergraduates were members of either club and which were non-members. Since, however, all undergraduates at the College were members of the Amalgamated Clubs, the Clubs could be sued. This meant that about

400 men were equally liable for the damage to the motor-launch; but the appearance of such a large number of defendants in court at once would have caused congestion. It was therefore agreed that I should appear as representative defendant.

There were other entertaining features of the action. The legal authorities decided, for instance, that since the bump (called a 'collision' in the pleadings) had been an aquatic affair, the case should be heard in an Admiralty Court; and, since an Admiralty Court must (apparently) sit within the smell of salt water, it sat at Ipswich. Anyone present in court without knowing the background of the case might well have thought that the racing eights concerned in the 'collision' were ocean-going liners; and a titter went round the court when an official solemnly read out, 'Direction and force of the wind at the time of the collision – unknown; state of the tide – unknown.'

The case lasted all day, with only a short interval for lunch. Despite the advocacy of that robust old Jesus man, Sir Godfrey Russell Vick, Q.C., on our behalf, the townsman won his action.

University clubs of which I was elected senior treasurer included the Judo Club, the Heraldic Society, the Musical Comedy Club, and the Pantomime Club. The Pantomime Club was founded in my rooms. Its first production was a kind of cross between *Cinderella* and *Jack and the Beanstalk*. The book was by Wendy Joyce, an undergraduate at Girton, who was also the producer. I played the part of the Dame, which I must confess is my favourite stage role. I had played the same part two years earlier in a village pantomime at South Mimms, where I appeared as the Widow Twankey in Gertrude Jennings's version of *Aladdin*. On the eve of the Cambridge production I was stricken with lumbago and could hardly crawl. It looked as though I should be unable to perform. Conrad Skinner, however, who had now retired from office at the Leys School and was reported to possess healing powers, came and treated me – not by touch, but by merely holding his outspread hands a few inches away from me for about twenty minutes. Whether *propter hoc* or merely *post hoc*, it is a fact that I was not merely able to take part in all three performances of the pantomime without feeling a twinge but even to dance a hilarious (but decent) Can-Can with no unpleasant after-effects. We gave three performances at Girton. My part included the singing of a song, 'Don't send your daughter to Girton', the words of which were by Robert Gittings. The audience included the Vice-Chancellor, Sir Henry Willink, whose alleged early love-affair with me I revealed across the footlights.

Another society founded in my rooms and meeting there from time to time — a society of a very different kind, and not limited to members of the University or to residents at Cambridge — was the Friends of Little Gidding. Its objects were to maintain the parish church of Little Gidding and to perpetuate the memory of the saintly Nicholas Ferrar, who lived at Gidding early in the seventeenth century, as readers of *John Inglesant* will remember. The Friends' annual pilgrimage, in July, is led by the Bishop of Ely. The tiny church stands in charming isolation in a remote part of Huntingdonshire, miles from any town. The only approach to it is by a cart-track, through a farmyard, and then across a meadow. Corn grows up to the very walls of the church and its diminutive graveyard, where Nicholas Ferrar lies buried just outside the west door. The nave, with its seats arranged as in a college chapel, holds only thirty people. The rest of the pilgrims have to stand outside. Even so, the church has more than enough seats to accommodate the whole parish on ordinary occasions, since the combined population of the three Giddings, which are served by one incumbent, is little more than three hundred. Of these, there are less than thirty in Little Gidding, fifty or so in Steeple Gidding, and about 240 in Great Gidding.

My love for Ely made me join the Friends of Ely Cathedral some years before the war began, and after the war I was elected to the Council of the Friends. Early in the nineteen-fifties some of the parts of the cathedral, including the famous fourteenth-century lantern, were found to be in an alarming condition and a large sum of money had to be raised to carry out the necessary treatment. With the approval of Dean Hankey I formed a Cambridge committee to raise funds from that part of the diocese. We held a number of public meetings and lantern lectures, organized street collections, and held garden parties in various colleges.

We were particularly fortunate in getting the valuable help of Mrs Camille Prior, the widow of my old teacher, Professor Oliver Prior. Mrs Prior, affectionately known as 'Pop' to her friends, had a genius for producing plays and other theatrical performances. She had done a great work for years in producing plays in English, French, German, Spanish and Russian on behalf of societies in the University and Town; and her valuable services to education in this sphere were recognized by the conferment of an honorary degree on her by the University. She came to the help of Ely cathedral by producing a number of historical pageants which attracted large audiences. She found many willing helpers who would do anything for 'Pop.'

When the cathedral had been made safe and sound 'Pop' took no more rest than before. She continued to produce plays, telling her friends that each of them was to be her last production, and acting in them herself. I had the pleasure of appearing with her in 'A Victorian Evening', which was produced in costume. We gave one performance at King's College and another at the Union Society. The book was by the Reverend M. J. Plumley, Professor of Egyptology, who played the part of the father of a Victorian family, with Pop as grandmother.

A great deal of my spare time during term after the war was given up to showing people round the College – sometimes our own undergraduates, at other times visitors to the University. Few things were more striking in post-war Cambridge than the great increase in the number of sightseers, particularly of the working class. Before the war, vast numbers of working men and women, even whole towns, were unemployed and underfed and never left their home towns. In the summer of 1936, for instance, some Jesus undergraduates ran a camp for unemployed men in the north of England. It was recorded in the college magazine that over a hundred such men stayed at the camp, and it is pathetic to read that they 'were given an opportunity to enjoy themselves in a country atmosphere, with an unusual amount of food and work.'

Things were very different after the war, when whole coach-loads of manual workers came to Cambridge every day of the spring, summer, and autumn. Where they came in hundreds before the war they now came in thousands, and from much greater distances. The increase was no doubt due to the institution of the Welfare State, the introduction of a five-day week in many occupations, and above all to full employment and holidays with pay. Whatever the cause, I soon began to spend hundreds of hours every year guiding visitors round the College, sometimes conducting two and even three tours a day. The amount of time taken by a tour varied with the interest (or lack of it) shown by the audience. Sometimes it lasted as long as three hours, while I tried to bring the tourists into the life of the College, by making them sit down for a while in Chapel, Hall, and Combination Room, or among the cockerels in my rooms. They usually asked intelligent and even searching questions; though once when I invited questions a woman asked, 'How far is it to Woolworth's?' and on another tour a man started the questions with, 'Where is the nearest public-house?'

There is nothing that gives me more enjoyment in life than entertaining, and nothing costs me more in time or money. I feel at times that, if I could, I would have a trestle-table circling the earth and lined with guests on both sides.

If a don keeps open house, and if entertaining is part of his work (as I believe it is), he works a·seven-day week, and his day lasts from early morning until late at night, often far into the night.

So at least I have found. Undergraduates, whether Jesus men or men and women from other colleges, pay social calls at any time — weekdays and Sundays, between meals or during meals, even during breakfast. Old members of the College are also apt to call at any hour, whether they are merely passing through Cambridge by car on business, or whether they are touring England when home on furlough from distant lands. If they have their wives and children with them they may perhaps stop only long enough for a cup of coffee and a talk, or they may stay to lunch or dinner. If they come alone they may stay a night or longer.

Some of my guests have been complete strangers to me when I first entertained them. Mr Phelp of Watford was one of these. He stopped me one afternoon on King's Parade to ask me to explain something in the guide-book that he was holding. Discovering that this was his first visit to Cambridge, I invited him to tea with me at the College, and he came. He was so interested in all he saw that I invited him to stay to dinner in Hall, and he stayed. Finding that he had not reserved a bed at any hotel in Cambridge, I invited him to stay the night in College, and he stayed. He enjoyed his visit so much that next morning I felt I must invite him to stay for a week, and he stayed. I have seldom known a guest to be so enraptured with the place as he was, or one whom it has given me so much pleasure to entertain.

Most stranger-guests have not stayed as long as Mr Phelp. Some of them have been casual sightseers (British or foreign) who have attached themselves to parties of visitors whom I was showing round the College and have come to my rooms afterwards for a drink. Others have been sorrowful-looking couples, weary with sightseeing, whose eyes (after a momentary look of surprise) have sparkled with acceptance when I have suddenly accosted them in the College courts with an invitation to tea in my rooms.

Gillie Potter, the well-known comedian and creator of the Hogsnorton saga, was no stranger when he first stayed with me at Jesus. I had met him some years before, at South Mimms, where he had dropped in at church for morning service one Sunday when I was home for the vacation. He became a fairly frequent visitor to me at Jesus, generally staying a night and entertaining my friends with his humour. As he was a tireless non-stop talker I preferred not to have him staying with me more than twenty-four hours at a time. I could seldom persuade him to stop talking before two o'clock in the morning. Once, when he had kept me out of bed until three, he appeared in my bedroom next morning at seven o'clock, asking to be taken to chapel, and giving me no peace until I took him.

I had several visits from the well-known company of professional entertainers called the Roosters' Concert Party, who had been founded by Percy Merriman in France during the first World War. They first got into touch with the College through reading about the Jesus Roosters in a newspaper. As a result, I invited Percy Merriman to stay a night and attend a Roost, and he enjoyed it. The whole company came to Cambridge later in the year to give a performance in the town, and when the performance was over I had them all to a late supper in my rooms. Most of them had never been inside a college before in their lives. After supper I took them round the Fellows' Garden by twilight. It was July, and the still air was perfumed with half-visible roses, night-scented stocks and lime blossom. To me, even after years of familiarity with the garden, it seemed very beautiful; but to them, visiting it for the first time, it was fairy land. It was pathetic to see one of the company pinching his arm, and to hear him murmuring, 'It can't be real. I must be dreaming.'

Sometimes I have much younger guests. One hot afternoon in August, for instance, when I was letting myself into the Fellows' Garden from Jesus Lane by the private door, five children (a girl and four boys) who were passing by stopped and peeped through the open doorway. They were of various ages, from about eight to twelve, I should say.

'Coo! that's a nice garden,' one of them said.

'Yes,' I answered, 'would you like to come in and look round?'

'Would that be all right?' one of them asked.

'Yes,' I said, and they came in.

'Do you live here?' one asked.

'Yes.'

'Do your father and mother live here, too?'

'No. Fathers and mothers don't live here. Only men live here.'

'Only men? Do you hear that, George? Only men live here. I never heard of such a thing, did you, George?'

'No,' George answered firmly. 'Never.'

I took them round the garden, showed them the flowers, and then remembered that the mulberries were ripe.

'Do you like mulberries?' I asked.

'Mulberries? What are they? We don't know mulberries.'

'Come with me,' I said, 'and I'll show you'; and I took them to the ancient mulberry-tree, reputed to have been planted by King James I.

'Oh! they're strawberries,' George said.

'You may call them strawberries if you like,' I answered, 'but we call them mulberries. Would you like some?'

There was a chorus of 'Yes.'

'Very well,' I said. 'Help yourselves.'

They did so, with no delay at all. Complete silence fell, lasting for some minutes. At last one of them, the girl, said, 'Can we take some home to mum?'

'Yes,' I said, 'and if you come to where I live I will give you a little box to put them in.'

I took them to my rooms and gave them the box. When they had admired my collection of what they naturally called chickens I suggested that they should wash their hands and faces, which were red all over with mulberry juice, before going home. My suggestion did not meet with approval. To use the language of wartime notices at railway booking-offices, they did not think that washing was really necessary. One of the bigger boys, in fact, closed the discussion with irrefutable logic by saying, 'Besides, we shall look just the same when we've had some more of those strawberries.'

'What!' I said in astonishment. 'Do you mean to say you could eat some more?'

There was a unanimous answer of 'Yes.'

'Very well,' I said.

They were down the four flights of stairs, across the court, and back in the Fellows' Garden in a flash. A quarter of an hour later I let them out into Jesus Lane and they went home, gory but happy, clutching their box of mulberries for mum.

35

One of my visitors for several years, until he resigned his see in 1947, was Claude Blagden, Bishop of Peterborough. Having been an Oxford don in earlier life he enjoyed an occasional brief return to academic surroundings, and he and the Bishop of Ely, together with John Grimes, Archdeacon of Northampton, used to dine with me about once a year at college, in the Prioress's Room. The party usually also included my friends Mr and Mrs F. G. Mitchell, through whom I had first met Bishop Blagden, when they had a wartime home at Norman Cross, near Peterborough. Mr Mitchell, being about the biggest man to be seen in a very long day's march, was commonly called 'Tiny', and his wife 'Blackie', which had been her nickname from girlhood. In Rooster circles she was called 'the Dame', being the only woman ever elected to membership of the Roost and having the further distinction of being created D.R.H. (Dame of the Order of the Red Herring).

After dinner on one of these occasions, when the Bishop of Peterborough had been admiring Nicholson's portrait of Q in my rooms, Tiny Mitchell stirred me up to tell a few Q stories. I told them how annoyed Q used to be if anyone called on him before lunch without an appointment. At first, I said, the caller would not hear a sound in answer to his knocking. After a third or fourth knock he would hear a mutter through the very thin door. After another knock or two, he would invariably hear Q call twice on the Almighty and then exclaim dramatically, 'Is there no peace in this blasted college?'

The Bishop was amused at the story. After his return to Peterborough he sent me a letter which I shall always keep, characteristic as it is of its writer, with his delightful sense of humour. It is quite brief, expressing his thanks, and ending:

> We at any rate, apparently unlike Q, found peace in your blasted college.
>
> Yours very sincerely,
> Claude Petriburg.

In the summer of 1948 I had an episcopal guest who stayed with me for some time. This was my uncle, Henry Daniels, who had been Bishop of Montana for nearly ten years and had come over from the United

States to attend the first post-war Lambeth Conference. It was a great pleasure to entertain him at College; to go with him to St John's College, where he confirmed some undergraduates for the Dean, my former proctorial colleague, Edward Raven; to Ely, where we stayed with the diocesan for the patronal festival; to Peterborough, where we were entertained by Archdeacon and Mrs Grimes; and to Clopton Manor in Northamptonshire, where Tiny and Dame Mitchell entertained us in the generous style for which they were famous. I had enjoyed their princely hospitality many times before, both at Clopton and at their former beautiful old Essex home, 'Albyns', which was unfortunately destroyed by bombs just before the end of the war. Staying with them, whether in Essex or Northamptonshire, was like stepping back three centuries in English rural life. The whole life of the village centred on them, as it had done on Sir Roger de Coverley; but they had no touch of Sir Roger's autocratic ways.

Tiny, the Dame and I had many interests in common, including devotion to the Church of England and to Jesus College, where their younger son had been a pupil of mine. They also shared my keen interest in theatricals, in which they were in fact my chief aiders and abettors. I gave many performances (mostly of music-hall turns) in their spacious hall at 'Albyns' and their almost equally spacious drawing-room at Clopton Manor, in which the whole parish could and often did assemble. At these performances (as often elsewhere) the Dame used to be my accompanist; and Tiny, who was an adept at the art, would make me up with equal skill for a male or female part.

When I went home for a day and a night in February 1946 to celebrate my father's eightieth birthday he was as acute mentally as he had ever been, almost as vigorous physically as twenty years before, and certainly as industrious as ever. His passion for gardening was undiminished. He had been a possessor of 'green fingers' all his life, and his crops were still the envy of his neighbours. Like William the Conqueror with his tall deer, he loved small plants as though he were their father. He loved everything (weeds excepted) that came up from the ground; and perhaps for that reason, he strongly disliked cats, dogs, and birds. His habits were unchanged. He was still as economical as early poverty and a frugal mind had taught him to be. He wore the most ragged clothes he could find, except sometimes in the evenings and always when he went out shopping. On those great occasions he wore a pair of kid gloves and carried a silver-mounted walking-stick.

We celebrated my mother's eightieth birthday two years after my father's. She had long been a semi-invalid but kept full control of household affairs from her couch. It was a great grief to her that her infirmities prevented her from reading much and from listening to musical programmes on the wireless as often as she would have liked. Her mind, on the other hand, had lost none of its clearness, and her interest in political and intellectual subjects was undiminished.

We had already celebrated Allen Hay's eightieth birthday in June 1946, as he was only a few months younger than my father. I naturally went home for the celebration.

Like my father, he had changed very little, except that he moved more slowly than before. His mind was as acute as ever, his humour as overflowing as it had always been. He was assiduous in his visits to London for various diocesan committees, in the business of which he was very far from being a cipher. In church, he had his choir and servers so well in hand that one ordinary Sunday morning, just after he had turned eighty, I counted twenty-four men and boys in the chancel. On Good Friday evenings, when services seemed to have been going on most of the day, he used to reduce us almost to despair by adding yet another hymn and a few more prayers to the end of Evensong – and there was *Tenebrae* to follow in a few minutes, with its uninterrupted chanting for about an hour and a quarter.

He was as happy-go-lucky as ever, picking the office hymn at Evensong during the reading of the first Lesson and the other hymns when the time came for them to be sung. When the organ stopped playing after the psalms and I stood at the lectern to start reading the First Lesson I could hear him – everyone in church could hear him – taking snuff as he sat inside the altar rails in his cope, so that the announcement of the Lesson ran something like this: 'Here beginneth the fifth chapter of the Second Book of Kings' (*sniff*) 'at the twenty-second verse' (*long sniff*). If someone else was preaching he sat during the sermon in his stall just inside the chancel screen, taking snuff as soon as the text was given out and offering his open snuff-box to any choirman who was sitting within reach.

At the Easter Vestry of 1948, when he was in his fiftieth year as Vicar of South Mimms, he appointed me his warden, as he was determined that I should be in office during the celebration of his golden jubilee. I accordingly presided over the celebrations in October that year, together with my colleague, Mr F. W. Gowar, the people's warden, who had been headmaster of the village school for many years. The jubilee was naturally a great occasion, both because very few parish priests can ever have served half a century in one parish, and also because Allen Hay as a character was unique. There were special thanksgiving services in church, with a tea in the village hall, followed by speeches and by the reading of messages from the Archbishop of Canterbury and the diocesan.

One of the special preachers at the celebration of Allen Hay's jubilee was Philip Loyd, Bishop of St Albans. Although we were not in his diocese he visited us and preached once a year during his short episcopate of five years. He had inherited this practice from his predecessor, Michael Furse, who, like all Bishops of St Albans, found that the shortest way to the parishes in the extreme south of his diocese lay through South Mimms. Motoring through the village one day, and seeing Allen Hay walking along the road, he had stopped his car and asked him how he dared to thrust his parish into the diocese of St Albans. Allen Hay retorted that the boot was on the other foot – that the Bishops of St Albans were intruders in his parish. He would nevertheless allow them free passage, he added, on payment of a toll. The toll was fixed at a sermon a year and was duly paid by Bishop Furse and his two successors until Allen Hay died.

I admired Bishop Furse greatly as a churchman but must confess that I had been slow to like him as a man. This was because I had absorbed some of the prejudices that Q had nourished against him ever since his Oxford days. (They were both Trinity men, Q being the senior of the two by six or seven years.) When I came to know him better, however, my prejudices were speedily replaced by a keen appreciation of his great personal qualities no less than of his robust Anglicanism.

I had no such prejudices to overcome against Bishop Loyd, whom I both admired and liked from my first meeting with him. I have always regretted that his reign at St Albans was too brief to enable me to get to know him well. Like his predecessor, he had been distinguished in the mission field before he went to St Albans. I knew him well enough to realize the truth of the description given of him after his death by a convert from Hinduism. Bishop Loyd, he said, 'was the embodiment of all that was best and beautiful in Anglicanism. His personal charm and infectious holiness were his unfailing weapons; and it spelled disaster to the existing allegiance of any non-Anglican who drew very close to him.'

By the time that Philip Loyd became Bishop, I was an almost daily visitor to St Albans when home from Cambridge during vacations. The ancient city which I had known all my life attracted me more than ever, and its grand cathedral had an increasing fascination. I spent hundreds of blissful hours lingering within its venerable walls, where

> the hollow past
> Half yields the dead that never
> More than half hidden lie,

gazing at the lofty Norman arches that carry the great central tower, visiting in turn the transepts with their Saxon work, the Chapel of the Four Tapers with its brightly coloured altar, the spacious retro-choir, the Lady Chapel opening straight out of it, St Michael's Chapel, and the Saint's Chapel and Shrine, then returning to the choir to watch a verger lighting the candles of the high altar, backed by its lofty statue-laden screen, like a great Spanish *retablo*, and to absorb the magic of Evensong from the stall of some absent honorary canon. At other times I would sit reflecting for hours in the vast building, leaving regretfully when it closed for the night.

In 1965 I was invited by Dean Noel Kennaby to conduct a Visitacioun of ye Cathedrall and Abbey Chirche of Saynt Alban by ye William Dowsing Societye, and these are some extracts from the Report:

> Imprimis we outerlie destroied all ye grene tinted glasse thorowout ye cathedrall, that men myght see ye goodlie trees & ye skie and no longer suffre from accidie.

> Item we did oute all copies of ye New Englishe Bible from ye lecternes, holdinge that boke to be nat goode for liturgicall reading, & did give them to a theological seminarie for studying.

> We liked not to see ye Subdeane & ye Precentor in one stalle, like unto Tweedledum & Tweedledee. We gave ordre that they sholde eche one have his owne stalle and that on ye northe syde.

> Ye singinge of ye quire is exquisite. We gave high prayse unto Master Hurford that, when he beteth tyme in ye presence of ye people, he leapeth not about (as ye maner of divers quiremastersis) like unto a monkey on an Italian organ in ye strete, as it sayeth in ye classicks.

> Yet when, in an hymne in ye Englisshe tongue, ye quire singeth ye Italian Ah-lay-loo-ya, it is an abhomination. That goode papiste, Adrian Fortescue, ryghtly sayth that a boke sholde be writ in one language at a tyme. Lykwyse an hymne sholde be songe in one language at a tyme.

> It is likewise abhominable to singe of temp-tay-ci-on & gene-ray-ci-ons. When men telle us that those wordes were utterde thus in tymes past we answere, Go ye & telle that to ye Marines.

Item, we waited upon ye Deane & said unto him, Very Reverende Sir, we beseech thee not to take our narracioun amiss, for verily our hert rejoiceth whenas we entre thy beauteous cathedrall & it is lifted up whenas divyne service beginneth. For whether it be said without note or whether it be songe it is performed with excedynge grete reverence & beautie, such as is outdone by no othere cathedrall in ye londe. Verily when men come hither from any londe & see & heare such services they will say hertily This is none othere but ye house of God & this is ye gate of heaven.

My South Mimms ties and duties have usually prevented me from being at St Albans on Sundays during vacations, except on very rare occasions, but on week-days I am there as often as possible. I have always disliked London, which I seldom visit if I can help it. To me it is a monstrous octopus, for ever stretching out its tentacles to grasp and swallow more and more of the country which I love; and St Paul's, nominally my cathedral (though it may not be so much longer, owing to changes in diocesan boundaries), is vast, grand and impressive, but cold, and I feel a stranger in it. St Albans Cathedral, on the other hand, I have always loved; and when I came to know Cuthbert Thicknesse, who became Dean in 1936, he made me feel at home in the Cathedral at once. Added to that, the Sub-Dean, Douglas Feaver, and his wife Katharine, who lived under the very shadow of the Cathedral, threw their house wide open to me and became two of my closest friends.

Bishop Loyd's biographer describes Dean Thicknesse as 'somewhat formidable but golden-hearted'. I would agree most warmly with the second of these epithets, but not with the first. I, at least, never found him at all formidable. I would accept 'firm', even 'blunt', as a fair description of him, but even so shall always think of him with admiration and affection. As Dean he was wonderfully successful, and the cathedral services under his ordering were most inspiring. He took as much care about the rendering of Evensong on an ordinary week-day as of an ordination or a diocesan pilgrimage to the shrine of St Alban, when a huge congregation packed the cathedral from end to end. I am thankful to say that his successors in the deanship have maintained his traditions, with equally inspiring results.

One of the Dean's numerous duties was to be chairman of the council of the St Albans High School for Girls, an independent church public school refounded in 1908 by Bishop Jacob. At the Dean's invitation I joined the council and enjoyed the work very much. When setting out from Cambridge for council meetings I used to amuse (and at first startle) my colleagues by telling them that I was going to St Albans to see my thirty or forty mistresses and 527 children.

The council was a highly gaitered assembly, seeing that it included the Bishop of Bedford and the Archdeacon of St Albans in addition to the Dean and sometimes the diocesan. The two outstanding figures at our meetings were the Dean, who ruled us as firmly and efficiently as he ruled the Abbey, and the headmistress, Miss Edith Archibald, who during years of service to the school had gained for it a high reputation in educational circles. She was an ardent Scotch Episcopalian, a Highlander, and in politics a Jacobite. When her pupils produced a programme of *tableaux vivants* at the school one could be certain that Prince Charles Edward and Flora Macdonald would be included in it. She was a most hospitable person, and I was her guest at many a pleasant dinner party at Borogate, one of the boarding houses of the school.

36

My almost annual expeditions to the Continent, interrupted in 1939 by the outbreak of war, were resumed in 1949, when I began to make up for lost time. I took particular pleasure in exploring Provence and Languedoc, for which Avignon made a very good centre. I renewed my acquaintance with Aix and its beautiful Cours Mirabeau, where the magnificent double avenue of plane-trees rises to the house-tops and dapples the wide promenade with a myriad patches of light and shade. I went to Cavaillon, Carpentras, Vacqueras, Les Baux, Montpellier, Béziers, Carcassonne, and Toulouse, with their memories of the troubadours; to the grand Roman remains at Orange, Vaison, St Rémy, Nîmes, Arles and the Pont du Gard; to Vaucluse, with its springs beloved of Petrarch; to Tarascon, with its memories of Aucassin and Nicolette and its modern memories of Daudet; to Saint-Gilles, where I visited the tomb of St Giles; thence to the silent walled town of Aigues-Mortes, built on a Mediterranean lagoon by St Louis as a port from which to launch Crusades; and back through Les-Saintes-Maries, where the Mediterranean Sea washes the walls of the church in which Mistral's heroine died, and where the gipsies gather from all over Europe every year to venerate the tomb of the black saint, Sarah, the alleged servant of Lazarus, Martha and Mary.

My stay at Avignon in 1955 was one of the most enjoyable that I have ever had in any foreign country. I went there with Frederic Raby to attend the 'Congrès International de Langue et Littérature du Midi de la France', the first of its kind.

There were 180 members of the Congress, under the presidency of the octogenarian Mario Roques, the doyen of Provençal scholars, who was a voluble speaker. France contributed just over a third of the 180. Britain came honourably second with twenty-three, Germany third with eighteen, Belgium, Holland, and Spain contributed ten each, Italy eight, and the three Scandinavian countries seven between them. Other European countries represented were Finland, Poland, Switzerland, Austria, the Irish Republic, and Yugoslavia. There were also representatives from the Argentine, Brazil, Canada, and Japan.

Most of our meetings were held in the fifteenth-century Palais du Roure, formerly the residence of a Florentine patrician family. This charming building, with a fig-tree and two tall ailanthus trees in its inner court, had been set apart a few years previously to be the head-quarters of the Institut d'Etudes Méditerranéennes, founded under the joint auspices of the Universities of Aix and Montpellier. Papers were read on both Old Provençal and Modern Provençal subjects, literary and linguistic. Most of them were delivered in French, a few in Provençal or Catalan. As two papers were being delivered simultaneously, we some-times had to choose between such themes as the pre-history of Petrarch's Laura (in Arnaut Daniel's poems), the palatalization of the final *n* in certain Gascon dialects, imagery in Mistral's *Mireio*, the legend of Judas Iscariot in Catalan and Provençal plays, Bernart de Ventadour's vocabulary, and the interpretation of Marcabrun's crusade poem.

One of the two highlights of the Congress was an expedition to Mistral's native village of Maillane on the 125th anniversary of his birth. The little village church was packed for the Sung Mass. The front part of the nave was occupied by a choir of women and girls in Provençal costume — a long gathered skirt, a tight-sleeved black bodice draped with a shawl coming to a point half-way down the back, and either a white lace bonnet with flowing ribbons or else a little Arlesien cap. An orchestra of men and boys, wearing white shirts and black broad-brimmed felt hats, sat in a side chapel, playing the primitive three-holed pipe (*galoubet*) with one hand and beating a tabor simultaneously with the other.

The reredos was outlined with electric lights of various colours. They seemed more in keeping with the celebrant's baroque laced alb and the six inches of shoe and sock visible below it than with his flowing Gothic chasuble. The small acolytes, dressed in cassocks of scarlet or Cam-bridge blue, were given the signal to move by a loud cracking noise, as though someone were shattering a stone slab with a pickaxe. It was impossible to hear more than twelve words of the Mass, because prac-tically the whole time either the choir was singing or the orchestra was playing. I enjoyed the service very much; but my companion Gonzalez-Llubera, the Catalan Professor of Spanish at Belfast, disliked it intensely. 'I came to church to hear the liturgy,' he said, 'not this beastly row.' The singing was entirely in Provençal. It consisted of versified paraphrases of the liturgy or of simple didactic hymns, written by Mistral and others and set mostly to music of the eighteenth and nineteenth centuries. The parish priest afterwards presented me with one of the very few remaining copies of the hymn-book, published in

1887 by the firm of the poet Aubanel. I was interested to find in it a hymn in praise of St Radegund.

When the Mass was over we followed the band and the choir in procession through the village to the cemetery. There we were able to admire the bold (perhaps even blasphemous) interpolation into Holy Writ inscribed over Mistral's tomb: 'Non nobis Domine sed nomini tuo et *Provinciae nostrae* da gloriam.' A wreath was laid, a *De profundis* was recited, a speech was delivered, and all who were capable of doing so joined in singing Mistral's *Coupo santo*, which might be called the Provençal-Catalan national anthem.

After three-quarters of an hour in the hot sun we moved away from the cemetery to Mistral's house, where we stood under the trees and listened to more speeches in French and Provençal, and more singing of *Coupo santo*.

From there we adjourned to St Rémy, where we were received at the Hôtel de Ville by the blind Mayor and (not for the first time during the Congress) were given *vin d'honneur* to drink. The Mayor made a brief speech in French and then a much longer one in Provençal. The tone of the latter reminded me of the saying — I forget its author, and I may have retouched it — that the Provençal regards the Catalan as a brother, the Spaniard as a half-brother, the Italian as a cousin, and the Frenchman as a foreigner. His remarks were not well received by the Parisians present.

The rest of the day was occupied by a lunch of several courses in the local school, by visits to Les Baux and Glanum, and by Provençal dances, songs, and plays in the open air at St Rémy in the evening. Those who stayed the whole course arrived back at Avignon about half-past one next morning.

The other highlight of the Congress programme was a grand dinner served by candle-light in the great hall of the Papal Palace. I unfortunately missed it, being stricken down with food poisoning.

In August 1950, when I was in Northern Italy, a cable reached me at Cernobbio to say that my mother was dangerously ill. I began to pack immediately, but even before I could leave a second cable arrived to say that she was dead. I reached home in time for the funeral at South Mimms, which Allen Hay conducted. I assisted him, and read the Lesson, but could not finish it. After cremation her ashes were buried in the shadow of the church tower. I cannot possibly express what I owe to her, except that it is more than to anyone else.

My old headmaster, John Brown, died about six months after my mother, at the age of ninety-one. I was allowed the great privilege of giving an address at his funeral service at Christ Church, Barnet, and the even greater privilege (seeing that I am a layman) of officiating at the graveside.

Edwin Abbott, one of the most unselfish men I have ever known, who had long been Senior Fellow of my college, died a year later, in the spring of 1952. He had made his home at Barnet with his sister for the past twenty years, and he and I had gone for innumerable walks together. Trains were his hobby, and he spent many happy hours sitting on a fence beside the railway line in Hadley Wood, watch in hand, timing the Flying Scotsman or some other express. A few years before he died he had a mental breakdown. When he had recovered a little he lived for a time at Knightsland, where we had helped in the haymaking together in previous years, and later returned to his own house. Even then, he was at times in such a nervous state that he was unable to move hand or foot or look after himself physically. More than once I took off my jacket, turned up my sleeves, and gave him a thorough bed-bath, for which I had fortunately not lost the technique.

When Abbott died at the age of eighty-four Allen Hay, who was two years his senior, was still going strong. He did not look anything like his age. One day when he was going into church a stranger accosted him in the porch. 'I have just been admiring the way you keep your beautiful church,' he said, 'and am therefore all the more astonished to see such negligence in the porch.' He pointed to the list of Vicars of South Mimms throughout the centuries which hung there. 'Look!' he said, 'nobody has taken the trouble to add any names to that list since 1898.' Allen Hay took a pinch of snuff, offered some to the stranger, and answered, 'I'm afraid I am to blame, but the matter will soon be attended to. You see,' he added, to the stranger's astonishment and embarrassment, 'I'm the 1898 man.' He was so pleased with this incident that he told it many times afterwards. Unlike most people, he always enjoyed a joke against himself quite as much as a joke at the expense of someone else.

His humour continued to run in a never-failing stream until he died. His mental faculties were unblunted; and his physical strength, though he inevitably moved at a slower pace than formerly, was little impaired until late in 1953, when he met with an accident at a London Underground station. This undoubtedly hastened his end, as a coroner afterwards found, but his iron will kept him going throughout the winter and spring. With some help, he officiated at the services of Holy

Week, Easter Day, and Low Sunday. Four days later he was admitted to hospital, where he died peacefully on May 8th. He was nearly eighty-eight years old, and had been Vicar of South Mimms for over fifty-five years.

Allen Hay's personality was so forceful, so distinctive, that no one who met him even on a single occasion could ever forget him or confuse him in memory with anyone else. My debt to him is enormous. No one gave me more encouragement, treated me with greater indulgence, or helped me to enjoy life more than he. Few people can have got so much innocent enjoyment out of life as he did: he enjoyed almost every minute of it, and the study of human relationships never ceased to fascinate him. Much of his happiness sprang from his incurable optimism: all his geese were swans. He loved the beautiful, and he made the services of the church a thing of beauty and a lasting joy to us. Even strong men wept when he died; yet we could not be sad for long, because he had given us so much enjoyment in life, so much happiness, so much laughter; and so, even on the day of his funeral, we laughed, and laughed aloud, when we were talking about him. How could we have done otherwise, when thinking of one who for so long, and so unfailingly, had given us 'beauty for ashes, the oil of joy for mourning, the garment of praise for the spirit of heaviness'?

Considering that my father was a couple of years older than my mother, and that he had been devoted to her from the day they first met, I was naturally anxious about the effect that her death might have on him. He took it very philosophically, however, and rapidly adapted himself to the change, adding housekeeping to his other activities. 'Il faut cultiver notre jardin,' in every meaning of the phrase, might have been his motto all his life, and it continued to be so now. About the time of his ninetieth birthday in 1956 he complained that an hour's digging was as much as he felt capable of doing at a time. During the next few weeks, however, he painted all the woodwork and stonework on the outside of the house, both back and front, upstairs as well as down, including the attic, mounted on a somewhat flimsy ladder. In the summer after his ninetieth birthday he fell from a ladder when sawing a branch off a laburnum, but suffered no worse injury than a few bruises. He still refused (as he had done ever since my mother's death) to have the gas fire turned on in his bedroom while he was dressing or undressing, even on the coldest days in winter.

His favourite indoor recreations were card games, at which he had been a first-class player all his life, and the collecting and storing of junk. There was so much heavy junk in the attic that my brother used to assert that the house was top-heavy and might overturn at any time.

In the autumn of 1958, when he was picking pears, he fell from a ladder and broke a thigh-bone. All he said on being carried to hospital on a stretcher was that the accident was a nuisance, because he had intended to mow the lawn that afternoon and bottle the pears in the evening. Although he recovered from the accident it was the beginning of the end. He died in October 1959 at the age of ninety-three, in the home for old people at St Albans, to which he had retired in the spring of that year, and his ashes were buried with my mother's at South Mimms.

37

On July 25th, 1959, a few months before my father died, I married Muriel Cunnington, of Ingham Lodge, South Mimms. She was a native of the village, much younger than I, and I had known her ever since she was born. I had known her parents too, but they were now dead and Muriel had been their only child.

Before going to Queen Elizabeth's Grammar School for Girls — the companion establishment to my old school — she had been taught at home by an elderly lady, Miss Jacobina Tweedie Griffiths, who lived in the village with her sister, Mary Christine Griffiths. The sisters were a charming, kind-hearted couple, but decidedly odd, Jacobina particularly so. They were women of culture, sincerity and goodwill to all men — except perhaps to Mr Winston Churchill; for they were out-and-out pacifists.

'Don't speak of that terrible man, Mr Cunnington,' Jacobina had said to Muriel's father one day some years after the war of 1914-18. 'Do you know what he did when he heard that war had been declared? He put his hands in his pockets and — WHISTLED.'

Both sisters wore clothes which were several generations out of fashion. Their pince-nez were tilted diagonally and generally had at least one cracked lens. Jacobina sometimes wore two hats at a time, and even in the bitterest weather she often wore very dilapidated rubber-soled canvas shoes, one of them with an untied shoe-lace, the other with no shoe-lace at all. The sisters loved to entertain their friends to tea; but, when sugar was unobtainable in wartime, they had a disconcerting habit of popping some of their sweet ration (usually peppermint bulls-eyes) into their visitors' tea. Embarrassment was caused, too, when Dr Johnson (the Griffithian cat) was seen to lick the cake or the butter before settling down comfortably on the tea-table as a spectator for the rest of the meal.

On leaving school Muriel trained to be a pharmacist. At the time of our marriage she was chief pharmacist at Westminster Children's Hospital, to which she made the long journey by car every week-day from South Mimms.

Both of us wanted a quiet wedding, at South Mimms; but there was little chance of our getting it if we announced it in advance, because, as is inevitable in a village, practically everyone in South Mimms knew us and we had a large number of friends elsewhere too, including the men who had been at Jesus College during the previous forty years. We therefore told as few people as possible and were married by licence at eight o'clock in the morning – the earliest canonical hour. Only two of my colleagues at Cambridge knew about it in advance – Trevor Jones and Frederic Raby, who was my best man. In addition to the Vicar and his wife, only two residents in the village knew. These were our old friend, Mrs Florence Blake, and Dorothy Philpot, headmistress of the village school, who lived with her. Only ten persons were present in church at the ceremony. Not even Mrs Finch, the daily help at the vicarage, knew anything until it was all over. On arrival at the vicarage at about 8.40 that morning she informed the Vicar that she had seen 'Dr Brittain and Miss Cunnington' driving away from the church. The Vicar, with some difficulty, convinced her that she was mistaken, and that she had seen Dr and Mrs Brittain.

For our honeymoon, we spent the next day (Sunday) at St Albans, then one day at Peterborough, and later on several days with my friend and former pupil, Alan Wyndham Green, at his stately Kentish home, Godinton Park, near Ashford. I had stayed there with him many times since 1945, revelling in the beauty of the great Jacobean house, with its exquisite carvings, its collections of *objets d'art*, its pictures, its lovely gardens and its spacious parkland, part of which is carpeted in spring with a million daffodils. In the summer before I married I had arrived at Godinton, to my host's astonishment, in a car with two nuns from John Mason Neale's foundation at East Grinstead. Alan had risen to the occasion and had shown them over the house and entertained them to tea before they left. He chaffed me a good deal afterwards.

When Muriel and I arrived at Godinton a year later, for her first visit, we had no sooner got inside the park gates than we stopped the car and I dressed her up as a nun. We then drove up to the front of the house. Leaving her in the car I got out, fetched Alan to the door and told him that Muriel had not been able to come after all.

'However', I said, 'I haven't come alone. You remember the two nuns who came with me last year?'

'I should think I do', he answered, laughing.

'Well,' I said, 'one of them has come again this year – Sister Monica.'

He looked up and there Sister Monica apparently was, looking very demure at the steering-wheel of the car.

He grasped the reality of the situation after a few seconds; but, to this day, he generally addresses Muriel as 'Sister Monica' whenever we go to Godinton.

The rest of our honeymoon was spent at Ingham Lodge. We did much entertaining there that summer, as indeed we have done ever since, no less than at Cambridge, because Muriel revels in entertaining as much as I do.

The Venerable B. C. Snell, Archdeacon of St Albans, well-known for his wit, asked me, when attending one of our parties, 'Have you always lived in this house?'

'No,' I answered, 'only since I got married; but Muriel was born and bred in it, her parents lived and died in it, and her grandparents lived and died in it.'

'Oh! I see,' he said, 'you took her on with the house' – a joke which Muriel has enjoyed as much as anyone on the numerous occasions when she has heard me repeat it.

One difficulty about the house was to find short names for some of the rooms, so as to avoid having to use such circumlocutions as 'the smaller front bedroom' or 'the left-hand room at the back of the house upstairs'. We solved the problem for three of the rooms by naming them after persons connected with the history of the house. One of them we named 'Jacobina', after the good Miss Griffiths. The other two, which stand side by side, we named 'Augustus' and 'Florence', after our dear friends, Charles Augustus Blake and his wife, whose lives had been intimately connected with the Cunnington family and with Ingham Lodge from the time of Muriel's grandparents. They had known Muriel all her life and me for most of mine.

One drawback to the house was that it had no upstairs lavatory. Our architect friend, Ted Salter, of Ridge, remedied the defect by cutting a slice off Florence and converting it to the required use. I often think of Dr Nairne when I go into that lavatory, because I remember his saying once, in his naive way, 'Some of the best views in the world are those one gets from lavatory windows.'

Certainly ours commands an attractive view, well up to the standard of those we get from all the windows of the house. It is surrounded completely by fields. On one side we look across three miles of arable land and meadows to West Barnet, which has not come an inch nearer for fifty years. The eye moves on to the long line of trees fringing Wrotham Park, where the Byngs have lived for over 200 years, from the time of the ill-fated admiral until now. Then come Dancers Hill, Mimms Wash and Bridgefoot. Potters Bar, except for three or four houses, is mercifully concealed from view by woodland. To the north-east stretches Mimms Wood, as vast and as beautiful as ever. The lovely ash-trees, elms, and cherries planted by Muriel's grandfather in our garden prevent us from seeing the main part of the village and even the parish church; but the haunting sound of its six bells is wafted to us, unless the wind is in the wrong direction, over the house-tops of the village and along Greyhound Lane twice on Sundays and on Thursday evenings, when the ringers practise.

The Michaelmas Term 1959, the first term after my marriage, began at Jesus with the installation of a new Master. We had pre-elected him during the summer to succeed Eustace Tillyard, who had had to vacate office on September 30th on reaching the retiring age. Our new Master was Denys Lionel Page, Regius Professor of Greek and a Fellow of Trinity, formerly in turn Scholar and Student of Christ Church, Oxford. We settled down quickly under his benevolent leadership. The number of undergraduates and of graduate researchers from our own and other Cambridge colleges, and from other universities, continued to grow, as also did the number of Fellows, and the need for a new building became pressing.

At the end of the term I was carried to a nursing home suffering from a combined attack of pneumonia, bronchitis, and asthma. I spent Christmas there. When I came out in January, Muriel and I went on a cruise, during which we spent about a fortnight in Madeira and another fortnight in Tenerife.

I had been warned by my doctor that the state of my heart and lungs was such that I must not return to the top floor of C Staircase but must have rooms where there were fewer steps to climb. My colleague Derek Taunt very kindly offered to exchange rooms with me. I accepted his offer and benefited greatly by the exchange. In view of what was to come later, I could not have done so well by moving into any other set of rooms in the college.

I was sorry to leave C Staircase, where I had kept for twenty-eight years. It held for me so many happy memories of Nairne, of Q, of our good bedmakers, Mrs Mitchley and Mrs Patten, and of the innumerable undergraduates and Old Jesuans whom I had entertained there. I was leaving Raby behind, too; but he came to my new rooms at least twice every day, for lunch and again in the evening, before we moved on to chapel or hall together. Trevor Jones, who had taught his pupils in my dining-room for many years, moved across with me to do the same thing and to carry on with the compilation of his great German and

English dictionary in several volumes. When it is finished it will represent the labour of thirty years or more.

So, in the May Term of 1960, I returned to Chapel Court, which I had left in 1932. I did not, however, move back into Staircase 8, but into a first-floor set of rooms on Staircase 13. I felt at home at once, for I had been into those rooms hundreds of times before. They had been occupied by Bernard Manning from 1930 until he died in 1941, and I had visited him there practically every day.

I had never known such luxury before. I now had a hall with a spacious cupboard in it, a keeping-room, a dining-room, a bedroom, a gyp-room, a lavatory, and a bathroom, all to myself. The keeping-room looked on to the chapel and the Master's garden, with its secluded corner where Steve Fairbairn's ashes lay buried. The dining-room looked towards Jesus Lane and that part of the Close where Soccer was played. The bathroom looked across Chapel Court to the Angel Gate. The gyp-room looked right down the long axis of Chapel Court to the cricketing part of the Close and the pavilion.

The same year saw the publication of my revision and continuation of Arthur Gray's *History of Jesus College.*

In the summer of 1961, when Muriel and I were on the point of going to Henley for the regatta, I was struck down by a coronary thrombosis and had to spend about six weeks in hospital. This was unfortunate, because I had intended to devote the Long Vacation that year to writing a second volume of the history of the Jesus Boat Club, of which the first volume had been published in 1928. However, after about a fortnight, although I was not yet allowed to write, I was allowed to dictate. Muriel came to the rescue, and spent many hours at the hospital day by day, while I dictated to her. It was interesting to see the startled or even shocked expressions on the faces of members of the hospital staff, unfamiliar with Cambridge terminology, when they heard me say that Sidney beat Lady Margaret or that Jesus bumped Emmanuel, and their puzzled expression if I said that First and Third Trinity five started ninth in the fourth division. I was also dictating part of my *Penguin Book of Latin Verse* to Muriel about that time. By our combined efforts both books appeared in 1962. We were able to relax during the following Easter vacation, when we went on a cruise to Greece and the Aegean Islands. It was delightful to renew my acquaintance with places which I had known nearly fifty years before in less pleasant circumstances.

By this time the College Council had decided to appeal to old members for their financial help in building a new court. I thereupon devoted all my spare time for some months to the writing of 1,600 letters to Jesus men of many generations. The response to the appeal was a generous one, and the new court was opened in 1965. It accommodated seventy-three undergraduates and two Fellows and was called North Court.

A few months later my colleagues, in view of the state of my health, took the unprecedented step, without my asking for it, of allowing my wife to live in college with me during term. She was, in all probability, the first woman to be allowed to live in rooms in Jesus or any other men's college in the University. She took to the life like a duck to water and seemed to become part of the College immediately. It would be unbecoming for me to praise my wife here; but I am confident that my colleagues would agree with what I have just said about her.

Cambridge is a cold place, and a fire is welcome during the greater part of the year in the Combination Room, to which the dons withdraw after dining in Hall. When we had comparatively few Fellowships we were so accustomed to sitting round the fire in a semicircle that we continued to sit round the empty grate in a semicircle even on the hottest summer day, no matter how many or how few of us there might be. On some nights there might be only half-a-dozen of us, forming a tiny semicircle. On ordinary nights we were from a dozen to sixteen in number. When our numbers expanded, there were sometimes so many of us that the semicircle became almost a complete circle, filling the whole room. There might even be an overflow into the Little Combination Room next door. When our numbers became even greater, we divided up into sets of eight at 'sep. tab.', like paying guests at a seaside boarding-house. This was unfortunate, but we could find no other solution to the difficulty.

Those who do not frequent Combination Rooms sometimes have strange ideas about what goes on in them after dinner. They picture the dons sitting there for hours, drinking large quantities of port every night of the year. Some of them probably imagine that St Radegund endowed the Combination Room with perpetual port. When they discover that she died in the sixth century, half a millennium before even the nunnery named after her was founded, they are inclined to think, perhaps, that at least John Alcock endowed the dons with a free supply of wine – but unfortunately he did not.

Those who wish to smoke in the Combination Room do so, but nowadays only about one in six is a smoker. We all join, of course, in intellectual conversation, on such subjects as the Annals of Tacitus, the geology of the West Indies, the flora and fauna of Borneo, Newmarket Races, rowing, or the Test Match. When we have had enough of the conversation we go — if we have not had to leave already to attend a committee, to read a paper to some society, or to prepare a lecture. Engagements of that sort, indeed, prevent us from going into the Combination Room at all on many evenings during the course of a term.

Portraits of departed worthies look down on us from the walls. There are three ways of getting one's portrait hung in a Combination Room (or Senior Common Room, as all other universities call it). One is to be a distinguished member of a college. A second way is to be an undistinguished member but to have one's portrait painted by a distinguished artist, and so get in on his merits. A third way is open to everyone, even to outsiders — the simple expedient of leaving enough money to the college in one's will.

S. T. Coleridge, whose portrait by Northcote hangs over the fire-place, qualified on both the first and second counts. It is true that as an undergraduate he wasted his time on drink, drugs, and unprofitable reading. It is true that he did not pay his bills, and consequently was brought into this very room more than once and threatened with expulsion, but he managed to twist the dons round his finger and stay in residence. It is true also that he made so much noise in college at night that — perhaps this was the worst of all his offences — he kept the dons awake, and that in the end he went down without a degree; but he made good in after years, as all the world knows.

Tobias Rustat, an official at the court of Charles II, who faces Coleridge from the other side of the room, was not a member of the College, though his father was. He qualifies under the second and third counts, because his portrait was painted by Lely and he bequeathed his property to the College, mostly to found scholarships for the education of sons of the clergy. He also founded a feast, still held at the College every year in May and named after him. Under the terms of his will, every Fellow who attends the feast receives a five-shilling piece at table. This was an excellent provision; for whereas a handful of small silver and copper, even with a total value of five shillings, might.to-day look insulting, when the bequest takes the form of a beautiful five-shilling piece, a 'waggon-wheel', one pockets the insult very readily, as do also the god-children to whom I pass mine on.

Snapdragon grows on the walls of Jesus College, Cambridge, as it grew on the walls of John Henry Newman's first college at Oxford. Towards the end of his *Apologia*, when recalling his last sad farewell to Oxford, he says, 'There used to be so much snapdragon growing on the walls opposite my freshman's rooms there, and I had for years taken it as the emblem of my own perpetual residence even unto death in my University.' That reference to the snapdragon is well known and frequently quoted, but his poem about the same flower seems to be almost unknown. I often think of its opening lines:

> I am rooted in the wall
> of buttressed tower and ancient hall,

and its ending:

> Well might I
> In college cloister live and die.

When I die I should like my ashes to be divided into two parts, one of them to be buried (if it were allowed) in Jesus College, the other part to be buried in the churchyard at South Mimms.

———————

The Master and Fellows graciously gave permission for F.B.'s ashes to be buried in the consecrated ground outside the east end of the Chapel. A simple inscription of his initials and dates is cut into the Chapel wall above the spot.

Index

256 INDEX

F.B. (Frederick Brittain)—*contd*
  Keeper of the Records at Jesus
    College 225
  marriage 245
  rooms at Jesus College 94, 104,
    163, 174, 181, 249
  politics 53-4
  acting 10, 28, 43, 88, 182
  singing 14, 166, 182-3
  countryside, love of 10, 15, 30-3,
    142
  smoking, giving up 200-1
  writing, 28, 85, 98, 125-8, 164-5,
    174, 182, 199
Feaver, Canon D. and Mrs K. 237
Fens 54, 85, 221
Ferrar, N. 227
'ff', origin of 21
Figgis, N. 197
Finch, Mrs F. 246
First World War, F.B.'s service in
  55-68
Fisher Unwin 97
Fitzwilliam Museum 112, 113
Flitt 1
Floyd, H. 22
Foakes Jackson, Dr F. J. 113,
  176-7
Footlights Club 165, 169
  May Week Revue 94, 169, 171,
    220
Fowey 185, 208
France, 239-41
Fraser, W. 153
Freeman, W. A. 27
French language 26
Frere, Rt. Rev. W. H. (Bishop of
  Truro) 135, 208
Frowykes 51
Furtado, E. 120
Furse, Rt. Rev. Michael (Bishop of
  St Albans) 235

Gade 21, 22
Gainford 73, 135
'Gaiters' *see Archdeacon's Horse,
  The*
Gardner, Rev. R. 196

Gaselee, S. 197
Gaylor, Arthur 160-1
Genoa 89
Gerken, J. 34
German language 26
Gill, Eric 163
Girton College 214-15, 226
  Mistress of 222
Gittings, Dr R. 179, 182, 226
Glossa Ordinaria 165
Glover, T. R. 86
Godmanchester 195-6
Gonzales-Llubera 240
Good Shepherd, Oratory of the 83
Gowar, F. W. 234
Grant, B. 64
Granta 55
Granta, The 85, *quoted* 86
Grantchester 55
Gray, Arthur 67, 69-70, *quoted*
  100, 176, 182, 183-5, 190,
  224
Gray, A. Beales 97
Great St Mary's Church, Cam-
  bridge 203, 205, 209, 213
Griffiths, Miss J. T. 245, 247
Grimes, The Ven. Dr 232, 233
'Grinds' 123
Grosjean, Paul 126
Guyatt, T. 26

Hall, H. R. Wilton 21, 54
Hankey, Very Rev. C. P. 193, 227
Harmer, Prof. L. C. 115
Harmsworth
  C. M. H. ('Joe') 95, 97, 109, 117,
    118
  Lady 109
  Sir Hildebrand 95
Harris, Wilson, 200, 201
Harrison, G. W. N. 26, 27, 35
Havard, 'Claude' 198
Hay, Rev. Allen 30, 32, 34, 39-42,
  49, 70-1, 92, 142-9, 150, 152,
  154, 161-2, 182-3, 202, 234-5,
  242-3
Heffer, E. 197-8